International Socialism 106

International Socialism 106

Quarterly journal of socialist theory

Editor: Chris Harman   Assistant editor: Sally Campbell

Published April 2005

Distribution/subscriptions:
International Socialism, PO Box 82, London E3 3LH
Phone: 020 7538 3308
E-mail: isj@swp.org.uk
American distribution: B de Boer, 113 East Center Street,
Nutley, New Jersey 07110

ISBN 1 905192 01 0

Printed by Cambridge Printing
Typeset by Sally Campbell
Cover by Noel Douglas (info@noeldouglas.net)
Cover photo: Ramzi Haidar/Getty

Subscription rates for one year (four issues) are:
Britain and overseas (surface):

individual	£22
institutional	£30
North America/Europe	£24
Rest of world	£26

International Socialism is associated with the Socialist Workers Party, but articles express the opinions of individual authors unless otherwise stated. We welcome proposals for articles and reviews for *International Socialism*. If you have a suggestion, please phone or e-mail as above.

Contents

Notes on contributors

Anne Alexander is author of *The New Intifada* and wrote, with Simon Assaf, 'The Rise of the Iraqi Resistance' in our last issue

Kieren Allen is a member of Socialist Workers Party of Ireland and author of books on James Connolly and Max Weber

Simon Assaf is a Lebanese socialist living in London

Angus Calder wrote *The People's War* and *Revolutionary Empire*

Alex Callinicos is a member of the Socialist Workers Party and author, most recently, of *An Anti-Capitalist Manifesto*

Esme Choonara is a supporter of the Socialist Worker platform in the Scottish Socialist Party

Andy Durgan is a member of the En Lucha socialist group in Spain and was a historical advisor on the film *Land and Freedom*

John Game is doing research on popular politics in Mumbai

Mike Gonzalez is on the executive of the Scottish Socialist Party and author of *Che Guevara and the Cuban Revolution*

Jane Hardy teaches at the University of Hertfordshire

John Holloway is a lecturer in Puebla, Mexico and author of *Change the World Without Taking Power*

Charlie Kimber is a journalist on *Socialist Worker*

Alex Law teaches at the University of Abertay Dundee

Daphne Lawless is in the Socialist Workers Organisation of New Zealand and a former member of the Alliance Party

Fernando Lizárrago lives in Argentina

John Molyneux wrote *Marxism and the Party* and *Rembrandt*

Gerry Mooney lectures in social policy at the Open University

John Rose is author of *The Myths of Zionism*

Terry Wrigley is editor of the journal *Improving Schools* and author of *Schools of Hope: A New Agenda for School Improvement*

Imperialism's new facade

Chris Harman

The supporters of US imperialism were crowing as we began to put this journal to press early in March. By the time we put the final touches to it their crowing looked increasingly misplaced.

They claimed that things were at last going their way two years after their conquest of Baghdad. Elections in Iraq had been followed by the election in occupied Palestine of a president willing to end hostilities with Israel. And then came a week of demonstrations against the Syrian presence in Lebanon. 'Maybe, just maybe, those neo-cons weren't so nutty after all,' crowed Max Boot in the *Los Angeles Times* (3 March). Bush's 'declaration of the cause of Middle East democracy is producing earth-shaking results', crowed Rupert Murdoch's *New York Post*. 'Many of those who have once again called a Republican president a stupid cowboy will be forced to eat their words and admit that it was the war in Iraq that began to change the political face of the Middle East,' crowed Angelo Panebianco in *Corriere della Sera*.

The crowing of the warmongers was matched by expressions of self-doubt by liberal opponents of the war. Typical was the reaction of Jonathan Friedland of the *Guardian* (2 March): 'We ought to admit that the dark cloud of the Iraq war may have carried a silver lining... It could yet have at least one good outcome. We have to say that the call for freedom throughout the Arab and Muslim world is a sound and just one—even if it is a Bush slogan and arguably code for the installation of malleable regimes.'

According to the euphoric theorists of a US triumphant, the Bush administration was guaranteed to succeed in the Middle East with methods used in Serbia, Georgia, Haiti and Ukraine. The demand for 'democracy' would sweep away regimes that reject US strategic objectives and replace them with governments with democratic legitimacy abiding by these objectives. All the US had to do was deploy its money and its own NGOs to court and finance internal opposition forces, and the regimes would simply collapse through rainbow-coloured peaceful 'revolutions'. A domino effect would lead to stable pro-US regimes sprouting up right across the Middle East, in a supposed rerun of the wave of political revolutions which swept Eastern Europe in 1989-90. The US, it is assumed, could not fail to cement its hegemony in this way.

But any such comparisons are very superficial and very glib. The funeral of the assassinated former Lebanese prime minister Rafik Hariri may have been immense, but the demonstrations afterwards were small affairs, made up mainly of upper class members of the Maronite minority (only about 20 percent of the population). This, Al Jazeera television said, was the 'Gucci revolution', not the cedar revolution. The huge anti-US demonstration organised by Hizbullah, the party of the Lebanese Shias (with 40 percent of the population, the country's largest religious group) a few days later put the anti-Syria demonstrations in the shade.

The Iraq miscalculation

What is more, the attention the US administration is now directing towards Syria is a symptom of weakness on its part, not strength. It is a product of the continuing problems it faces in Iraq.

The elections in Iraq do not mean that the resistance has gone away (as Anne Alexander and Simon Assaf show in the next article), or that the US has somehow miraculously escaped from the morass it blundered into two years ago. Its assumption then was that not only could it easily overthrow Saddam Hussein, but also it could just as easily set up a stable puppet regime within a matter of weeks. Rumsfeld insisted this could be done with a mere 130,000 troops, most not needing to be in Iraq long, ignoring the advice of army chief of staff General Eric Shinseki that hundreds of thousands of US troops would be needed to ensure security in Iraq, including the security necessary to rebuild and operate the country's oil industry. The relatively small number of troops used fitted into the neocons' wider assumption that the US's overwhelming technical superiority in armaments would enable it to move straight on from Iraq to threaten any other country physically, waging two or more wars at a time if necessary.

No amount of chest beating can conceal how wrong these assumptions were. The death toll of US troops is now over 1,500, creating discontent among the families of service personnel. The financial cost is predicted by Anthony Cordesman, former Middle East adviser to US administrations, to reach $232 billion by the end of this year, and $308 billion by the end 2007. Occupying Iraq accounts for about 15 percent of the $427 billion US budget deficit which threatens to destabilise the US and world economies.[1]

Just as serious for US imperialism's overall global goals is the cost in terms of military overstretch. Far from being ready for further Iraq-type wars, the US barely has enough troops to sustain its position in Iraq. When it invaded Haiti last year, it sent 2,000 troops, not the 20,000 sent by Clinton a decade ago, and has since done its best to replace them with forces from countries like Brazil and Argentina. Bogged down in Iraq, the administration has been forced to go softly on North Korea and to sit back while Chávez in Venezuela—as important a source of US oil imports as the Middle East—steps up his anti-imperialist rhetoric and plans to diversify his oil sales through deals with China and other countries.

The election result in Iraq is not, by itself, going to change any of this. The privileged strata among the Shias who dominate the most successful electoral slate already show signs of trying to do a deal with the US to advance their own class interests by bringing the insurgency to an end, and their equivalents among the Sunnis will hope for some offer that enables them to do the same. But it will be difficult for them to gain widespread support among the population at large for such an approach and isolate the armed resistance unless they are seen to use oil revenues to rebuild shattered infrastructure and economy. And this means putting up resistance to US pressures for the oil to serve simply as a tool for US economic and strategic interests when it comes to bargaining with the other great powers.

The US then faces the dilemma that to stabilise the country after the elections it needs to loosen the economic control which was a central part of its rationale for going to war in the first place. Cordesman summed up the problem in an article last November. 'The odds on lasting US success in Iraq are at best even, and may well be worse,' he wrote. 'The US can almost certainly win every military battle and clash; it is far less certain to win the political and economic war... The US faces too much Iraqi anger and resentment to try to hold on in the face of clear failure, and achieving any lasting success in terms of Iraqi political acceptance means that the US must seek to withdraw over the next two years...' Among the preconditions for the US getting out without risking a very visible defeat were to stop using 'Iraq as a lever for changing the region' and to stop interfering with 'Iraq's independence in terms of its politics, economics and above all oil'.[2]

The Bush administration shows no sign of doing this. It will be distrustful of the main forces in the new Iraqi assembly, since they are dominated by Shia politicians who in the past have shown some degree of allegiance to Iran. And so it will insist on keeping US troops in the country, even if the price of doing so is to ensure that resistance to the occupation continues in one form or another. It may well end up in the situation which has occurred in other such colonial occupations, where sections of the collaborationist government play a double game, encouraging some degree of resistance so as to increase their own credibility with the masses and their bargaining power in relation to the occupiers. It will not develop a solid foundation of pro-American rule, the only way the US can get out of the morass.

The Cambodian syndrome

How does a great capitalist power react when it is bogged down in one small, even if strategically central, country? If it cannot retreat, it is forced to get involved in more adventures in order to try to shift the overall strategic balance in its favour. This is what Nixon and Kissinger did in 1970s when they extended their war in Vietnam across the border into Cambodia, causing another million deaths.

None other than the architect of the Cambodia attacks 35 years ago, Henry Kissinger, joined with George Shultz to urge this policy on Bush in late January, calling for a 'strategy for eliminating the sanctuaries in Syria and Iran from which the enemy can be instructed, supplied, and given refuge in time to regroup'.[3]

The US was already making scarcely veiled threats against Iran last autumn, with widespread talk of the Israeli air force bombing Iran's nuclear facilities. The US administration may eventually give the go-ahead to that scenario. But a direct confrontation with Iran is full of dangers to the US position in Iraq. Representatives of the Iranian regime have boasted privately to journalists that they have more 'assets'—armed supporters—on the ground in Iraq than the US. And the Shia politicians elected to the new assembly cannot expect to maintain their influence for long if they back US attacks on the Shias of Iran.

This explains the shift in focus to Lebanon and Syria.

But this tactic can rebound in the US administration's face just as its move against Iraq did two years ago. The US could only get its anti-Syrian demonstrations in Lebanon by relying on the leaders of some of the sectarian factions who waged the civil war of 1975-90. Yet Syrian troops entered the country, in the first place, to help one of them, the Maronite Falangists, avoid defeat at the hands of the forces of the left and the Palestinians. Then the US (and France) relied on the Syrian presence to stabilise the country after US intervention (shelling Beirut) had made things worse and 250 marines had been blown up in 1983. Now the US is risking reigniting civil war, without any guarantee that the outcome would be favourable to it.

An explicit part of the US agenda (embodied in the resolution it pushed through the UN) is to disarm and curtail the influence of Hizbullah. But Hizbullah is well armed and skilled at fighting. It is, after all, the only Arab force that has ever won a significant victory over the Israeli army, forcing it out of southern Lebanon five years ago, and it has massive support among the impoverished Shias of the south. The assumption that it will accept humiliation is naive in the extreme. So is any assumption that the US can make such moves in Lebanon without upsetting high ranking Shia religious notables in Iraq with close links with Lebanon.

The most likely outcome for the neo-cons if they proceed with their 'strategy' is that they will simply spread the chaos in Iraq more widely across the region. If pressure on Syria were to lead to the regime's collapse all sorts of uncontrollable forces might be released. After all, it has been the Syrian regime which has been clamping down on guerrilla attacks on Israel from southern Lebanon for the last five years, and more recently on the movement of resistance fighters and arms into Iraq. In their blind fury that its regime will not do 100 percent of what US imperialism wants, the neo-cons would be destroying a force which has done 90 percent of that for 30 years and more.

Opening the pressure cooker

Those euphoric about the 'spread' of democracy extend their argument to Saudi Arabia, where the first ever local elections have taken place, and to

Egypt, whose dictator, Mubarak, has decreed that more than one candidate will be allowed to stand in the presidential election in the autumn. As the neo-cons see it, this is part of one great process of stabilising the region through replacing autocratic regimes by capitalist democracies—ideally, as in the American model, with elections confined to competition between different pro-capitalist and pro-imperialist parties.

But in reality the processes at work are very different in each case. Lebanon already had a long established democratic structure, even if distorted by bargaining between the leaders of different religious sects, and the 'cedar' revolution was about bending this to suit US interests. Palestine under Yasser Arafat already had elections, even if they produced a corrupt government, and the so called 'democratic' change merely amounted to the Western states exerting pressures on a war-weary and half-defeated people to vote for a president who would give in to many of the demands of the occupying power. It will in no way lessen the bitterness of the terms imposed by Israel, or the sense of anger against the pro-US rulers in the Arab world for failing to lift a finger for the Palestinians.

The turn towards elections in Saudi Arabia and Egypt is designed to provide a safety valve lest enormous discontent among the mass of people explodes violently. The aim has been to do what was done, for instance, by the South Korean military dictatorship after it was faced with mass demonstrations and strikes in 1987-88. It relaxed repression against the moderate pro-capitalist elements in the opposition (although not against more radical groups) while promising them an elected government four years later. In this way it drew their leaders into acceptance of its framework for a 'transition' which, under the guise of change, left untouched the central features of Korean society. It helped them ward off the chances of sudden explosive change (and kept intact the repression against the radicals when the opposition eventually took office). Essentially the same approach was followed in dismantling many of the Latin American dictatorships in the 1980s. Known as 'apertura' ('opening') it was a slow, carefully controlled process of allowing the bourgeois opposition parties to begin to play a role in parliamentary and other electoral institutions, so that when full democracy came about they were hegemonic within it.

But it is a tactic which always contains a danger for those using it. If the discontent below is too great, even the smallest opening can create an uncontrollable movement of people to express their feelings. The very attempt to save a regime through reform can unleash the forces of revolution. After all, it was Gorbachev's attempt to prop up the Soviet Union's regime through 'openness' ('glasnost') that allowed the popular discontent to emerge that so rapidly brought it crashing down.

There have been several times when the US State Department encouraged one of its client states to reform so as to increase stability—and unwittingly helped its enemies on the road to power. So it withdrew support from the Cuban dictator Batista late in 1958 and from the Nicaraguan dictator Somoza in 1979 in order to pressure them to accept reform, but by doing so hastened their fall to forces opposed to US imperialism.

The neo-con assumption in the Middle East today is that any instability will rapidly be brought under control by powerful local forces that accept the US's agenda. After all, this did happen in most of the east European countries after 1989.

But it is an over-optimistic view for them to hold today, particularly in the Middle East. It was still possible in the early 1990s to convince the mass of people who had suffered under the rigours of Stalinist state capitalism that privatisation and the unleashing of market forces would produce a dramatic improvement in their livelihoods: I remember arguing with dissidents in Poznan in Poland in 1988 who assured me that the market would give them Scandinavian-level living standards.[4] You do not find such over-inflated expectations about market capitalism anywhere today. Neo-liberalism and privatisation are not something new in the Middle East. They have been the core policies of the existing dictatorships for at least a decade (see the interview on Egypt below). And they have been accompanied by a worsening economic situation.

The Korean 'opening' of the late 1980s took place in a country with a very rapidly expanding economy and full employment, where the ruling class could concede very large wage increases so as to reduce the political pressure on it. The situation in the big Middle Eastern countries is very different. National income per head in Egypt, for instance, is one fifth of the South Korean level.

Countries which knew considerable economic growth and some reduction in poverty in the 1960s and 1970s are now faced with the lowest growth rates in the world after sub-Saharan Africa, growing poverty and massive levels of unemployment, especially among the young. In Egypt official unemployment figures of 9 percent hide a real figure of 15 to 30 percent; more than one-third of Morocco's youth are unemployed; while in Syria youth unemployment is a staggering 73 percent. Such a situation creates massive bitterness—and not only among workers. The economic squeeze hits the old petty bourgeoisie, and the lack of jobs is devastating for hundreds of thousands of university graduates who aspire to join the new middle class. They do not respond by looking to the US version of capitalism as an alternative. Very large numbers are drawn towards Islamist organisations, which blame 'cultural imperialism' for their problems. The secular intelligentsia, feeling themselves to be heirs to a tradition of fighting Western colonialism and moved by a sense of solidarity with Palestine, are not going to jump into the American camp as easily as the East European intelligentsia so stupidly did 16 years ago. If the genie escapes from the bottle in Egypt or Saudi Arabia it will not simply bow down to US hegemony.

The one group the US can rely on, at least to some extent, is the local bourgeoisie—including the state bourgeoisie running the remaining nationalised industries. Their turn to neo-liberalism has been part of a process of trying to find niches for themselves within multinational capitalism. They can identify with the untrammelled capitalism of the official American vision of the world. Even in the midst of the miseries of Israeli-occupied Palestine there are bourgeois PLO leaders prepared to put their faith in US promises. But in societies where economic growth has been slow in recent years they are quite cut off from wider social layers.

The days are long gone in which any national bourgeoisie anywhere would throw down a revolutionary challenge to those who run the world system. Even in the 1960s the ruling classes in the supposedly 'progressive' Arab countries put preservation of their class positions within their own states above rhetoric of fighting to unite the whole Arab world from the Atlantic to the Gulf in opposition to imperialism.[5] But this does not mean they will always automatically dance to the American tune. They all want to advance their own positions in the global pecking order, and they will occasionally exploit to this end both popular discontent with imperialism and divisions between the great imperialist powers. They do not provide a foolproof means of imposing US hegemony in the midst of movements of mass protest. Even in the Serbian prototype for the US manipulation of mass movements, the government which emerged at the end, that of Kostunica, is a nationalist one which resists certain US demands.

Madness in great ones

The optimism of the neo-cons—and of gullible liberals like Friedland—consists in believing that if they encourage the break-up of the existing Middle Eastern regimes and throw all the bits up in the air, they will land in the pattern that US imperialism needs. It may be that such unlikely things happen occasionally, but only a desperate bunch of people would gamble $308 billion on it. That is why the neo-cons' approach is causing unease within the US political establishment, with conservative 'realists' deeply unhappy with it. One former CIA analyst complains, 'Bush administration policy toward the Middle East is being run by men who were routinely referred to in high circles in Washington during the 1980s as the "crazies".'[6]

However, what is at issue is not the psychology of the individuals in key positions. Their approach follows, as we have argued in this journal over the last two years,[7] from the position of US capitalism. Its overwhelming military superiority over the other big powers is not matched by a similarly unchangeable economic dominance. This creates a pressure to engage in military adventures that will secure its global hegemony against all comers for the foreseeable future—to ensure a 'New American Century'. Moves in such a direction began under the Clinton administration, and the Bush team saw the invasion of Iraq as the means to bring them to fruition. Now, having embarked so far into the morass, they feel compelled to go further. But if they do so, they risk compounding their problems many times.

NOTES

1: Figures from M Sieff, UPI, 27 January 2005.

2: A Cordesman, 'Playing the Course: A Strategy for Reshaping US Policy in Iraq and the Middle East', www.csis.org/features/iraq_playingcourse.pdf

3: *Washington Post*, 25 January 2005.

4: A transcript of some of the discussions is contained in 'Which Road for Polish Socialists?', in *International Socialism* 41 (Winter 1988).

5: See Tony Cliff's analysis after the defeat of the Arab armies by Israel in the 'Six Day War' of 1967, reprinted in T Cliff, *International Struggle and the Marxist Tradition* (London, 2001), pp43-57.

6: Ray McGovern, who served as a CIA analyst for 27 years, *Asia Times*, www.atimes.com

7: See, for instance, A Callinicos, 'The Grand Strategy of the American Empire', in *International Socialism* 97 (Winter 2002), and my own 'Analysing Imperialism', in *International Socialism* 99 (Summer 2003).

The elections and the resistance in Iraq

Anne Alexander and Simon Assaf

The day after Iraqis went to the polls, George Bush and Tony Blair declared that Iraq had 'turned the corner'. Pro-war commentators were quick to demand that the anti-war camp apologise for opposing the war and some who had been against the war conceded that invasion was a price worth paying for 'democracy', even if there were no weapons of mass destruction. Yet the positive gloss on the elections hides deepening problems for the occupation. The resistance has not lost its mass support. There are continuing attacks on US troops and their Iraqi allies, while the parties that won the elections cannot deliver on promises over a timetable for withdrawal of US troops and an end to neo-liberal policies.

Why the elections?

US officials have consistently talked of 'democracy' in Iraq, but they want an electoral system which gives them scope to control the process. Thus in 2003 they championed the idea of indirect elections from regional caucuses instead of direct, national elections. The timing of the polls was a crucial feature of US strategy. They wanted to delay so as to allow their local allies time to entrench themselves in the machinery of the state. It was this combination of delay and indirect elections that led the most influential Shia cleric, Ali Al Sistani, to call on his supporters to take to the streets in a show of strength in January 2004.

The US finally felt compelled to concede direct elections. But they tried to prepare the ground by what they thought would be a crushing blow against the resistance. Their previous assault against Fallujah in April 2004 had taken place as the same time as they faced armed opposition from the supporters of the more radical of the Shia clerics, Muqtada Al Sadr in Baghdad and many cities in the South. This time they relied upon Sistani's desire for elections to keep the Shias quiet while they crushed Fallujah.

Continued resistance

But the resistance was not destroyed with Fallujah. The focus simply shifted to Mosul, Ramadi and other cities, while Baghdad continues to record the highest number of daily attacks on US troops and their Iraqi allies. The growing potency of the resistance can been seen by the levels of attacks on occupation forces. In December 2003 there were 510 attacks on US troops; in December 2004 there were 3,000. They have also grown in sophistication, with well planned ambushes and deadly roadside bombs replacing the 'spray and pray' tactics that characterised the first months of the resistance. A bleak assessment by the Washington-based Centre for Strategic and International Studies in December 2004 noted with alarm that 77 percent of all attacks targeted US troops. The report warns of a failure to recognise the growth and character of the insurgency and accuses the US military of using 'denial as a method of counter-insurgency warfare'.[1] Despite US claims, the report says, these were not regime diehards and foreign Jihadis, but a well entrenched national movement with widespread popular support.

Central to the strategy behind the all-out assault on Fallujah was that the US needs to build up reliable local security structures—army, police, prisons and intelligence services. But these plans are seriously adrift. The local forces are in constant danger of collapse. The Brooking Institution in its weekly update on the occupation continues to track severe problems with the Iraqi security services. The US has failed to reach its stated aim for Iraqi security personnel. By January 2005 they planned for a force of 272,566 men trained and equipped to combat the resistance; they recruited only 141,761, of which only 41 percent had weapons, 25 percent access to vehicles and 17 percent radio equipment. Furthermore the security forces are heavily infiltrated by the resistance: 'Developments in Iraq indicate that the US faces a repetition of its experience in Vietnam in the sense that as various insurgent factions organise, they steadily improve their intelligence'.[2]

A *New York Times* report in February 2005 described the quality of the intelligence available to the resistance: 'Attacks by insurgents to disrupt Baghdad's supplies of crude oil, gasoline, heating oil, water and electricity have reached a degree of co-ordination and sophistication not seen before. The new pattern shows that the insurgents have a deep understanding of the complex network of pipelines, power cables and reservoirs feeding Baghdad'.[3]

What the elections showed

A major factor behind the continuation of the insurgency is the high levels of hostility to the occupation across Iraq. A poll conducted on the eve of the elections found 80 percent in Sunni areas and 69 percent in Shia areas wanted the occupying forces to leave.[4] Moreover, other opinion polls suggest that the US vision of a neo-liberal Iraq is at odds with the view most Iraqis have of the kind of society they want. In November 2004 only 5 percent said they would support political parties calling for a reduced role for the state in the economy, while over 65 percent wanted to see the state playing a greater economic role.[5] In June 2004 an overwhelming 85 percent agreed with the statement that 'wealth must be fairly and equally divided among the public by the state'.[6]

Such feelings found some expression in the election results. Iyad Allawi's election campaign alone should have put paid to any claims that the Iraqi elections were 'free and fair'. The interim prime minister, a former CIA asset who was hand-picked by US officials to lead the cabinet in June 2004, used every dirty trick to maximise his vote. The fact that he failed to win tells us more about the weakness of the Iraqi state machinery, and Allawi's failure to build a base of support outside it, than it proves the strength of Iraqi 'democracy'. Glossy posters, showing just the prime minister's eyes, promised to crack down on 'terrorism'. The US-funded TV channel, Al-Iraqiya, churned out endless footage of Allawi kissing babies, Allawi giving pep talks to the National Guard, Allawi announcing the government's tough security measures for the election. Reporters invited to a press conference organised by the Iraqi National Accord, Allawi's party, were handed envelopes containing a $100 bill as a 'gift'. In some areas Iraqi National Guardsmen were handing out election leaflets calling for a vote for Allawi.[7]

Allawi was not the only one to be accused of manipulating the polls. Turkoman and Christian leaders accused the leading Kurdish parties of ballot-rigging in Ninawa governorate, claiming that in many areas ballot boxes arrived late, or not at all. Turkoman parties also accused the Kurdish parties of bussing in thousands of Kurdish former residents of Kirkuk to vote in the city, ensuring a majority for the Kurdish-dominated Brotherhood list in the local elections. No wonder then, that journalists from the Institute of War and Peace Reporting (IWPR) found many voters took part in the polls with the memory of Saddam Hussein's rigged elections fresh in their minds, reporting that rumours were circulating in Karbala that anyone who didn't vote would be arrested.[8] Yet Iyad Allawi, interim prime minister since June 2004, did badly in the elections, as did many of the rest of the former exiles who dominated the Governing Council.

The electoral success of Shia Islamists, such as Abd-al-Aziz Al Hakim from the Supreme Council for the Islamic Revolution in Iraq (SCIRI), allied to the US was due to the blessing of Ayatollah Ali Al Sistani for their United Iraqi Alliance (UIA) list. It won half the seats in the new parliament standing on a platform which includes a specific commitment to set a timetable for US withdrawal, plus a raft of measures including full employment and universal healthcare.

Throughout their time on the Governing Council, Abd-al-Aziz Al Hakim from SCIRI and Ibrahim Al Ja'afari from the Daawah Party did not show the slightest interest in challenging the occupying forces.

However, if the UIA eventually forms a government (at the time of writing, nearly six weeks after the elections, the parties had still not even agreed on a prime minister), it will be more vulnerable to pressure from below than the former exiles. The UIA's appeal rests on an anti-occupation platform, even if its most important leaders are committed to working with the US. But if they abandon the hopes of those who voted for them, they risk losing support to their more radical rivals, such as Muqtada Al Sadr.

Two faces of Shia Iraq

The relationship between Muqtada Al Sadr and Sistani exposes the contradictions among 'the Shia'. Far from being the kind of monolithic bloc pictured by the Western media, Shia Iraqis are divided by class and by geography, as well as by language and ethnic identity, as much as they are united by faith. Even among the relatively narrow layer of Iraqi Shia who actively support an Islamist approach to politics, there are huge contradictions. Muqtada Al Sadr, for example, took an ambiguous approach to the elections. His spokesmen announced they would not be standing candidates, arguing that genuine elections could not be held under occupation. They also stressed the need for solidarity with the boycott called by Sunni clerics in protest at the assault on Fallujah. However, they stopped short of urging Iraqis not to vote, as this would have placed Sadr in direct opposition to Sistani. Some of Sadr's supporters, including the former editor of one of his newspapers, *Ishraqat*, stood as an independent electoral list which apparently drew most of its support from Sadr City. Meanwhile the UIA leadership claimed that their list included other associates of the young cleric.

Muqtada Al Sadr's attitude to the elections may well reflect the genuine contradictions in his organisation. On the one hand, his main base of support lies in Sadr City among the Shia urban poor of Baghdad. Sadr City's residents have experienced the brutality of occupation at first hand, and have risen in rebellion against US troops several times in the past two years. In April 2004 protesters from Sadr City sparked a mutiny among Iraqi National Guardsmen bound for the fighting in Fallujah as they begged them not to join the US-led assault.[9] They have little in common with the Shia clerical hierarchy in Najaf and Karbala, which has traditionally allied itself with Shia landowners and merchants. Yet Al Sadr's constant appeals to the Hawzah, the Shia seminary in Najaf, tie him to this same clerical hierarchy and make it difficult for him to openly defy Sistani.

Falah Jabar, in his authoritative account of the Shia movement in Iraq, issues a warning about characterising religious groups in Iraq with distinct political outlooks: 'The terms Shia and Shiaism cannot and should not be deployed as sociological categories. Using terms to signify a monolithic type of compact community imbued with unity of purpose and monodimensional political orientation is a naive stereotype created by an ignorant world media'.[10]

For many pro-war commentators, the election results were a victory for the Shia majority over the Sunni-dominated Ba'athist regime. This not only ignores class divisions in Iraqi society, but also hides the ambiguity of US policy towards Iraqi Shias. The success of the insurgency has forced US officials to rely on powerful clerical leaders such as Sistani, but they have always hoped to balance their influence by constructing a coalition of allies from different religious and ethnic groups. In the early days of the occupation, when US commanders thought they were only mopping up 'Ba'athist remnants', the warnings from Washington were all about the dangers of Shia radicalism and the pitfalls of majority rule.[11]

Jabar argues that 'each social group among the Shia is characterised by a definite form of social organisation, specific lifestyle, distinct value system and independent economic activity and interest'.[12] The poor peasants who began settling Sadr City (or Revolution City, as it was then called) over the last 30 years were fleeing Shia landlords, clerics and grain merchants. While the Shia merchants in Najaf and Karbala merged into the upper echelons of clerical hierarchy that made up the great religious and land-owning families, Sadr City has long been the focus of radical movements of the dispossessed, from the Communist Party to Muqtada Al Sadr's militia, the Mahdi Army. Many tribes in Iraq also have Sunni and Shia branches, while the rate of intermarriage is high, especially in urban areas.

For the clerics and merchants who dominate Najaf and Karbala, the occupation has provided the opportunity to develop the trade in pilgrims and build hotels, but for Sadr City the loss of the oil revenues that once provided for the health service and education means the fate of the occupation will determine if they sink deeper into poverty or regain some of the economic securities they enjoyed in the past. Ahmad Hashim describes what is at stake for the Najafi merchants:

> After the collapse of Saddam's regime, these holy cities witnessed a massive revival in commercial activity and the construction of housing and hotels to accommodate pilgrim traffic from Iran and the wider Shia world. Despite tension between native Iraqis in these towns and the recent and richer Iranian inhabitants (many Iraqis blamed the dramatic increase in prices and rents on the Iranians), a large proportion of the population was benefiting from the economic upsurge.[13]
>
> Class tensions between Shias were revealed when the petty bourgeoisie and commercial class of Najaf and Karbala responded angrily to the loss of business because of the fighting [in September 2004].[14]

The boycott campaign

Sunni Islamist groups were the main supporters of the campaign to boycott the elections, although several other organisations opposing the occupation also took part, such as the Iraqi National Constituent Congress. The Association of Muslim Scholars, a Sunni Islamist group, took the lead as preparations for an attack on Fallujah were revealed in October 2004. The scholars rejected the idea that fair and representative elections could be held under occupation. Sunnis were divided over the issue of the elections. Sunni politicians who joined the Governing Council under Paul Bremer, such as Adnan Pachachi and Ghazi Al Yawir, expressed reservations about the timing of the polls, but did not join the boycott. The Iraqi Islamic Party, another Sunni Islamist party, at first put forward a list of candidates and then withdrew from the polls.

The extremely low turnout for the elections in the largely Sunni areas confirms that the boycott had solid support. Press reports suggest that while many were concerned about security during polling, many stayed away on principle.[15] Those calling for a boycott did not all use violence to try and deter voters, although there were numerous attacks on polling stations. Boycott campaigners put up posters urging people not to vote in Baqubah and Ramadi. Young activists leafleted the streets and mosques in Mosul.

Political and tactical difference inside the resistance

The resistance is not only being tested on the battlefield, but also politically. The elections brought into sharp relief political and ideological differences inside the resistance. The pressure to build a national movement is reflected in the diverse groups involved in the armed resistance. A breakdown of groups found organisations ranging from Islamist to Nationalist and left wing organisations—including a radical split from the Communist Party and the military wing of the long established Iraqi opposition group, the Nasserite Organisation. It may be possible for a resistance to emerge with Islamic leadership, but it could not achieve unity on a specifically Islamist agenda.

There are Sunni fundamentalist tendencies based on Salafism and Wahabism, extreme puritan versions of Islam, and often claiming affiliation to Al Qaida. These number between 300 and 1,000 out of 20,000 estimated resistance fighters, but their attacks on coalition forces through deadly suicide bombings act as a 'force multiplier'. Although many of the groups are admired for the effective suicide attacks, especially against tanks and armoured columns, there is growing opposition to indiscriminate bombings. Recent reports from the resistance found growing hostility towards Salafist or Al Qaida inspired groups.[16] Tensions between local resistance organisations and Salafist groups almost spilled over into fighting in Fallujah on the eve of the US assault in November 2004. After the 28 February car bombing on a police recruitment office in Hillah that killed over 100 locals, one umbrella organisation, the Islamic Front for the Iraqi Resistance, based in the Ninawa and Diyala provinces, ordered its members not to co-operate with Salafist groups involved in killing civilians.[17] The Association of Muslim Scholars, the public face for the Sunni-based resistance groups, called for an immediate halt to attacks that could endanger civilians. Many of the mainstream Iraqi resistance groups fear such attacks could alienate popular support for the insurgency.

The Salafist interpretation of Sunni orthodoxy sees Shias as heretics, and so the overtly sectarian attacks on Shias, including deadly attacks on mosques and religious festivals, are blamed on these groups by some, although there is no direct evidence. Many others blame US 'Black Ops' for the attacks, which are seen as a danger to a unified national movement by presenting the insurgency as exclusively Sunni.[18]

The resistance is entering a new post-election phase. There could be the development of a more unified movement similar to the PLO, which attempts to narrow the scope of military resistance so as not to undermine popular support, while appealing for national unity.

The Kurds

The Kurdistan Alliance—a joint list of the two major Kurdish parties, the Kurdistan Democratic Party and the Patriotic Union of Kurdistan—won just under 26 percent of the vote and controls the second largest bloc in the new parliament. It lays claim to the city of Kirkuk, which under Saddam Hussein was 'Arabised' by encouraging Arabs to settle there. Kurdish leaders are clear that Kurdish influence over Kirkuk and its oil is a condition of remaining within Iraq. And if the Kurds decide to secede and create an independent Kurdistan, Kirkuk's oil will be crucial to the new country's economic viability.

There are no easy answers in Kirkuk, however, as many of the Arabs who settled in the area were poor farmers from the south. Uprooting up to 200,000 people to restore land and property to those forced to move by the Ba'athist regime will not right the injustice done in the past. Turkoman and Arab residents now fear that returning Kurdish former residents will displace them and the city has already seen protests organised by Muqtada Al Sadr's representative in Kirkuk, Abd-al-Fattah Al Musawi, described by local news reports as a Turkoman.[19] The future of Kirkuk will test the unity of the Iraqi state—possibly to destruction.

The Lebanon option?

Some common threads emerge in the US strategy in the face of continued insurgency and popular hostility to the occupation. It does not rely entirely on either a 'strongman' neo-Ba'ath type government, nor in straightforward 'majority rule democracy'. Over the past two years US policy has generally favoured the creation of a 'consociational democracy'[20] in Iraq: the kind of power-sharing agreement on which the Dayton Peace Accord in Bosnia is based.

Under this system different ethnic, religious or linguistic groups are represented in government according to their demographic size, while civil service jobs are allocated according to ethnic quotas. Minority groups are given a veto over government decisions, and the power of the central state is redistributed away from the centre, through a system of regional autonomy or federalism.[21]

At a superficial level this appears to offer a mechanism for balancing the demands of competing ethnic groups by ensuring that everyone has a place in the sun. In reality, the system entrenches and institutionalises the vertical cleavages in society, whether ethnic, religious or linguistic. It gives those at the top of each 'community' a share in the spoils of state power, which they can then dispense as patronage to those further down. Immense power concentrates in the hands of politicians who have a vested interest in maintaining the ties which bind together workers and bosses, rich and poor, within their 'community', while encouraging members of different groups to see other ethnicities or sects as their main competitors for jobs, services and housing.

The US created the Iraqi Governing Council following a such a framework.[22] The Governing Council was dominated by groups which have a sectarian or ethnic character, such SCIRI, the Daawah Party and the two major Kurdish parties. Individual members appear to have been selected as 'representatives' of their 'community'.[23] A similar process was applied to the interim cabinet, and there have been persistent claims in the Iraqi press that the interim government has been operating what is by default a quota system for civil service jobs, with the major parties turning the ministries into private fiefdoms.[24] A particularly ominous form of the parcelling out of the state has been the institutionalisation of party militias through their incorporation into the security forces. Meanwhile, the Transitional Administrative Law (TAL), Iraq's temporary constitution (agreed by US administrator Paul Bremer and the Governing Council in March 2004) effectively gives the Kurds a veto over a permanent constitution, and potentially also allows the creation of autonomous regions for the Turkoman and Chaldo-Assyrian (Iraqi Christian) minorities.[25] Such a system could have disastrous consequences in a society as fragmented and impoverished as Iraq, and adds to the urgency of ending the occupation. The occupying forces are playing the politics of divide and rule, hoping to manipulate ethnic and religious strife by institutionalising it.[26]

Contrary to the picture presented by some, sectarian conflict is not ingrained in Iraqi society, with occupying forces necessary as impartial 'referees' to prevent squabbling Iraqis from fighting among themselves. Intermarriage between different sects and religious groups is common. There is no history of sustained ethnic or religious conflict comparable with Lebanon. The state has often engaged in discrimination or tried to stir up sectarianism, but this has rarely been successful in motivating ordinary Iraqis to attack their neighbours. Hundreds of thousands of Kurds remained living in Baghdad, despite Saddam Hussein's murderous campaign against their relatives in the north.

Yet the longer the occupation continues, the greater the danger that sectarianism will put down deep roots, as the experience of Lebanon shows. It endured 15 years of civil war in the 1970s and 1980s thanks in large part to a 'consociational' system of government imposed during the period of French rule between the wars.

If there is a dark cloud hanging over the future of the occupation, there are also grim warnings over the future of the country. US policy is creating the conditions for a rise in sectarianism, religious strife and ethnic conflict. The occupation faces a determined and growing opposition—the resistance. Over the last two years the diverse groups that have taken up arms against the occupation have faced internal as well as external battles. Now the pressure is growing on them to adopt a national agenda, rather than a narrowly Islamist one. If they do so they can counter the immense harm the occupation is doing and deal a blow to US imperialism of global significance. That is why the struggle against the occupation is a priority everywhere.

NOTES

1: *The Developing Iraqi Insurgency: Status at End-2004* (Centre for Strategic and International Studies, Washington DC).

2: 'Iraq Index: Tracking Variables of Reconstruction & Security in Post-Saddam Iraq', http://www.brookings.edu/iraqindex Updated 4 March 2005.

3: J Glanz, 'Insurgents Increasingly Sophisticated in Targeting', *The New York Times*, 21 February 2005.

4: 'Survey Finds Deep Divisions in Iraq; Sunni Arabs Overwhelmingly Reject

Sunday Elections; Majority of Sunnis, Shiites Favor US Withdrawal', New Abu Dhabi TV/Zogby Poll Reveals, 28 January 2005, http://www.zogby.com/news/ReadNews.dbm?ID=957

5: 'Survey of Iraqi Public Opinion', International Republican Institute, 24 November-5 December 2004, http://www.iri.org/1-20-05-IraqiElection.asp

6: As above, 24 July-2 August 2004.

7: Institute for War and Peace Reporting, *Iraq Crisis Report* no 99, 25 January 2005.

8: Institute for War and Peace Reporting, *Iraq Crisis Report* no 108, 2 February 2005.

9: See A Alexander and S Assaf, 'Iraq: The Rise of the Resistance', *International Socialism* 105 (Winter 2005).

10: F A Jabar, *The Shiite Movement in Iraq* (Saqi Books, 2003), p20.

11: Amatzia Baram provides an example of this type of analysis in 'Post-Saddam Iraq: The Shiite Factor', *Iraq Memo* 15, Brookings Institution, 30 April 2003 http://www.brookings.edu/views/op-ed/fellows/baram20030430.htm

12: F A Jabar, as above.

13: A S Hashim, 'Iraq's Chaos: Why the Insurgency Won't Go Away', *Boston Review* (October/November 2004). Ahmad S Hashim is a professor of strategic studies at the Naval War College in Newport, Rhode Island.

14: As above.

15: Institute for War and Peace Reporting, *Iraq Crisis Report* no 99, 25 January 2005.

16: Hashim writes of one incident, 'The different agendas and modi operandi of the nationalist Iraqi insurgents and their ostensible religious Arab allies have caused considerable tensions. In early summer, nationalist insurgents in Fallujah were about to assault a group of foreign jihadists based in the Jolan suburb and who were led by a Saudi with the nom de guerre Abu Abdullah. Later in the summer the insurgent authorities in Fallujah, largely made up of former military personnel and Iraqi police and led by clerics, succeeded in kicking out a number of non-Iraqi terrorists. But this did not resolve the tensions between them and native-born extremists who have the solid backing of a number of Salafi clerics within the city.'

17: S Haddad, 'Iraqi Resistance Distances Itself From Civilian Blood', 7 March 2005, IslamOnline.net. The report states that 'on Sunday 27 February Iraqi resistance fighters decided to withdraw from the city of Al-Hadytha, following the US wide-scale crackdown thereon, to spare civilian lives. [The group] also reaffirmed in the statements that it was out of the question for its members to target civilian foreigners, such as reporters, drivers and relief workers. It also pressed for not attacking Iraqi infrastructure facilities, such as oil pipelines, government institutions and public utilities.'

18: Many resistance groups make their declarations in leaflets distributed at Friday prayers, but other sources include the left wing *Free Arab Voice* which compiles daily reports of resistance attacks and declarations. Report can be found on www.albasra.net

19: Institute for War and Peace Reporting, *Iraqi Crisis Report* no 68, 16 June 2004.

20: A Lijphart, *Democracy in Plural Societies: A Comparative Exploration* (Yale University Press, 1977).

21: A Wimmer, 'Democracy and Ethno-Religious Conflict in Iraq', International Institute of Strategic Studies, *Survival* vol 45, no 4 (Winter 2003-04), p121. See also B O'Leary, 'Multi-Nationalism, Power-Sharing and the Kurds in a New Iraq', Cafritz Foundation Conference Center (George Washington University), 12 September 2003, available online at http://old.krg.org/docs/federalism/federalism-iraqi-kurds-paper-sep03.pdf

22: B O'Leary, as above.

23: One example was Songul Chapuk, who

was appointed to the Governing Council ostensibly as a representative of the Turkoman community. According to *Christian Science Monitor* she was asked to select the minister of science and technology, and chose Rashad Mandan 'at random' from 50 other Turkoman candidates for the post.

24: Interview with Haifa Zanganah, 11 March 2004.

25: Law of Administration for the State of Iraq for the Transitional Period, Coalition Provisional Authority website, 8 March 2004 http://www.iraqcoalition.org/government/TAL.html

26: See W A Terrill, 'Strategic Implications of Intercommunal Warfare in Iraq', February 2005, http://www.carlisle.army.mil/ssi/pdffiles/PUB595.pdf from the Strategic Studies Institute at the US Army War College for a recent US military assessment of the possibility of civil war.

Egypt: the pressures build up

Egypt's ruler, Mubarak, shocked the country at the end of February by suddenly announcing a change in the constitution to allow more than one candidate to stand in this autumn's planned presidential election. There has never been such a multi-candidate election before and only a couple of weeks earlier Mubarak had ruled out any change.

A state of emergency has existed since 1981, when Mubarak became president after the assassination of his predecessor, Sadat. Oppositionists of all sorts are routinely harassed, imprisoned and tortured by the security police. This has applied in recent weeks even to the liberal pro-Western politicians, like Ayman Nour of the Ghad Party who was imprisoned and, he alleges, tortured a few weeks before Mubarak's announcement. And in late January three supporters of the Socialist Research Centre were arrested at the Cairo book fair for selling a book calling for the removal of Mubarak.

The very weekend that Mubarak made his announcement, the Socialist Research Centre organised the first public conference about socialism to take place in Cairo for at least 50 years. Supporters of the centre spoke to Chris Harman, who was one of the speakers, about the political crisis.

The origins of the crisis

There has been a big change in people's attitude to the regime in the last five or six years. Ten years ago there were still some hopes in the Mubarak regime—maybe the peace process in Palestine would work, maybe the economic reforms would improve things. There was still space for such beliefs. In the last five or six years all this has collapsed.

Wide sections of people have become openly opposed to the regime.

There has been rising anger because of price increases. There has also been rising anger due to increasing repression. The latest incident was in the Sinai town Al-Arish after the bombing of the Taba Hilton hotel used by Israeli tourists. There were mass arrests. Thousands of people were arrested and tortured—I think 2,000 are still in jail in terrible conditions—and this has caused a lot of anger.

This is happening at a time of extreme economic stagnation. On top of this there has been an unprecedented level of corruption. Billions of Egyptian pounds have been siphoned off through privatisation and bank loans with all kinds of corrupt deals.

And then Mubarak made it clear that he intended to give himself—or possibly his son—a mandate for another six years. That has magnified the anger.

The new radicalisation

As in other countries, there has been an important political shift in Egypt since the year 2000. First the Palestinian intifada and then the situation in Iraq have created a new wave of politicisation.

What happened with the intifada was very significant and a surprise to many of us. Within a few days of the outbreak of the intifada in September-October 2000 students in the universities began a big wave of more or less spontaneous demonstrations, involving hundreds of thousands, which went on for three or four weeks. This was something unprecedented in Egypt. We haven't seen anything like it in the last 20 years. And again very significant was that school students took part in the demonstrations—perhaps a million school students participated in demonstrations all over Egypt. A new generation was radicalised because of the Palestinian events.

This led to the forming of new solidarity committees involving many disillusioned leftists from the 1970s who had disappeared from the political scene wanting to be part of the movements. The committees attracted hundreds of newcomers.

Then a few months later the preparations for the war against Iraq began and there was a new wave of activity. The most significant demonstration in recent Egyptian history occurred on 20 and 21 March 2002 when the war started. A committee in solidarity with the Iraqi people and against aggression called for people to gather in Al-Tahrir Square, the biggest square in Cairo, on the first day of the war. Perhaps 50,000 people gathered in the square and occupied it for the whole day. The next day they gathered again and there were confrontations with the police. And it attracted not just students, as before, but ordinary people from the city. They were very militant. The demonstration was called against the aggression. But within a few minutes people began focusing their anger against the regime, tearing down the pictures of Mubarak which filled the square and chanting slogans against the regime itself. One of the police chiefs said that without the harsh repression it could have developed into a national riot.

The economy and the crisis of the regime

In May 1991 the regime did a deal with the IMF. In the mid-1990s there was propaganda that this programme was beginning to succeed, with the IMF and the neo-liberal institutions in the world claiming that the government was solving its economic problems, reducing the budget deficit and so on. There was something like a state of ecstasy among government people that they were succeeding in moving towards neo-liberalism.

After two or three years, in 1998, the economic situation worsened. The attempts to increase exports failed completely. The attempts to bring in serious foreign investments failed completely—investment fell significantly. The stagnation began which is still with us now, after seven years. The one thing the government claimed as a success through the 1990s is now seen by many people as a failure. People's practical experience is of unemployment, of being sacked from jobs, of increasing prices. This feeds the political disillusionment with the regime. One significant point was that just a month or two before the US attack on Iraq the government had floated the currency, which led to the rise in prices which still continues.

The government's response over the last year and a half has been to shift to a more radical neo-liberal policy. The failure of its neo-liberal policies has pushed it further towards rapid privatisation, getting rid of all the state banks as fast as possible, reducing subsidies. There is a new team of radical neo-liberals around Gamal Mubarak, the president's son, who are getting into the main positions of power as regards economic policy.

This is creating tension within the ruling party. You have these younger, less experienced people who want to push very rapidly, and you have the older ones who want to keep things as they are. And you have an ailing dictator who is beginning to go senile and who is losing his grip, with the beginnings of struggles over who is going to take over.

So you have a new push on the neo-liberal economic front at the same time as a panicking state security apparatus, subject to contradictory pressures. The most recent incident was that a liberal opposition party was given the right to start activity and then the leader was shoved in jail. So the different sections of the apparatus are not as synchronised as they used to be. And people can see these discrepancies. To take an example, one day the regime put up a huge poster of Mubarak's son shaking hands with an Egyptian Olympic medal winner; the next day they took it down. They are not sure of how to deal with things and everyone on the street talks about these things: why did they put up the poster? why did they take it down?

The popular mood

Our impression is that there is a significant change in the mood among the people. Four or five years ago when you got into discussions with people about what's going on and what they think of the regime, you might find some who were not interested in politics; you might find others saying the regime is good, or that Mubarak is good but those surrounding him are not. Today nine out of ten people will say the reason everything is going wrong in Egypt is Mubarak himself.

For the first time, we are seeing public attacks on Mubarak. One of the opposition newspapers, the Nasserist party newspaper (*Al-Arabi*), focuses only on attacking Mubarak and his son. This has never happened in Egypt in the last 20 years. Sections of the liberal intellectuals are attacking Mubarak. So two months ago one of the high-ranking intellectuals attacked Mubarak at a meeting between Mubarak and some of the intellectuals, and the intellectuals are very proud that this attack happened. So the regime is under attack, not only from below, but from within the higher ranks of the middle class.

One expression of this is the Campaign for Change. It is attracting new people, including some influential people. One of the country's most prominent ex-judges has written an article in the Nasserist newspaper calling upon people 'to organise civil disobedience' against the government.

What is happening may seem small and insignificant. But if you look at it in the context of how the ruling class has operated in Egypt for the last 20 years, you can see the significance of what is going on.

There are two sorts of demonstrations. The spontaneous demonstrations are basically student demonstrations. The organised demonstrations are by smallish numbers of activists. There will be a small number of leftist worker activists on them, but they are not normal working class people, but leftist activists who happen to be workers.

The regime for its own reasons feels compelled to allow demonstrations. But it dare not allow the demonstrations to reach outwards. The only demonstration to reach out beyond the activists to involve wide numbers of people in the city centre was that on the first day of the Iraq war two years ago. It was because that drew in vast numbers of people that the regime has become more intolerant, believing that if it does not contain the demonstrations with vast numbers of police, they can spread, particularly with the anger caused by the increase in prices. People are ready, if they are given the chance, to join such a movement. So the police actions against protests are much bigger than in the past.

To take one small but telling example, we had a small meeting of 15 people in the apartment that serves as the headquarters of the Socialist Research Centre a few weeks ago. Outside there were eight big vehicles, each with 70 or 80 riot police inside, besieging the centre and stopping people coming in. They surround 15 people with a thousand police because they feel if they do not things will explode.

The mood among workers

The way the regime uses repression to stop the protests reaching out to the popular areas makes what is happening on the economic front very important. For this is accelerating changes under the surface. There have been growing protests among the working class. The number of protests in the last six months alone is already equal to a third of what happened in the previous five years. Socialists who are active in working class areas can see that anger is accumulating and that things can explode at any time now.

Economic stagnation means many factories are closing or attacking the benefits of workers. This is mainly happening in the new industrial areas, in the private sector. And then there is the acceleration of privatisation in the last year. The remaining factories in the public sector are being sold and this is causing trouble in these factories. At the moment there are three or four strikes or potential strikes due to privatisation.

One of the important strikes is the asbestos workers' strike. They have been sitting in for more than two months now. Asbestos is a dangerous material causing cancer—many of the workers have cancer. There are no safety measures taken in the factory. It is now prohibited to use asbestos in Egypt. The government allows factory owners who already have asbestos to use it, but has banned further imports, and so the factory is no longer working. Fifty workers are involved in the sit-in.

The most significant strike was by cement workers. Their three-day strike wrecked a deal to sell their factory. It shows what can happen in the near future in response to the government's privatisation drive.

At another factory the owner was a businessman who fled because he could not pay his debts to the banks. The workers organised a sit-in and strike and they kept the factory going under their own management, using the material left in the factory. They had done this for more than two years and then they failed to continue.

The weak point in the struggles is that they do not usually manage to go beyond the individual factory. We are attempting to overcome this through participating in a co-ordinating committee for the defence of workers. It has started to be really active in the past year, drawing together worker leaders from several factories in the industrial areas, and trying to build small committees in these industrial areas so as to become a focal point for the strikes. But it has only had limited successes so far. Generally the movement is still localised and defensive and it is very difficult to build a network of activists or a solidarity movement as long as the dictatorship is intact. There needs to be a change in the political atmosphere to make this possible.

The peasant protests

The peasants tended to be a conservative force after the land reforms of the 1950s not only reduced the maximum size of land holdings, but the government also subsidised the seeds and other inputs necessary for cultivation. These things have been taken from them over the last ten years. Land rents have been liberalised, the rights to inherit tenancies have been taken away, so owners can get rid of tenant peasants completely or increase the rents, and this has recreated a rebellious peasantry that wants the land.

One of us was involved in the 1997 movement and was arrested, and has been active in several peasant struggles in recent months, involving 300 or 400 peasants in various villages.

The process of rent liberalisation was split into stages. The first stage in 1997 involved only tenants on land that was not part of the land reform redistribution. Around 7,000 peasants were arrested and about 100 were killed in clashes with the police. But the movement as a whole was not successful and rents increased dramatically.

What is happening now is the second stage. The old owners are being allowed to take back the land redistributed in the land reform. The issue can potentially be much bigger than in 1997. That involved only one sector of the peasants. Now the issues affect all different kinds of peasants—small landowners, tenants, agricultural labourers and so on. It is part of the wider liberalisation process that involves the state giving up its control over the provision of inputs and buying crops at fixed prices. At the same time, whole villages are in debt, with many peasants running away to avoid having to pay. The new wave of struggle is just beginning to take off. In two villages, the peasants succeeded last month in keeping the land, using arms against the landowners.

The opposition: the Muslim Brotherhood

The Muslim Brotherhood is still the largest opposition. It is estimated to have hundreds of thousand of members, with a very strong presence in all parts of the country. They have played a significant role in the movement for solidarity with Palestine and Iraq. But all the time they are involved in a balancing act with the state. So if the part of the opposition we are connected with organises a demonstration they will say they will take part but will not mobilise for it. They will only mobilise in agreement with the state. For example, during the Gulf War, they organised a joint demonstration with the ruling National Democratic Party. But they were able to bring 100,000 people to that demonstration. So they have an agreement with the state that there are certain lines they will not cross. Despite that the state continues to jail their members, especially the middle and higher ranking cadres. They are in and out of jail. Their student activists are arrested on a regular basis all over the country.

There are signs of tension within the organisation, not only between the older generation—the entourage of the founder, Hassan Bana (who died in 1949) continued to run the organisation until now—and the younger generation, but there are also tensions due to their attempts to hold the movement back. You can see this whenever there is a big potentiality for mobilisation and they refuse to move. This is apparent in their newspaper. There have been lots of articles talking about these tensions—'Why didn't we mobilise for this?'—from younger members; the leadership replying we have to do this in stages, there are external threats on the nation, we should not divide the nation now, and so on.

The higher ranks of the Muslim Brothers are getting more bourgeois, in the sense of accepting totally reformist methods, refusing any mass mobilisation against the state. In our magazine at the time of the Iraq war we asked a leading member of the Muslim Brotherhood to write an article for us. One of the things he wrote clearly that they totally would not accept was revolution or mass public protests, and further that they were in agreement with the state so long as there was an external threat. The higher ranks of the Muslim Brothers have over the last three decades got more and more into mainstream politics.

They see themselves as competing to run the state, something like the Turkish scenario, where the Islamic Party runs a mainstream capitalist government. They think that, if they are respectable enough, they can win things at the end of the day.

In the peasant struggle in 1997 they sided with the state to break up the land reform rules, because of the idea of private property. The strata that are related to them in the countryside are the middle owning peasants. They ignored the solidarity movement with the intifada for a while. There were general elections and they wanted the state to leave them alone. They even criticised the demonstrations led by socialists and Nasserists.

But at the same time, although they are not active and are not against the state, they attract hundreds of thousands of people. We see this as a potential tension that can explode if the class struggle rises, because many of their younger members think that they are an alternative, that they can deliver.

They adopted a tactic in the late 1980s and 1990s of taking over the professional associations and the student unions. They succeeded tremendously in this. They have been losing some ground recently to other forces because of their attitude to the movement of the last two or three years—although they remain much bigger than the others. People see that they are not mobilising, that they are aligned with the state. So the signs are that they are going to lose some of their seats in the election for the Bar Association.

They have a group in parliament which is obsessed with religious issues, like video clips being shown on television, advertisements for alcoholic drinks, books which are too secular or critical of Islam. There were big demonstrations recently by the Coptic Christians. The position of the Muslim Brotherhood paper was terrible, reactionary. One of the articles said, 'We wish we had as many rights as the Christians who were able to have this demonstration without it being smashed.'

At the same time, their group in parliament will put forward demands for legislation of workers' rights and in some cases against privatisation. They are very strong in attacking corruption, and on Palestine and Iraq. They are also very active in running Islamic charity provision for poor people.

On women, on alcohol, on the Copts, they have very hard attitudes. But they mix that with relatively good positions on Palestine, on Iraq, on corruption, against price rises. Their central issue now is ending the emergency laws, the democratic demands, against the press laws. So you get these contradictions.

The Muslim Brotherhood have adapted their position on women to new conditions. They could never talk to the petty bourgeois now and say women should not work—this would make life hard for thousands of people. So they say they are for women going to university, for women working and for women being politically active. They are the organisation with the highest number of women in it. On their demonstrations there are rows of men in the front, then rows of thousands of politically active women in the back. They go round houses during elections talking with women about how to vote. But over the issue of women wearing the veil and of women on television, the issue of morality, they are extremely hard.

They are no longer openly hostile to the left. We do not hide our positions at all on the issues where we disagree with the Muslim Brotherhood, whether it's Copts or whatever. But we cannot refuse to work with them over issues like Palestine or Iraq or the Cairo conference against imperialism, which is due to take place in late March. Other sections of the left hate us for this, saying we are making a mistake. We say we have to work with the Muslim Brotherhood over specific issues.

The more radical Islamist groups have been obliterated physically. The regime has killed off most of their leadership between 1992 and the present. It has jailed 20,000 or 30,000 of them. Most of these are still in jail and the remaining leaders in jail have given up the struggle and have published books explaining how wrong they were to take up arms against the state. The only sections that are still active are the ones that are outside Egypt, that are connected to Osama Bin Laden.

The Nasserists

The other important oppositional force is the Nasserists, who look back to the time in the 1950s and 1960s when Abdel Nasser as president followed an Arab nationalist policy abroad and state capitalism at home, nationalising 85 percent of industry. They argue centrally against the neo-liberal policies and for a harder line against imperialism and Israel. But if they are against privatisation it is because it opens the economy to foreigners. They are for the national capitalists—and a few capitalists back them.

The main opposition newspaper campaigning against Mubarak is the Nasserist paper. And there are several Nasserist figures—writers and so on—who are becoming prominent in the movement against Mubarak. They are not that significant in terms of numbers. They are not much bigger than the left. But because of the history, they have a wider pull—and they have members of parliament and a legal weekly newspaper. In the last two or three months it has sold out within two or three hours of being published.

Their support comes from the middle class, intellectuals, and students. Until now they have not had real roots as an organisational force. But wider sections of people, everyone who wants change in Egypt, who hates the status quo, more and more look to the Nasserists and their newspaper, because they are the most direct and courageous in their attacks on Mubarak. We think that, if the class struggle rises and the political situation changes, they can build influence quickly, because Nasserist ideology has influence. You can hear people say that the situation under Nasser was much better. People put pictures of Nasser up in their houses and shops and so on.

The way ahead

There are two sorts of movements in Egypt at the moment and they move parallel to each other—the political struggles by the activists, and the economic struggles. One of our aims is to find ways to unite the two movements. This means winning the activists to try to organise among the workers and peasants. It also means trying to convince sections of the workers, especially their leaders, that their struggles are totally connected with the political struggle.

As socialists we have been able to participate in many strikes and sit-ins and to involve ourselves in many things. So at the Socialist Research Centre conference this weekend there are workers from two or three factories who we have worked with in the last few months, who are prepared to come and talk about their own grievances and their own struggles.

At the time of the intifada protests there was an attempt to organise a demonstration in a workers' district. Some 30 people began the demonstration and it succeeded in attracting hundreds. This showed the connection between the political aspect and the class anger among workers. Due to our limited numbers and influence we were not able to build on this. But now things are changing. We are more able to intervene politically because of the new developments on the economic front.

Britain after eight years of Blair

Chris Harman

Britain was on the eve of an election as we prepared this issue of the journal. The articles in this section deal with changes that have occurred under New Labour. Most readers will see them a few weeks before voting. Some will not do so until afterwards.

This election is different to the usual pattern in Britain. Over the past 80 years the performance of Labour governments in office has caused greater (1929-31, 1964-70 and 1974-79) or lesser (1945-51) degrees of disillusion among working class voters, allowing the Tories to return to office after six years at the most. This time all forecasters were expecting a third term of Labour when it began its campaign in February, even though the *Guardian*'s Jackie Ashley writes, 'The early weeks of the pre-election campaign appear to have brilliantly cut a Labour lead of seven points to three' (3 March).

Blair's supporters boast he has been prime minister longer than any previous Labour leader. His top collaborator and rival, Gordon Brown, boasts that Britain is leading Europe in the adoption of US-style workforce flexibility and has enjoyed a period of economic and employment growth unparalleled for decades. Certainly the registered jobless figures are far below those of a dozen years ago (although still two or three times the figures of the 1950s and 1960s) and there has been growth in total employment, especially in London and the south east. And until recently take-home pay for most employed workers was just about keeping ahead of price increases.

Yet disillusion with Labour is massive. Everyone expects turnout in the election to be even less than the record low of 59 percent four years ago. The Labour Party's membership has slumped more than at any time in the past, as Charlie Kimber shows in his piece, and for the first time since the First World War some unions have voluntarily disaffiliated from the party. The war against Iraq has played a big part in this. But it is worth remembering that disenchantment with New Labour began in its first term, with Blair and Brown's continuation of the Thatcher-Major path towards what we now call 'neo-liberalism'. It was in the first term that they cut benefits for single parents and disabled people, allowed the head of schools inspection, Chris Woodhead, to launch a vicious ideological onslaught on teachers, pushed ahead with the privatisation of air traffic control and council estates, and joined with Clinton in bombing Belgrade. The disillusionment was already sufficient for the Scottish Socialist Party to do well enough in the only election in Britain then involving proportional representation to win a seat in the Scottish Parliament in 1999, and socialists in England to pick up respectable, if modest, votes in the Greater London election of 2000 and the general election of 2001. The disillusionment fed the forces of the far right, with the Nazi British National Party beginning to win council seats after racist riots they provoked in the decaying former textile towns of the north west and West Yorkshire, so emerging from the extreme margin of political life.

It is against this background that the rise of the anti-war movement after 11 September 2001 is so important. The 50,000 and 100,000 strong demonstrations against the Afghan war in October and November 2001 were the first real expression in Britain of the anti-capitalist feeling that burst onto the world scene at Seattle two years before. They laid the ground for the biggest anti-war movement Britain has ever seen, with four demonstrations in the 300,000 to 500,000 range (September 2002, March, April and November 2003) and one, on 15 February 2003, of up to 2 million. The demonstrations since against the occupation of Iraq have varied in size, and so far have come nowhere near matching 15 February. But the movement against the war has by no means gone away, as has been shown by big rallies in London suburbs and in provincial towns, and by two demonstrations in 2004 in the 60,000 to 100,000 range (big by the standards of any protest in Britain in the last century, except for those of 2002-03). Another demonstration is due as this journal is being printed.

But it has not only been the demonstrations that have expressed hostility to the war. The anti-war movement has been the spearhead of a radicalisation over other issues. There is now a level of politics among students in some universities, like LSE, SOAS and UCL, which has not been matched since the mid-1970s. There are also signs of that mood spreading to other places as the school students who took part in the walkouts the day the war started move into higher education. And in the unions, the war has provided the issue above all which has focused hostility of activists against New Labour. There too the hostility was already growing during Labour's first term, with the unexpected victory of anti-Blair candidates in a number of small unions, especially the train drivers' union ASLEF. But it has been during the last four years that the left has won victories in major unions like the civil servants' PCS, the rail workers' RMT, the postal and telecom workers' CWU and the newly created Amicus, leading to a lot of media talk of an 'awkward squad' of union leaders with influence on the Trades Union Congress. The biggest sign of the change of mood in the unions was when the 2002 TUC conference voted against the war—although vacillation by key union leaders allowed the Labour leadership to avoid defeat (or even a proper debate) over the issue at the party's conferences in 2002, 2003 and 2004.

The growth of a new anti-capitalist left in the anti-war movement and the unions has not yet been matched by any general upsurge of industrial struggle. At least three factors are important in explaining this.

The first is that the election of the 'awkward squad' union leaders has not broken the tendency of the union bureaucracy to vacillate and retreat once major confrontation becomes possible. This was shown in the one long-running national dispute to occur in either of New Labour's terms, that in the fire service in 2002-03. The union's newly elected 'awkward squad' general secretary, Andy Gilchrist, waged an exemplary campaign through the summer of 2002 to persuade firefighters that they should struggle over pay, creating a momentum for action not known in the union for a quarter of a century. But he then restricted the dispute to a series of short strikes, before calling it off out of fear of seeming to damage the war effort (even though Gilchrist himself was a public opponent of the war). Instead of breaking the long spell of demoralisation prevalent in the trade union movement since the bitter defeats of the miners and print workers in the mid-1980s, the fire dispute served to prolong it—although a very successful unofficial strike of postal workers in November 2003 showed how militancy can achieve quick victories.

The second factor has been the way the restructuring of British capitalism has led to wave after wave of factory closures and a haemorrhaging of jobs in sections of industry where rank and file trade union activism expressed through shop steward organisation was once strongest. Jane Hardy's article provides a thorough breakdown of what has happened. The overall result is that there are now fewer than half the numbers of workers in manufacturing than during the last great advance of class struggle in the early 1970s, while the number of miners has fallen from 246,000 to 6,000 since then. The industries with traditions of militancy that once countered the backsliding and cowardice of the trade union bureaucracy have been decimated.

Thirdly, New Labour itself has usually been able to avoid measures that would provoke industrial action—or at least industrial action that goes beyond one-day protests. Important here has been its approach to pay. In the 1960s and 1970s both Labour and Conservative governments provoked anger among sections of workers with few or no previous traditions of struggle by incomes policies that held wages down at a time of rising prices. After initial successes, these provoked massive rebellions both from groups of workers with militant traditions and from new groups of workers without any such traditions. So, we saw the wave of unofficial strikes in the car industry, clothing, glassmaking, buses and elsewhere in 1969-70, the successful miners' strikes in 1972 and 1974 and then the 'winter of discontent' in 1979.

Blair's governments, by contrast, have followed the pattern set by Thatcher and Major of relying on a combination of the 'market' (with historically high levels of unemployment) and anti-union laws to keep the unions in check while the wages of most workers just about keep ahead of inflation. At no point have real wages been slashed, as they were at least temporarily during the 1964-70 and 1974-79 Labour governments. The attacks which have taken place have involved job losses through the restructuring of industry, increased pressure for people to work harder and longer, the subjection of public sector employees to 'market testing' and cuts in certain welfare benefits. They have created a deep, growing bitterness among very wide sections of workers, which will explode at some point. But they have not yet provoked sustained mass industrial action.

This has led commentators on both the right and the left to see class as declining in importance. Yet the reality is very different. The distribution of income and wealth has continued during New Labour's years to follow the trend of the Thatcher-Major years of moving in favour of capital. Gordon Brown's supposed 'redistributive' measures in favour of the poor have only touched a small portion of the massive increases in the incomes of the rich, but have, through measures like university fees, the council tax, insurance tax and so on, hit harder the slightly better paid sections of the working class (skilled manual workers, teachers and so on). The realities of class for the 70 to 75 percent of the population still in manual or middle-to-low grade white collar jobs is unchanged, as Jacob Middleton shows in detail. This divide finds vivid expression in the geography of cities, as Alex Law and Gerry Mooney show. And New Labour's vision of the educational system is based on reproducing the existing class divisions through shaping children to fit into capital's continuing, if changing, demand for labour power. Terry Wrigley's article shows how this is happening.

However, there is a widespread pessimism about the capacity of workers to struggle, even among those who accept the reality of class. This is to be found within the anti-capitalist movement, where there is a prevalence of 'autonomist' notions that see change as taking place through a spontaneous coming together of different sectionalised and localised movements, with no need to find a strategic axis in workplace struggles. It is also to be found within trade union structures and among their academic advisers, with the claim that there is little likelihood of any return of trade union strength unless somehow a government is persuaded to increase workers' rights to organise and strike without the threat of the sack. The debate between Martin Smith from the Socialist Workers Party and Gregor Gall in our last issue was essentially over this argument.

Here the findings of Jane Hardy's article are very important. She shows that restructuring has not just included the contraction of employment in much of manufacturing industry and mining. It has also involved the maintenance of absolute production levels in important parts of manufacturing and the growth in size and importance of new sectors of the economy just as important for capitalism as manufacturing and mining ever were. Such developments are ignored in much of the fashionable talk about 'deindustrialisation' and 'post-Fordism'.

Yet these help explain the limited revival of industrial militancy we have seen in certain industries. Postal services and urban transport, for instance, are even more important for capitalism today than they used to be. It has to be able to send and receive business documents (and for that matter to get to people's homes the things they buy through the internet), and it has to be able to get vast numbers of workers to and from their places of employment each day (something made more difficult by two decades of low investment in public transport). It's not surprising therefore that these are two sections of workers who have displayed much greater militancy than in the past, and provided an antidote to the 1980s-type demoralisation still afflicting activists in many other sectors.

The path taken by groups like the postal workers and London tube workers today can be that taken by workers in other expanding sectors in the future. Union organisation is weak or non-existent in many of them. But this was once true of what we now think of as the traditionally strong sectors.

There have been recurrent waves of restructuring of British capitalism over the last 150 years. Each has involved the relative decline of some established sectors and the rise of new ones. Along with this went, at each stage, a shift in the centres of organisation and militancy within the working class. So textiles predominated in the first phase of the industrial revolution, and its workers played a predominant role in the greatest industrial struggle of the Chartist period, the general strike in the North West in 1842. After a lull of nearly half a century, the next great wave of struggle was focused on the very different industries that had grown in the interim, like match manufacture, gasworks, chemicals and the docks. Twenty years later it was the turn of the railways and the mines to show unprecedented militancy. Then from the 1930s to the early 1970s the growth industries were motors and light engineering, and it was with militancy and unofficial shopfloor organisation in these sectors that British capitalism was so concerned that the government set up a royal commission under a senior judge, Donovan, into industrial relations in 1968.

Union strength and class consciousness did not simply grow gradually with the development of new sectors of industry in such cases. They lagged behind the expansion of these sectors, sometimes by decades, as the majority of workers showed little inclination to struggle against employers who used intimidation and victimisation against the minority who tried to organise. Established activists were often dismissive of the new groups of workers, whose lifestyles were often different to those of older sections and who lacked their traditions of solidarity—and middle class experts concurred in judging them not to be real workers. So before the great wave of organising that occurred after 1889, the burgeoning unskilled workforce in London was dismissed as 'feckless' and 'undisciplinable', while in the early 1960s there was a serious academic debate about whether the rapidly growing numbers of workers in the motor industry were 'bourgeoisified'.

Yet each successive new group did in the end become organised. This rarely happened though the routine methods of normal trade unionism. Instead it depended upon some issue causing some group in one of the new sectors to enter into struggle and suddenly discover its power to shake the employers and win gains. Its example then inspired others to militancy of their own.

So it was with the match workers and dockers in the late 1880s, the railwaymen, dockers and miners in 1910-14, those who built trade unionism in the car and aircraft industries in the 1930s and with the spread of militant trade unionism to white collar workers in the public sector with strikes of teachers, civil servants, hospital and local authority workers in the 1970s.

There was a greater or lesser degree of spontaneity to all these cases. There had to be, since it is not until a group of workers takes action that it sees how strong it is. But something else was always involved—a body of activists both inside and outside the industry prepared to take the effort and initiative and shoulder the risks involved in encouraging such action. So the 'new unionism' of the late 1880s depended, in part, on outside activists like Annie Besant, Eleanor Marx, Tom Mann and John Burns. So the socialist revival of three or four years earlier with the foundation of the Social Democratic Federation and the Socialist League was a key element in the upsurge. In a similar way, networks of militant syndicalists (again including Tom Mann) were very important in laying the ground for the Great Unrest in the years before the First World War, and Communist Party activists were central to the spread of union organisation into motors, the aircraft industry and light engineering from the 1930s onwards.

Jane Hardy's article points to the growing sectors today where conditions, payments systems and managerial bullying operate along essentially the same lines as has been normal in manufacturing and mining, suggesting that 'global Fordism' is a better name for the present stage of capitalism than 'post-Fordism'. And it shows that these sectors are of strategic importance for British capitalism. Jacob Middleton's article shows how poorly paid many of the workers in these sectors are. Finance, for instance, is not mainly stockbrokers and market makers. It is routine office workers, mostly women, and large numbers of cleaners and maintenance workers, many new immigrants or from ethnic minorities. Such workers can get organised and show their class power—and at some point they will do so. But the process will require new networks of activists to take the initiative and the risks. It was not established national union leaders who initiated the struggles of the late 1880s, 1910-14, the 1930s or the 1970s—although some lower ranking officials seized the opportunity to expand their influence by identifying with the struggles. Left to themselves most national union officials are unlikely to spearhead the organisation of the unorganised in the expanding sectors in the years ahead. A new layer of socialist activists is required to relate to the newly expanding sections of the working class and to make older sections aware that they have strength if they care to use it.

This is where the politics of what has been happening becomes so important. The demoralisation caused by Labour in office can go in two directions. Previous Labour governments created a cynicism which ate into traditions of class solidarity and provided an opening for right wing forces to gain an influence in some working class areas. Labourism historically held the organised sectors of the working class together as well as holding them back, and its erosion has always made it easier for reactionary and racist moods to spread—particularly as Labour politicians try to protect their voting base by pandering to these moods. The way in which hysteria over asylum seekers and 'anti-social behaviour' has affected wide layers of people in recent months is a sign of how quickly the poison can work. But the disillusion can also open the way the creation of new left networks in workplaces and localities. The impact of the anti-capitalist movement since Seattle, and especially the anti-war movement, has been to provide a national focus to the left, able to inspire and draw together those wanting an alternative.

But the focus needs to be sharper. There are attempts by Britain's traditional second capitalist party, the Liberal Democrats, to exploit the anti-war feeling for their own ends (which include a sharp move towards neo-liberalism in economic policies), and mere cynicism with New Labour's lies over the war can even help the Tories, the right wing populists of the UK Independence Party and the Nazis. This is what makes the

Respect coalition (along with the SSP in Scotland) so important. It has enabled revolutionary socialists to work together with wide numbers of anti-war activists, disillusioned former Labour stalwarts and Muslim activists to provide a strong focus to the left. We do not dare predict how it will do in the general election, but it did manage to get 10 percent and more votes in several inner city areas in the European and London elections last June, and has done well since in parliamentary by-elections in the Midlands and council by-elections in east London (getting more votes than New Labour in two cases). For these reasons, it hopes to give New Labour at least a couple of shocks.

But Respect's real importance lies in preparing the ground for what happens after the election. British capitalism has enjoyed a great deal of luck over the last decade. Its enforced departure from the European Exchange Rate Mechanism under the Major government had the by-product of insulating it from the stagnation that has afflicted the biggest European economy, Germany, while it benefited from the American boom (and bubble) of the late 1990s. This has been particularly true of its financial sector in the City of London—hence the upsurge in employment in the south east. But it has not solved important underlying problems. Working hours may be longer than those in continental Europe, as Jacob Middleton shows, but they are still substantially shorter than those of the US. And UK productivity levels per hour are nearly 20 percent behind those of both Europe and the US. This creates a lag in competitiveness, expressed in big trade deficits and the dependence of continued economic growth on increased levels of private indebtedness.

The British economy today accounts for a relatively small part of the world system, with about 5 percent of world trade, as Jane Hardy shows. It is a smallish boat in a big expanse of water. This has enabled it, accidentally, to find havens to shelter in as the two great storms in the world economy over the last eight years hit—the Asian crisis and the US recession. But it may not be nearly so lucky when the next wave of crisis sweeps the globe, for instance if an ending of the Chinese boom bursts the new economic bubble in the US.

It has only one way to prepare for such dangers. That is to press ahead with more neo-liberal measures designed to increase 'flexibility' and, especially, to cut its costs by further trimming what it sees as unnecessary expenditure. And that is not possible without confronting large sections of employed workers over key matters at some point. Such is the logic behind New Labour's decision to push ahead with attacks on the pension entitlements in the public sector in the run-up to the election. In the process it is stirring some of the least militant groups of workers to protest, as has been shown by mass yes votes in the unions over calls for one-day strikes in late March and early April. Again, we do not know at the time of writing whether these strikes will actually take place. What we do know is that underlying pressures pushing to a revival of class struggle in Britain will break through in an unexpected way at some point, and that we have to build networks of activists to face up to them. The anti-war movement has helped to create such networks. Respect's electoral campaign can help further.

The changing structure of the British economy

Jane Hardy

Capitalism, according to Marx's analysis, is a dynamic system subject to continually changing forms. We bear witness to the 'permanently revolutionary' character of the system every day as it transforms, in some cases dramatically, all aspects of our lives: where we work and organise, our access to welfare services and pensions, how and where we spend our leisure time.

This is very much in evidence close to where I live and work in Hatfield. British Aerospace (formerly de Havilland) dominated the landscape in the post-war period, physically and in terms of the jobs and education on offer. Ten years after its closure in the early 1990s the British Aerospace buildings have been demolished and replaced with shiny new buildings which include gargantuan warehouses, a complex of six buildings owned by T-Mobile, the Ocado internet food order firm and a Royal Mail parcel depot. In 1998 *Saving Private Ryan* was filmed on the old airstrip. One of the biggest employers is the local university which was originally designed to train aerospace engineers, but now has a 'state of the art' new campus on the old British Aerospace site. It raises a huge amount of revenue from the large number of overseas students who pay exorbitant fees. Across the road is a giant shopping centre with a cinema (showing exactly the same films as the other three multiplexes within a ten mile radius), bars and fast food restaurants. Many of the shops in Hatfield town centre are either boarded up or charity shops. When Wal-Mart bought Asda and closed it for 'refurbishment' in 2002 the nearest place to buy food was three miles away.

Academics have seized upon such changes under the banner of the 'new economy' to suggest that we are living in an entirely new phase of capitalism. We were told in the mid-1970s that we were moving into a post-Fordist phase, with the end of mass production, flexible employment and apparently more satisfying work. A report from the Work Foundation proclaimed the advent of the 'weightless economy' in 2002,[1] where 'creating value depends less and less on physical mass, and more and more on intangibles such as human intelligence, creativity and even personal warmth'. Hardt and Negri have jumped on this bandwagon by suggesting that we live in a 'post-industrial economy, an informational economy'.[2]

Will Hutton argues that mass production in the UK is dead and that there is a new global division of labour. Production will move to China and other parts of South East Asia, while Britain concentrates on goods that 'are tailored, customised, niche products, exploiting research; in other words knowledge goods'.[3] New Labour has tried to sell the 'creative industries' as a panacea for the UK economy. In the same vein the terrain of academic discussion has shifted to an obsession with the knowledge economy, innovation, networked economies[4] and clusters.[5]

Others with a more critical perspective who have distanced themselves from overtly corporate agendas have emphasised the role of finance as a malign influence on British growth and productivity, and in some cases it has been elevated to a new phase of capitalism. Boyer and Aglietta talk about finance-led capitalism as a new epoch. Others talk about financialisation as a fundamental change driving the restructuring of the system.[6]

Taken together all these claims about 'weightlessness', 'knowledge economies' and 'creativity' are used to suggest that the working class has disappeared.

'The present society is no solid crystal, but an organism capable of change, and constantly engaged in processes of change.' So writes Marx in

Table 1: Changing structure of industry

Source: A Griffiths and A Wall, *Applied Economics: An Introductory Course*, tenth edition (London, 2004), p6

(All figures are percentages)	1964	1969	1973	1979	1990	2001
Primary	**5.8**	**4.3**	**4.2**	**6.9**	**3.9**	**3.9**
Agriculture, forestry and fishing	1.9	1.8	2.9	2.2	1.8	1.0
Mining and quarrying	3.9	2.5	1.1	4.5	2.1	2.9
Manufacturing	**40.8**	**42.0**	**40.9**	**36.7**	**31.5**	**24.8**
Manufacturing	30.0	31.2	30.4	27.9	22.5	17.6
Construction	8.4	8.4	7.3	6.2	6.9	5.4
Electricity, gas and water	2.4	2.4	2.8	2.6	2.1	1.8
Tertiary	**53.8**	**53.0**	**54.9**	**56.5**	**64.4**	**71.3**
Distribution, hotels and catering	14.0	13.3	13.1	12.7	13.5	15.6
Transport, storage, post & telecommunications	6.0	6.3	7.0	7.3	7.6	8.0
Financial intermediation, real estate, Renting and business activities (including ownership of dwellings)	13.7	14.1	17.7	18.3	22.6	24.7
Public administration, national defence and social security	7.6	7.0	6.1	6.1	6.3	4.8
Education, health and social work	6.9	7.1	7.7	8.1	8.9	13.0
Other services	5.6	5.2	5.1	5.7	5.5	5.2

Table 2: Workforce jobs by industry in the UK, 2004

Source: *UK 2005: The Official Yearbook of the United Kingdom of Great Britain and Northern Ireland* (Office for National Statistics, 2005), p147

	Jobs (thousands)	Jobs (percent)	Percentage change 1984-2004
Agriculture and fishing	420	1.4	-36.5
Energy and water	203	0.7	-64.3
Manufacturing	3,654	12.1	-32.4
Construction	2,111	7.0	+15.5
Services	23,939	78.9	+37.6
Of which:			
Distribution, hotels and catering	7,040	23.2	+25.3
Transport and communication	1,813	6.0	+13.5
Finance and business services	5,828	19.2	+80.0
Public administration Education, health	7,362	24.3	+28.3
Other services	1,893	6.2	+57.3

his preface to *Capital*. We have to concentrate not simply on the form that capitalism takes but on its underlying driving forces if we are to understand its complexities and contradictions and how these are manifested in concrete phenomena. As David Harvey puts it:

> The geographical landscape of capitalist activity is riddled with contradictions and tensions and it is perpetually unstable in the face of all manner of technical and economic pressures operating upon it. These...all arise out of the molecular processes of endless capitalism in time and space. And these tensions are caught up in the general expansionary logic of a capitalist system in which the endless accumulation of capital and the never ending search for profits dominates... Capitalism perpetually seeks to create a geographical landscape to facilitate its activities at one point in time only to have to destroy it and build a wholly different landscape at a later point in time to accommodate its perpetual thirst for endless capital accumulation.[8]

This article tries to capture some of the changes which are shaping the structure of UK capitalism as it responds to its insertion into the world economy and place in the global division of labour.

Changes in the structure of production in the UK

The most outstanding trend between 1964 and 2001 (shown in Table 1) is the falling share of total production of the secondary sector, especially manufacturing, and the increase in the tertiary sector, especially finance. By 2001 manufacturing in the UK accounted for only 17.6 percent of output, while the financial sector's output had grown to make it the largest sector of production with 24.7 percent of total output.

By 2004 only 12.1 percent of workers were employed in manufacturing, with their numbers having fallen by 32 percent in 20 years. Finance and business services employment grew by 80 percent over the same period, until they accounted for 19 percent of workers (see Table 2).

Such figures provide a broad sketch of the changes taking place, but exaggerate them. As Harman points out, some of the shift from the 'industry' to the 'service' sector amounts to no more than a change in name for essentially similar jobs.[9]

> Someone who works in a factory putting food in a tin so that people can

> warm it up to eat at home is a 'manufacturing worker'; someone who toils in a fast food shop to provide near-identical food to people who do not have time to warm it up at home is a 'service worker'.[10]

This distinction between the sectors has been further blurred by the way many manufacturing firms have responded to competition by transforming themselves into service or part-service firms. For example, a large part of Xerox's activity is now in servicing as well as making and selling office equipment, and Volvo not only make buses but design local transport systems. The outsourcing of cleaning, computer programming, transport and a whole range of other functions which used to be carried out in-house inflates the scale of the shift from 'manufacturing'.

What is more, the concepts of 'tertiary' and 'services' lump together activities that play different roles in capitalist economies.[11] Some of them produce commodities just as much as does manufacturing, with which they are intertwined. As Marx saw it, anything that results from the use of capital and generates surplus value is a commodity. This would include marketed services such as airports, gyms and entertainment, and all those activities that aid the production of commodities such as cleaning and computer programming. Commodities have to be moved from their point of production to their final destination for consumption and these physical movements are also part of the material production process.

However, British capitalism has faced a more rapid fall in manufacturing than other advanced economies, even if conventional measures of economic activity overestimate the shift to the so called service sector.

The long term decline of British manufacturing

The relative economic decline of Britain, and manufacturing in particular, has been long in the making. Britain for much of the 19th century was the most advanced capitalist power. But the monopolistic stranglehold exerted on certain industries through the captive market of the colonies bred complacency and low rates of investment. The British ruling class had an inflated sense of its importance and delusions of grandeur which were increasingly disproportionate to its economic power by the middle of the 20th century. However, by the 1960s this spiral of relative decline was clearly evident. The growth in GDP in the UK between 1950 and 1973 was only 2.5 percent compared with 4.9 percent in Germany and 8 percent in Japan. Industrial employment fell by 14.8 percent in the UK between 1964 and 1979, while continuing to grow in certain other major economies (see Table 3). The rate of capital investment in machinery and factories was well below that of Japan or of other European countries. This had a cumulative impact and was reflected in an enormous productivity gap between the UK and other major centres of capital.

In the early 1970s Britain's final admission to the Common Market exposed inefficient capitals to ferocious competition, a situation compounded by the recession of the mid-1970s, and the state had to bail out British Leyland, shipbuilding and British Steel to slow down their decline. The recession of the early 1980s resulted in a serious bloodletting as inefficient firms went bankrupt, and there was a loss of nearly 19 percent of manufacturing jobs in four years.

Table 3: Changes in industrial employment in selected countries

Source: A Griffiths and A Wall, *Applied Economics: An Introductory Course*, tenth edition (London, 2004), p9

	1964-79	1979-83	1983-2001
UK	-14.8%	-18.9%	-10.4%
US	+27.2	-8.7	+6.7
Canada	+35.7	-8.7	+21.1
Japan	+28.3	+4.1	-1.9
Belgium	-18.6	-15.2	-13.4
France	+2.3	-7.4	-19.6
Germany	-10.6	-8.5	+11.4
Sweden	-10.9	-7.1	-20.2

The Single European Market in 1992 was a strategy of the European ruling class to restore the competitiveness of their economies in face of competition from the US and Japan. The reduction of barriers between countries meant that capital (but not workers) had free rein. This opened up to competition a whole tranche of industries such as telecoms, utilities and public contracts that had previously been protected by capitalist states and led to a massive restructuring of capital with unprecedented mergers and acquisitions on an international scale. US and Japanese capital sought to gain a foothold in fortress Europe, and a spate of national and European mergers were aimed at breeding and protecting European and national champions.

The recovery from the deep recession of the early 1980s was again highly uneven between countries. Between 1983 and 2001 the UK, France

Table 4: Leading exporters and importers in world merchandise trade

Source: *International Trade Statistics 2003* (WTO, 2003), p21

Rank	Exporters	Share %	Rank	Importers	Share %
1	US	17.4	1	US	13.3
2	Germany	7.8	2	Germany	9.6
3	Japan	6.3	3	UK	6.9
4	France	5.5	4	Japan	6.6
5	China	4.1	5	France	4.4
6	UK	4.0	6	China	4.0
7	Canada	3.8	7	Italy	3.6
8	Italy	3.4	8	Canada	3.0
9	Netherlands	2.9	9	Netherlands	2.7
10	Belgium	2.5	10	Hong Kong	2.6

Table 5: Gross value added in manufacturing, UK, 2003

Source: *United Kingdom National Accounts 2004: The Blue Book* (Office for National Statistics), p422

Standard Industrial Classification (SIC) category	% contribution	Rank
Food, drink and tobacco	14.5	1
Textiles, leather and clothing		
Textile and textile products	3.6	10
Leather and leather products	0.4	13
Wood and wood products	1.7	12
Paper and paper products; publishing and printing	13.3	2
Coke, refined petroleum products and nuclear fuel	2.0	5
Chemicals, chemical products and man-made fibres	10.1	5
Rubber and plastic products	5.2	8
Other non-metallic mineral products	3.6	10
Basic metals and fabricated metal products	10.0	6
Engineering and allied industries		
Other machinery and equipment	7.9	7
Electrical and optical equipment	11.0	4
Transport equipment	11.9	3
Other manufacturing	4.9	9

and Belgium underwent a contraction in their manufacturing bases. Germany,[12] Canada and the US had increases in industrial employment. Although the UK faced a further decline of 10.4 percent, it was less than that of France and Belgium. This can probably be accounted for by a sharp increase in UK productivity from an intensification of work. But the increase in competitiveness was insufficient to stave off a further haemorrhaging of manufacturing jobs under Labour as well as the Tories. Some 575,000 more manufacturing jobs were lost in the UK between 1997 and 2002—a fall of a further 18.6 percent.[13]

Contrary to Hutton's thesis that manufacturing jobs in Europe are being moved out to China and South East Asia, employment in Europe actually increased. According to the EU Commission employment in manufacturing went up by over 500,000 in Spain between 1997 and 2002, by over 400,000 in Italy, by nearly 120,000 in Germany, and by nearly 150,000 in France.[14] Although definitions of 'high tech' are problematic and arbitrary, the loss of UK jobs in this sector suggests Hutton's thesis of a knowledge economy may amount to little more than wishful thinking.

Real production still matters

The decline of industrial production in Britain has been greater than in other advanced capitalist economies. However, the picture of the collapse of manufacturing is simply a nonsense. Britain is still a significant exporter of goods, being ranked sixth in the global economy, with almost the same world share of exports as China, despite the popular notion that China is now the workshop of the world (see Table 4). To use a football analogy, it has fallen down the Premier League, but has not been relegated to the First Division.

There are significant variations as regards the profitability and dynamics of the different sectors of British manufacturing industry.

By far the biggest contributor to total production is the food and drinks industry, which is dominated by large transnational firms such as Nestlé and Unilever.[15] However, the industries which are hailed as the 'jewels in the crown' of British capitalism are car production, defence and pharmaceuticals (see Table 5).

Car production is expanding and competitive, despite the end of car assembly by Ford at Dagenham and Luton in 2002, and of Jaguar production in Coventry in 2004. The UK produced 1.7 million cars in 2004, which is the highest number for 30 years.[16] This is despite the significant relocation of auto production to Poland, the Czech Republic and Slovakia. The car industry has undergone massive restructuring and is dominated by foreign capital. There has been a clearout of inefficient capitals, usually the established older sites, in favour of greenfield production in new locations largely based on Japanese capital. Nissan in Sunderland and Toyota in Burnaston (West Midlands) are the most efficient car plants in Europe.[17]

The pharmaceutical industry is hailed as one of the great success stories of British capitalism, with two British firms, GlaxoSmithKline and Astrazeneca, occupying second and third place in the global league table of companies. The industry employs 83,000 people with about 250,000 in downstream related sectors, and fits with the image of the UK as doing 'high-tech' production based on innovation. Smallish biotechnology firms have come to be seen as the panacea for restoring competitiveness and comparative advantage in the high-tech sector. However, these are gobbled up by large pharmaceutical companies as soon as they make any (potentially) profitable discoveries, and quickly absorbed into the accumulation and competition strategies of the mega global firms. 83 percent of jobs in pharmaceuticals are involved in research. Government and bosses give this as a glowing example of 'high-tech', 'knowledge-based', 'research-oriented' jobs which are part of the 'new economy'. It rings all the right bells. However, science and research workers are subject to all of the same pressures as other workers. There have been rounds of redundancies as firms close or merge. Work is intensified and the plug pulled on projects as these giant firms look for the next money-spinning drug.[18]

The UK has one of largest defence manufacturing sectors in the Western world, producing minor and major weapons of destruction. Big firms such as British Aerospace and Rolls-Royce are no longer workshops of the Ministry of Defence.[19] They have moved from being manufacturing companies in the traditional sense to being assemblers of the components of subcontractors. In the process of this 'hollowing out' defence firms, BAe being a good example, have got rid of substantial numbers of workers and productive capacity.[20] Despite claiming to be global firms these companies are firmly tied to the national (or European in the case of Airbus) base, relying on the state as a major customer and to secure orders with other governments. Furthermore, defence firms rely on huge subsidies in the form of export guarantees to underwrite any deal.

Deeply enmeshed in the global economy

One legacy of imperialism is that Britain has been more enmeshed in the world economy than its competitors in terms of finance, trade and the internationalisation of capital. Table 6 shows that outflows of capital have been a major way for the British ruling class to deal with falling profits in the home economy and find new profitable outlets for capital.

Britain remains the recipient of the largest inflows of foreign capital in Europe. Outflows of capital are even more significant. It is by a wide margin the largest foreign investor in other economies in Europe, second only to the US. This explains the pro free market stance of the British ruling class, whose strategy and flow of profits is highly dependent on the opening up of new markets through the WTO or individual diplomacy. Witness the plane-loads of executives from large British firms and British civil servants that accompany politicians on overseas visits.

'Cathedrals in the desert': global outposts of foreign capital: A distinctive feature of British capitalism has been to cultivate itself as a low-cost site with 'flexible labour' for foreign firms, especially Korean and Japanese, jockeying for position within the European Union. Foreign-owned firms accounted for nearly 50 percent of manufacturing investment in the North East and 30 percent for the country as a whole between 1998 and 2001.[21] New Labour have followed the path of the Tories and have worked with their acolytes in the big business of regional regeneration to pump huge amounts of money into attracting foreign capital, despite the rhetoric of the market and competition. These firms have often had little impact on local economies. They are like 'cathedrals in the desert', largely screwdriver plants undertaking simple assembly operations. A *Financial Times* survey in 2003 reported that half of the £750 million of grants offered to 50 regional aid projects over the previous decade went to 16 companies which had either closed or fallen a long way short of job creation targets. In Scotland, Wales and the north east between 2000 and 2004 12,390 jobs were lost in the electronics industry as firms such as Motorola, Panasonic, Eriksson and Samsung, among many others, closed down or relocated elsewhere.[22] There were, however, a few exceptions outside the electronics sector, most notably the Nissan plant built in 1984 which employs 5,000 people.[23]

The finance sector: prophets, falling profits and swindlers

The number of people working in finance increased by 80 percent between 1984 and 2004, until finance and business activities accounted for nearly 25 percent of total output. We need to explain not only the enormous expansion of this sector, but its impact on and relationship with the real economy.

Circulating surplus value: Marx argued that credit plays a dual role in capitalist economies—that of a prophet and that of a swindler. As a prophet, credit ushers in new technologies, new industries and new forms of production. It brings together those capitalists that do not have an immediate outlet for their profits and those with an idea for productive investment but no capital. Financial capital acts as a sort of lubricant for the redistribution of surplus value created in the process of production.

Firms used to finance mergers and acquisitions mainly from their own funds or in conjunction with merchant banks. However, the massive mergers and acquisitions of the last 20 years would not have been be possible without syndicates of financial institutions or leveraged buyouts to underpin them. They have provided the means for capital constantly to restructure itself and survive in the face of competition and falling profit rates. The credit system makes capital more mobile geographically, allowing capitalists to shift from one sector to another and expand to other parts of the world. Marx could not have foreseen the mega-mergers of the last 15 years, but he was very prophetic in anticipating the role of finance in restructuring capitalism through the concentration and centralisation of firms:

> The credit system in its first stages furtively creeps in as the humble assistant of accumulation, drawing into the hands of individuals or associated capitalists, by invisible threads, the money resources which lie scattered over the surface of society in larger or smaller amount; but it soon becomes a new and terrible weapon in the battle for competition and its finally transformed into an enormous social mechanism for the centralisation of capitals.[24]

The massive 'money resources' that buy-out companies are now able to muster are financing increasingly large mergers and acquisitions. Big private equity groups are becoming big players in increasing the concentration in various sectors as they raise ever larger funds.

Financialisation: The financial system is critical to the dynamics of capital accumulation, but finance capital also embraces a vast range of unproductive activities which are simply a way of making more money, are purely speculative and have nothing whatsoever to do with facilitating investment in productive activities. However, finance and financial institutions have deep impacts on the overall dynamics of capital accumulation.

'Financialisation' and 'shareholder value' are the new buzz words. In short they mean that firms are increasingly driven to make short term, high profits to keep shareholders happy. This has become an important tool in disciplining capital and punishing firms that are not delivering a high enough rate of return. Share prices fall in firms which are not making enough profits, making them vulnerable to hostile takeovers by leaner, fitter firms. Firms try to rescue their falling shareholder values and profitability by downsizing and getting rid of their less profitable operations or through an endless series of financial dodges, ranging from raiding pension funds to the massive fraud of companies like Enron.

We are not in a new epoch of financial capitalism as some have suggested. However, financial markets now play an important role in accelerating the restructuring of capitalism by exposing firms with lower returns to the hostile predations of stronger capitals. This trend is much more pronounced in the UK and US than in other capitalist economies.

The growth of financial products: One reason for the growth of the finance and commercial sector that has been given little attention is the proliferation of so called 'financial products'. This is a swindle that workers face every day. Banks and building societies try and entice customers with a bewildering array of savings products, loans and insurance to deal with every eventuality. A new departure is that the non-financial sector has also jumped on the bandwagon to offer a panoply of store cards, loans and insurance. Leaflets at the Tesco checkout advertise everything from holiday insurance to pensions. Water and gas providers try to persuade people of the dire consequences of not taking out monthly insurance. Many of these activities are unnecessary, costly and play on the fears of workers, but they generate a whole new sphere of economic activity and employment, and are an outlet for capital in some parts of the real goods sector when profits levels are low or negative. Financial services provided 80 percent of profits for General Motors and 26 percent for Ford in

Table 6: Inflows and outflows of foreign investment (% of world total)

Source: *World Investment Report 2003: FDI Policies for Development: National and International Perspective* (UN Conference on Trade and Development, 2003)

	Inflows 1991-2002 annual average	Outflows 1991-2002 annual average
Belgium & Luxemburg	6.7	6.5
France	6.0	9.9
Germany	4.5	8.7
Ireland	1.2	2.1
Italy	1.2	2.0
Netherlands	4.0	3.5
Spain	3.0	2.5
UK	7.2	12.7
US	19.9	20.0

Table 7: Leading exporters and importers in world trade in commercial services

Source: *International Trade Statistics 2003* (WTO, 2003), p23

Rank	Exporters	Share %	Rank	Importers	Share %
1	US	17.4	1	US	13.3
2	UK	7.8	2	Germany	9.6
3	Germany	6.3	3	Japan	6.9
4	France	5.5	4	UK	6.6
5	Japan	4.1	5	France	4.4
6	Spain	4.0	6	Italy	4.0
7	Italy	3.8	7	Netherlands	3.6
8	Netherlands	3.4	8	China	3.0
9	Hong Kong	2.9	9	Canada	2.7
10	China	2.5	10	Ireland	2.6

1998.[25] In the electronic and consumer goods sectors significant profits are derived from exorbitant interest rates and costly guarantees. Such moves into finance by large multinationals blur the lines between the real economy and finance.

The City of London

The UK ranks second as an exporter of commercial services and accounts for 7.8 percent of world trade in this sector (see Table 7). The role of the City of London lies behind the expansion of finance generally, and specifically British capitalism has a competitive advantage in this sector.

The City's pivotal role in international finance and commerce originated in Britain's grip on world trade in the 18th and 19th centuries and the rise of British imperialism. But its international importance has long outlived the decline of the British economy. Up until 1945 it was the leading financial centre and sterling the dominant currency. This role passed to the US after the war, but the City assumed a new role in the 1950s and 1960s at the heart of the Eurodollar market, based on borrowing and lending dollars held outside the US, and fought to maintain its dominance in finance in the face of competition from other emerging financial centres in Japan and Germany. The so called 'Big Bang' of 1986 swept away many of the traditional restrictive practices which were driving business elsewhere, and it created LIFFE (London International Financial Futures Exchange) as a casino for large-scale betting on the future price of currencies, interest rates and derivatives (which are a combination of interest rates and currency).

The internationalisation of finance through the lifting of restrictions on the movement of capital in the 1980s opened up more profitable opportunities for the City. The *Business Times* estimated that the global value of derivatives rose from $2.9 trillion to $127 trillion between 1990 and 2002. The UK share of world turnover represented average daily turnover of $643 billion in April 2004 compared with $275 billion in 2001.[26]

The privatisation of pensions has hugely increased the funds available to the financial sector, with workers increasingly being forced to make their own pension provision as firms have closed their final salary schemes. The real value of insurance and pension funds has increased more than fivefold over 20 years and their surpluses, after paying out benefits, increased from £27.7 billion in 1990 to £43.3 billion in 1996.

GATS and the finance sector

Four out of the top ten global financial corporations are based in the UK (HSBC, Bank of Scotland, Barclays and Lloyds).[27] The importance of banking and finance in the UK economy means that the liberalisation of trade and investment is crucial to the profitability and expansion of this sector. Therefore the GATS (General Agreement on Trade in Services) implemented at the end of 2003 was particularly important for British capitalism. This meant an end to any national laws and regulations that were a barrier to trade in any form of 'services' from finance to old people's homes. The opening of markets for financial firms from the US and UK were key forces behind the GATS negotiations during the Uruguay talks (1986-1994) that created the WTO. US and European firms, including those from the UK, lobbied very hard for the prising open of new markets, especially the lucrative Chinese market during negotiations for its entry to the WTO.

The ability of the City to maintain profits and its central position in the global economy are highly dependent on the expansion of British financial capital and British global financial corporations being able to grab new markets. However, although financial services have not experienced the scale of restructuring of other sectors, competition is intensifying. There is particular pressure on labour costs and an incentive to look for low-wage locations to bolster profits.

Export of 'back-room jobs'

The press has been full of stories reporting job losses as a result of high-profile British firms in the financial sector uprooting and transferring some part of their service operations to India, the Philippines or China. Between December 2003 and August 2004 three British insurance companies (AVIVA/Norwich Union, Axa and Lloyds TSB) and HSBC relocated 9,000 jobs between them out of the UK.[28] In addition, the list of services that can be outsourced is being extended to legal work, medical reports and clinical trials. Firms facing intense competition find the idea of an un-unionised workforce who will work for longer hours and whose wages are less than one sixth of the amount they would pay in Britain an attractive quick fix.

But the hype does not reflect the reality. Call centres constitute the biggest part of this BPO (Business Process Offshoring) market in India. According to industry estimates, there were over 300,000 call centres worldwide at the end of 2002 employing around 18 million people.[29] Yet India had just 250 call centres, employing 33,800 people in the summer of 2004. A survey of US firms in 1996 showed that 26 percent were unhappy with the results of outsourcing and 51 percent of those had recalled their activities in-house.[30] Part of the answer for this is there is a limit to the rate of exploitation of labour. In India the employee turnover rate at call centres rose from 16 percent in 2002/03 to 35-45 percent in 2003/04.[31]

An Income Data Service survey of 107 companies in October 2004 suggested employment in UK call centres was likely to increase rather than contract: 58 percent of firms had increased staff levels and planned further expansion in the future.[32] Ironically in 2004 an Indian firm opened a call centre in Belfast.[33]

Logistics, distribution and transport

Marx wrote in the *Grundrisse* in 1857 that as capital sets out to 'conquer the whole earth for its markets, it strives to annihilate this space with time'.[34] Trade has taken place over vast geographical distances for thousands of years, but the crucial aspect now is the dimension of time. This idea of 'time compression'[35] not only applies to trying to get access to new markets quickly but to the production process itself.

Firms need to reduce the time they spend producing goods in order to turn over capital more quickly. This involves a whole raft of activities and research into new products, logistics, warehousing and transport. Intensified competition makes the nature and efficiency of distribution systems central. For the system as a whole the 'annihilation of space through time' means developments in transport, with parallel changes in flows of information through the postal system, radio, telecommunications and then the internet. For individual capitalists it means bringing goods to the market more quickly; eliminating waste in the form of time, effort, defective units and stocks in manufacturing-distribution systems; strategies such as just-in-time management, lean logistics, direct delivery, and the outsourcing of logistics services; and shortening the life cycle of products, so as soon as you have bought a new computer or mobile phone it is out of date and has been superseded by the next model. These methods all serve to speed up the realisation of surplus value and the starting of another round of accumulation.

Significant numbers of workers are employed in these sectors. Transport and logistics firms such as BOC are themselves large multinationals and big employers. Airports employed 180,000 workers directly (0.8 percent of total employment) and 200,000 indirectly in 1998. This amounted to 3.4 percent of total employment in London and the south east.[36] Such workers are not peripheral to capitalist production but central to it. A strike by those delivering components would bring production lines to a halt in a matter of hours in a just-in-time system. One by drivers delivering food to supermarkets would mean empty shelves in a short space of time.

Creative industries, creative accounting

The 'creative' and 'cultural' industries have been flagships of New Labour's economic policy. Chris Smith, when minister of culture in 1998, said they had 'moved from the fringes to the heart of the UK economy' and were 'a key economic driver, providing the jobs of the future and maintaining our position in the world'.[37]

Such industries are defined as those with 'their origin in individual creativity, skill and talent' and with 'the potential for job creation through the generation and exploitation of intellectual property'. They include 'advertising, architecture, the art and antiques market, crafts, design, designer fashion, film and video, interactive leisure software, music, the performing arts, software and computer services, television and radio'.[38]

Grandiose claims suggest that the creative industries generated around £112.5 billion of revenues in 2001 (double those of 1998), employed 1.3 million people (compared with 966,000 in 1998), made £10.3 billion of exports and accounted for over 5 percent of GDP.[39] But such figures rest on a completely spurious definition of 'creative', and lump together a disparate group of industries and economic activities. If software and computer services are left out (which arguably could be counted as science or business) then the numbers would immediately fall by half a million people and £36.4 billion. And to associate these industries with either small, innovative firms or some sort of individual creative endeavour is ludicrous.

The media is an area of economic activity completely dominated by huge global firms. Two pieces of legislation[40] by New Labour gave the green light for a spate of massive mergers and acquisitions and the emergence of mega media groups owning companies across television, radio and newspapers and magazines. AOL-Time Warner, News Corporation, General Electric, Sony, Vivendi and Viacom along with a few others control vast sections of the media. Close to 35 percent of newspapers in circulation in the UK belong to Murdoch's News Corporation.[41] At the other end of the scale many people working in these 'media' and 'creative' industries are often self-employed and badly paid, living from one short term contract to the next.

Supermarkets, super-concentration of capital

Supermarkets employed 1.02 million workers in 2004, making them the largest employment sector in the UK.

Tesco alone accounts for £1 out of every £8 spent in shops in the UK, its turnover accounts for 2.6 percent of gross domestic product and it employs 236,000 people, twice the number in the British army.[42]

New store expansion was the all-consuming engine of corporate growth by major UK food retailers in the 1980s and early 1990s. Profit margins were high and these cathedrals of consumption completely changed the urban landscape as the number of supermarkets and hypermarkets tripled. This 'golden age' came to an abrupt halt during 1993/94, when the major food retailers became engulfed by financial problems. Since then hyper-competition has led to firms battling for survival within the sector.

There has been huge investment in information technology to shorten the time from field to shelf. All operations from purchase to distribution have been centralised, with increased use of EPOS (electronic point of sale) units, enabling retailers to cut costs and stocks. These processes have been critical in ensuring the expansion of fresh and chilled products, which are the ranges on which supermarkets make the highest profits. In 2002 Tesco could replace depleted stock in eight to ten hours while Sainsbury's took 24 to 48 hours.

There has been a spate of mergers and acquisitions, Asda being taken over by Wal-Mart (2000) and Safeway by Morrisons (2004). A decision by the Competition Commission to categorise convenience stores and supermarkets as separate markets gave the green light to large food retailers to recolonise high streets through the new breed of convenience stores such as Tesco Metro and Sainsbury's Local, as well as petrol garage forecourt stores. The degree of concentration in this sector is enormous. The only small food shops that can survive the competition are family businesses based on self-exploitation and open for 15 hours a day. Meanwhile, the competition between giants had led to large-scale international acquisitions. Tesco is now the largest supermarket chain in Hungary and has 144 stores in the Czech Republic, Hungary and Poland. It has also expanded into the Far East with stores in Thailand, Singapore, South Korea and is currently moving into mainland China with the acquisition of a hypermarket chain in 2004.

There has also been warfare between different firms in the supply chain—the producers of fresh food, the packagers and processors, and the and retailers. Relationships between giant food-producing transnationals and giant supermarkets became increasingly adversarial, with Unilever, Kellogg and Heinz whining that they find themselves compelled to produce UK supermarket own brands or risk losing shelf space for their own products. From 2000 onwards major food retailers gained more power over their suppliers through the use of internet markets and Globalnetxchange, an electronic virtual marketplace. The large firms gain as suppliers are forced to drive down prices and middle wholesalers are cut out of the picture completely. As supermarkets make huge profits these lower prices are not passed on to consumers.

Finally, firms have concentrated on their largest single cost, namely labour. As opening hours have been extended large food retailers have used an array of different contracts to increase the flexibility of the workforce, from rolling schedules, seasonal work, flexitime, zero-hours contracts, annualised work and term time only. Since 2000 hyperflexibility has included giving a minimum of hours and expecting workers to 'flex' up to any number of additional hours; averaging hours; changing rotas every few weeks; and doing away with overtime and unsociable hours payments. A further attack on workers in 2004 involved supermarkets refusing to pay the first three days sick pay. Food retailing has the greatest number of part-time workers of any industrial sector in the UK—68 percent in 1994, an increasing proportion women.

The numbers employed in individual supermarkets now compare to those in factories historically. These new workplaces have exactly the same potential as the old for workers to talk, argue, share grievances and organise on questions of pay and working conditions.

Uneven landscape of British capitalism

Capitalism creates new landscapes at one point in time only to destroy them and build wholly different landscapes elsewhere. The changes in the structure of production have profound implications for the geography of British capitalism. As activities emerge within or are captured by particular places others go into decline. The growth of the City of London has not only created large numbers of jobs in finance, but is accompanied by a huge number of other workers to support them. A huge wave of construction of buildings and transport infrastructure in the City provides even more jobs and changes the physical landscape.

European regional economic statistics predicted that five out of the ten fastest growing European regions between 2004 and 2009 are expected to be in the south of England. Some of the slowest regions are also in the UK.[43] Changes in the structure of the production and particularly the huge expansion of finance has driven demographic changes. Most northern cities have suffered from falls in population, while the proportion of graduates living in London has increased from 16 percent to 20 percent.[44]

A report from researchers at the University of Sheffield argues, 'The country is being split in half... To the south is the metropolis of greater London, to the north and the west is the "archipelago of the provinces"—city islands that appear to be slowly sinking demographically, socially and economically'.[45] However, the unevenness is more complex than this. Gentrification is taking place in cities such as Manchester, Leeds, Liverpool and Edinburgh. The docklands of Liverpool (as in London) have turned into expensive flats, exclusive shops and wine bars. On the other hand, behind the glittering facades of places like Canary Wharf there is a whole world of low-paid workers in cleaning, catering, security and delivery work. Within a stone's throw is Tower Hamlets, one of the poorest areas in Britain. The superstar regions are characterised by extremes of poverty and wealth and provide a microcosm of the fundamental contradictions of global capitalism.

Conclusion

British capitalism has been involved in large-scale restructuring across international boundaries. The scale and depth of this restructuring has been greater than in other advanced European economies.

Despite the decline in manufacturing the apocalyptic picture of its collapse is far from true. Britain still retains a significant manufacturing core, and its share of global exports is equal to that of China. The claim that there is a new division of labour whereby all low-skilled jobs are being exported is highly exaggerated. Such claims are empirically selective and overestimate the potential for moving production (or parts of production) out of the country. The widely cited sectors of electronics and textiles have always been footloose. However, other important areas of production such as food retailing, transport and welfare services are firmly rooted in the home economy. Within a sea of poor productivity there are islands of efficiency in some sectors, with highly profitable global firms in car production, defence, pharmaceuticals and food retailing.

What is true is that British manufacturing employs far fewer workers. However, the automation and the just-in-time production methods used by bosses to restore profits or steal an advantage on competitors are also a source of weakness. A strike in one part of the production chain can bring the whole operation to a grinding halt in a matter of hours.

The openness of the British economy generally and its role in recycling global finance explains why New Labour and the ruling class have thrown themselves so enthusiastically behind and championed deregulation and liberalisation. Heavily dependent on foreign investment in manufacturing, and on being the second most important exporter of capital, the profitability of UK firms lies in the prising open of foreign markets. The pivotal role of the City in global capitalism and the need for expansion means that future profits are highly dependent on big new markets like China.

New Labour has played a significant role in the restructuring of the economy through its attitude to different sections of capital, despite the rhetoric of free markets.

There are important changes taking place in commodity production and where people work. There is the growing importance of the production of 'intangible' commodities which are classified as part of the service sector. There are larger numbers than before of workers in transport, logistics and computer programming who contribute to the production and productivity of goods. In a situation of hyper-competition these jobs are critical to the profits of individual firms. And there has been a huge growth of people working in the finance sector. The working class is not disappearing. It is working in different places. Neither is it turning into a privileged layer with better working conditions and wages. There is no more job satisfaction working in a call centre or inputting data into a computer than sitting on an assembly line. Although some people working in the City earn exorbitant salaries, many of the jobs in finance are repetitive, hard and badly paid.

The mantras of the 'new economy', 'creative industries' and 'weightlessness' implying a new era of better and more satisfying work are propaganda on the part of New Labour to give capitalism an acceptable face. The bottom line is that the interests of the vast majority of workers in the so called service sector lie in being organised to defend their wages, working conditions and pensions.

NOTES

1: D Coyle and D Quah, *Getting the Measure of the New Economy* (Industrial Society, May 2002).

2: M Hardt and A Negri, *Empire* (Harvard, 2001), p285.

3: W Hutton, 'Don't Weep for Our Lost Factories', *The Observer*, 19 December 2004.

4: The idea of networked economies was popularised by M Castells in *The Rise of the Network Society* (Oxford, 2000).

5: The notion of clusters of industries producing growth in local economies is very popular in academic circles and among policy makers. For a discussion and critique of this see F Currie and J Hardy, *Clustering, Knowledge and Locality: The Case of the Pharmaceutical and Film Industries in Hertfordshire* (report produced for the Association of Universities in the East of England, June 2002).

6: See articles by R Boyer and M Aglietta and others in a special edition of *Economy and Society*, vol 29, no 1, 'Shareholder Capitalism and the Political Economy of Late Capitalism' (February 2000).

7: M Haynes, 'Capitalism in Marx's Time and Ours', *International Socialism* 19 (spring 1983).

8: D Harvey, *The New Imperialism* (Oxford, 2003), pp100-101.

9: C Harman, 'The Workers of the World', *International Socialism* 96 (autumn 2002).

10: As above, p286.

11: There is no intention here to get into thorny debates about productive and unproductive labour (see S Freeman and B Vandesteeg, 'What is "Unproductive Labour"?', *International Socialism* 12 (1981), but to make the point that in Marxist terms the distinction between goods and services is an artificial one. Intangible goods are equally part of the process of production.

12: This may be partly explained by reunification.

13: EU Commission figures quoted in 'Manufacturing Now: Delivering the Manufacturing Strategy' (TUC, 2004). http://www.tuc.org.uk/economy/tuc-8248-f0.cfm

14: EU Commission, as above.

15: S Broadberry and N Crofts, as above, argue that the productivity gap in sectors such as food and tobacco was lower than other sectors. In particular British manufacturing was bad at implementing mass production methods and was disadvantaged (along with other European countries) relative to the US.

16: W Lyons, 'The Car in Front is British as UK Output Nears Record of 1972', *The Scotsman*, 15 September 2004.

17: 'UK Plants Most Efficient in Europe', BBC News, 26 June 2001.

http://news.bbc.co.uk/1/hi/business/1411386.stm.

18: K Randle, 'The White-Coated Worker: Professional Autonomy in a Period of Change', *Work, Employment and Society*, vol 10, no 4 (1996), pp737-753.

19: BAe (British Aerospace) supply armaments such as missile guidance systems, Rolls-Royce supply military engines across the global economy. Airbus UK is part of a European consortium where the scale of research and development is too large for one national capital.

20: P Dunne, 'Restructuring of the British Defence Industry', paper presented at ECAAR Panel on peace economics. AEA/ASSA meeting, Boston, January 2000.

21: Office for National Statistics, *Regional Competitiveness and State of Regions* (May 2004), p10.

22: C Tighe, 'Samsung to Quit UK Site in Quest for Cheaper Labour', *Financial Times*, 16 January 2004.

23: As above.

24: K Marx, *Capital*, vol 1 (Penguin, 1976), p778.

25: J Froud et al, as above.

26: 'The UK Foreign Exchange and Over the Counter Markets in April 2004', Bank of England, 2004.

27: M Vander Stichele, *Critical Issues in the Financial Industry: SOMO Financial Sector Report* (March 2004).

28: I Gordon, C Haslam, P McCann, B Scott-Quin, *Offshoring and the City of London* (report for the Corporation of London, 2005).

29: R Rao, 'How to Tap the Opportunities for Outsourcing', *Financial Times*, 25 August 2004.

30: As above.

31: As above.

32: J Moules, 'Call Centres Defy Threat of Overseas Competition', *Financial Times*, 5 October 2004.

33: J Moules, 'Indian Operator Taps Skills of Loyal Belfast Workforce', *Financial Times*, 5 October 2004.

34: K Marx, *Grundrisse*, 1957.

35: Not exclusively but extensively used by D Harvey, *Limits of Capital* (London, 1999).

36: *The Economic Contribution of Aviation to the UK: Part 2 Assessment of Regional Impact: Final Report* (Oxford Economic Forecasting, May 2002).

37: 'Britain's Creative Industries Booming' (BBC News, *UK Politics: Talking Politics*, 11 November 1998).

38: As above.

39: As above.

40: The Broadcasting Act 1996 and the Communications Act 2003.

41: 'Media Ownership Laws to be Relaxed' (BBC News, 8 May 2002). http://news.bbc.co.uk/1/hi/uk_politics/1972519.stm

42: N Pratley and J Finch, 'How Tesco Took Over Britain', *The Guardian*, 6 January 2005.

43: B Willis, 'North-South Divide "Set to Widen"', *Guardian Unlimited*, 13 August 2004. http//www.guardian.co.uk/northsouth/article/0,2763, 1282728,00.html

44: L Elliott, 'The United Kingdom of London', *The Guardian*, 5 July 2004, reviewing D Dorling and B Thomas, *People and Places: A 2001 Census Atlas of the UK* (Sheffield, 2004).

45: As above.

The working class

Jacob Middleton

It has become common to deny either the existence or relevance of class to Britain today. Yet the numbers of people who describe themselves as 'working class' grew from 51 percent in 1994 to 68 percent in 2002.[1] The staggering rise in inequalities of wealth and income under Thatcher ensured, by 1995, that Britain was among the most unequal societies anywhere in the world. For the richest 10 percent of the population, incomes rose by 68 percent between 1979 and 1995. For the poorest 10 percent, after housing costs, incomes fell by 8 percent, and the slow reduction in inequality of the post-war years was reversed.[2] The richest 10 percent of the population have increased their share of Britain's total wealth from around 50 percent in 1991 to 57 percent today.[3]

Some analysts have concluded that the only people really to suffer from this change in distribution and wealth have been an 'underclass' of the 'excluded'. So Will Hutton's popular book in the mid-1990s, *The State We're In*, talked of the '30:30:40' society—40 percent comfortable, 30 percent materially better off but insecure, and a bottom 30 percent left behind by any count. Liberal commentator Polly Toynbee sums up the attitude: 'We have seen the most rapid change in social class in recorded history: the 1977 mass working class, with two thirds of people in manual jobs, shrunk to one third, while the rest migrated upwards into a 70 percent home-owning, white collar middle class'.[4]

There has been a change in the distribution of employment with the restructuring of industry described by Jane Hardy in her article in this journal. In 1981 35 percent of the workforce were employed in industry as opposed to services; this had fallen to 20 percent by 2004. Nevertheless, one in five of the workforce—around 6 million people—are still in industry.[5] And of the people employed in 'services', very many are in jobs with a big 'manual' component: workers in 'distribution, hotels and restaurants' accounted for 7.1 million jobs and 'transport and communication' for 1.8 million in 2004.

'Deindustrialisation' has not brought the liberation from drudgery that its promoters spoke of: the transformations have led to a decrease in the quality of working life, and a reinforcement of basic class divisions.

'Job polarisation'

Recent research by Maarten Goos and Alan Manning found an increasing polarisation in the British labour force. They ranked jobs by average pay, from best paid to worst, and found a decline in employment in middle ranking occupations between 1979 and 1999. The numbers of those in both the worst and the best paid occupations increased significantly. In 1979 there were 926,000 people employed in the 21 lowest paid occupations, such as sales assistants, bar staff and waiters; by 1999, there were nearly 1.5 million people in the same jobs. The numbers in the very highest paid types of work, like engineers, hospital consultants and senior managers, increased from 90,000 in 1979 to 207,000 by 1999.[6]

The lowest-paid jobs are not mainly in the old manufacturing industries. The Joseph Rowntree Foundation notes that 'relatively few low-paid jobs are in production industries facing direct competition from low-wage producers abroad'.[7] Two fifths of 7 million workers in Britain who earn less than £6.50 per hour are in service industries, and a further quarter are in the public sector. Contrary to the great myth of the 'middle class' service worker, it is clear that class divisions are far *sharper* here than they are elsewhere.

The destruction of averagely-paid jobs in British industry has not led to the creation of equivalent work elsewhere in the economy. They have largely been replaced by lower-paid, less secure employment.

McGovern, Smeaton and Hill have identified a link between what they call 'non-standard employment' and poor-quality jobs:

> Between one quarter and a half of the working population in Britain are in jobs that have at least one bad characteristic. Approximately one quarter of all employees are low paid, just over one third have no pensions, a similar proportion have no sick pay, and half are in jobs that do not have a recognised promotion ladder... Only one in four of the British labour force are in jobs that are not bad in any respect![8]

They reveal a distinct tendency towards worse quality employment among those on 'non-standard' contracts (part time, temporary, or fixed term): 'Over half of those in various forms of part time employment...do not have sick pay compared to under one third of those in permanent, full time employment. Similarly, one in two of those in permanent part time positions are on low pay compared with one in five of those in standard jobs'.[9]

'Flexibilisation' allows costs and overheads to be reduced by squeezing the workforce. This is directly linked to the reduction of union power, as 'workers who lack collective representation are almost 50 percent more likely to have substandard conditions than those who have union representation'.[10] The great majority of jobs in Britain—92 percent in the year 2000[11]—remain permanent with traditional forms of contract, but the existence of a 'flexibilised' group of precariously employed workers acts as a significant drag on their conditions.

The impact of education

Inequalities along the traditional route to social mobility, education, have worsened. The numbers entering higher education have risen significantly over the last 20 years, from one in ten to nearly one in three of the age group in England. But the class division in education has also got worse: over a quarter of 18 to 19 year olds from the richest 20 percent of households attended university in 1979; this had risen to just under half by 1997. By contrast, only 8 percent of 18 to 19 year olds from the poorest 20 percent of households attended university in 1979 and just 15 percent by 1997. New university places were disproportionately allocated to the children of the rich relative to the poor.[12] Under New Labour this gap has widened. A Higher Education Funding Council for England (HEFCE) report found that between 1997 and 2000 'most of the new places in higher education have gone to those from already advantaged areas'.[13] The introduction of tuition fees had a limited impact on participation, but has significantly increased dropout rates among students from poorer households. The same HEFCE report concludes, 'Young people living in the most advantaged 20 percent of areas are five to six times more likely to enter higher education than those living in the least advantaged 20 percent of areas'.[14]

One study concluded, 'The social class of a person's parents actually has a greater impact on their educational attainment now than previously... Thus it is not the most able who have benefited from the expansion of the UK education system but rather the most privileged'.[15]

Much has been made of the significantly higher wages commanded by those with degrees compared to the average.[16] But those from poorer families gain much less in this respect than those with richer backgrounds. In other words, education acts to reproduce existing inequalities. Moreover, after a period during which the distribution of returns evened out, they are now becoming more dispersed, particularly at the top end of the income scale.[17] A recent study found that 22 percent of all graduates were employed in non-graduate jobs.[18] There is a substantial stock of educated workers available to exert downward pressure on an increasing number of jobs requiring degree-level education.

The net effect of the expansion of higher education has been to both raise the average level of education among the British workforce, and *simultaneously* harden class boundaries within British society.

The connection between an individual's income and their parents' is now much stronger than it was under the last Labour government. Stephen Machin shows that those born into the lowest income households in 1970 are more likely to remain in the lowest income group than those born in 1958. Conversely, fewer of the very rich now slip down the income scale.[19]

Working hours in Britain

Two workers in five have usual working weeks longer than 40 hours, compared to only one in five across France, Denmark and Sweden. The average working week for full time employees in the UK is 44 hours, four hours longer than the EU average.[20]

The figures show some 51 percent of those in industry working longer than 40 hours a week and 34 percent of those employed in 'services'. This probably overstates the differences between the sectors: excess hours worked in jobs like teaching are not recorded. But the presence of low-paid, insecure workers in manufacturing regions has acted as a further compulsion on manufacturing workers, leading them to accept working longer hours.[21]

Women workers

Female participation in the labour market has soared, while male participation rates have declined, reduced at one end by the larger numbers remaining in education, and at the other by larger numbers of retirees (voluntary or otherwise). The gap between women's and men's participation rates halved in two decades.[22]

However, women's participation is still dominated by childcare commitments, with 46 percent of women with a youngest child under five being defined as 'economically inactive'. This declines as the youngest child ages, to only 28 percent for women with no dependent children.

Women earn on average around a fifth less than men. But their pay has increased on average slightly faster than men's over the last 20 years, with the gap in full time pay closing slightly from 26 percent to 23 percent between 1994 and 2002.[23]

This has led some to conclude that women should no longer concern themselves with economic inequality. The transition to a service-based economy, it has been argued, has led to a transformation in the possibilities available to women, enabling them to compete on an equal basis with men in the market for work.

A 'privileged pole' of 20 percent of women have markedly improved their position, earning significantly more than two thirds of working men.[24] But the shift in employment and output in the economy has, in general, reinforced pre-existing trends. The income gap between female and male part time workers has remained static at 36 percent, reflecting the bias towards the employment of women in lower-paid service occupations.[25] And most women's experience of work is punctuated by periods of part time or non-employment.[26]

Workless households

The number of households in which no person is employed rose from 4 percent in 1968 to 8.2 percent in 1977, and peaked at just under 20 percent in 1992.[27] The rate of long term unemployment has fallen in recent years, as has the proportion of workless households with dependent children. Many households that would previously not have worked are now entering the labour market, with just under 60 percent of lone parent households with dependent children now in employment, usually in service sector jobs which offer low working hours. But there is a variation in the proportion of working-age men not in work[28] from 8 percent in some areas to 31 percent in others, with exceptional areas of unemployment existing alongside areas of very high employment rates.[29] This highlights 'the plight of many coastal towns and the former coal mining districts alongside major urban areas'.[30] And the numbers of childless workless households in poverty reached record levels over 2002-03.[31]

The existence of large numbers of workless households acts to depress wages. They are not an 'underclass', but a flexible 'reserve army of labour', available as a constant downward pressure on wages of the lowest paid and in areas of highest unemployment.[32]

During a period of economic recovery workers have been thrown between work and the dole, rather than moving directly into employment and staying there. This, along with a decline in long term unemployment rates, indicates an increased contact with the labour market, even where this was infrequent and poorly-paid: those on lower wages are more likely to leave employment, while those returning to employment are generally paid less than average.[33]

Migrant labour

The transformation of the British economy has depended on the use of exceptionally badly paid and insecure labour. One estimate suggests that 13 percent of UK GDP can be accounted for by the so called 'black' economy. Estimates of the number of foreign workers employed illicitly in the UK vary between 500,000 and 2 million, with another 500,000 British-born workers joining them. This is an enormous contribution to the British economy, hidden from conventional accounts of the working class.

The presence of huge numbers of unprotected migrant labourers ties closely with the experience of British-born ethnic minorities, who have formed an important part of the British working class since the 1950s. Non-white British workers are on average paid less and work longer hours than their white counterparts; though the gap in average incomes has closed slowly over the past 20 years or more, it remains wide. In certain cases, as with the Bangladeshi population, it has widened drastically in the past five years. The great majority of ethnic minority workers in Britain live in the large urban areas, accounting, for example, for 40 percent of inner London's population. The national figure is just 8 percent. The experience of race and racism remains critical to the British working class in significant areas of the economy, and the ability to rely on a (covertly) segregated labour market is important for many sectors.[34]

Trade unionism

One of Thatcher's greatest 'achievements' was to cripple and weaken the British trade union movement. A peak membership rate (usually called 'union density') in 1979 of 49 percent of all workers in a trade union declined steeply and has now stabilised at around 29 percent. Strike days remain at a historic low, despite some improvements over the last few years.[35] There was a slight increase in total membership and density over 2003, but the majority of the working class in Britain today is not organised and just 35.8 percent of workers are affected by collective bargaining.

Men and women are now equally likely to be trade union members. 34 percent of full time and 23 percent of part time women workers are in trade unions, as against only 31 percent of male full time workers and 12 percent of part time ones. It is the small number of male part time workers that prevents trade union density being lower among men.[36] So once women enter the workforce, they are more likely to join a union. This is symptomatic of the rise of female employment particularly in public sector services.[37]

Conclusion

Against the mythology of a flexible and contented labour force, the dramatic restructuring of the British economy over the last 20 to 30 years broke with tendencies towards equality and has dramatically reinforced the underlying divisions of class in society. The working class itself now looks different, though it retains a core of industrial workers in the 'traditional' mould. But its experience remains the same; of prevailing insecurity, of economic inequalities, and with a pronounced tendency for these features to worsen. Though the most basic, defensive institutions of the working class remain quiescent, the bad experiences and unmet expectations of the last two decades weigh heavily upon millions of people.

NOTES

1: MORI finding on numbers agreeing with statement, 'At the end of the day, I am working class and proud of it.' See R Mortimore, 'Working Class—And Proud Of It!', 16 August 2002, at http://www.mori.com/mrr/2002/c020816.shtml

2: J Hills, 'Income and Wealth: The Latest Evidence' (Joseph Rowntree Foundation, 1997).

3: As above.

4: *The Guardian*, 5 June 2002.

5: Annual Abstract of Statistics 2003.

6: M Goos and A Manning, 'McJobs and MacJobs: the growing polarisation of jobs in the UK', in R Dickens, P Gregg, J Wadsworth (eds), *The Labour Market Under New Labour* (Basingstoke, 2003), pp73-74.

7: 'Monitoring Poverty and Social Exclusion 2004', Joseph Rowntree Foundation.

8: P McGovern, D Smeaton, S Hill, 'Bad Jobs in Britain: Nonstandard Employment and Job Quality', in *Work and Occupations* 31:2 (May 2004), p235.

9: As above.

10: As above, p239.

11: Office for National Statistics, *Social Trends 2001*, Table 4.6, p88.

12: S Machin, 'Higher Education, Family Income, and Changes in Intergenerational Mobility', in R Dickens, P Gregg, J Wadsworth (eds), *The Labour Market Under New Labour* (Basingstoke, 2003), Tables 18.1 and 18.2, p284. The figure for *all* people entering higher education is higher than that for 18-21 year olds.

13: D MacLeod, 'Survey Says University Access Depends on Postcode', *The Guardian*, 19 January 2005.

14: As above.

15: F Galindo-Rueda and A Vignoles, 'Class Ridden or Meritocratic? An Economic Analysis of Recent Changes in Britain', Centre for the Economics of Education (January 2003), at http://cee.lse.ac.uk/cee%20dps/ceedp32.pdf

16: A Gosling, S Machin, C Meghir, 'The Changing Distribution of Male Wages in the UK', IFS Working Paper W98/9 (1998).

17: See C Harmon, H Oosterbeek and I Walker, 'The Returns to Education: A Review of Evidence, Issues and Deficiencies in the Data', Centre for the Economics of Education (December 2000), http://cee.lse.ac.uk/cee%20dps/CEEdp05.pdf (p15).

18: P Dolton and M Silles, 'Over-Education in the Graduate Labour Market: Some Evidence from Alumni Data', Centre for the Economics of Education (Spring 2001), at http://cee.lse.ac.uk/ceepercent20dps/ceedp9.pdf

19: S Machin, as above, Tables 18.4, 18.5a and 18.5b, pp287-288.

20: *Labour Market Trends*, March 2004, pp116-117.

21: See Centre for Economic Performance (LSE), *Centre Piece* 13 (Spring 2001).

22: *Social Trends* 2004, p52.

23: H Robinson, 'Gender and Labour Market Performance in the Recovery', in R Dickens, P Gregg, J Wadsworth (eds), as above, p232.

24: T Warren, 'A Privileged Pole? Diversity in Women's Pay, Pensions and Wealth in Britain', in *Gender, Work and Organisation* 10:5 (November 2003), p615.

25: H Robinson, as above, Table 15.5, p241.

26: As above.

27: R Dickens, P Gregg, J Wadsworth, 'Non-working Classes: Britain's Chronic New Unemployed', *Centre Piece* (Spring 2001), Tables 4 and 5.

28: This includes all those not in work, as well as the registered unemployed.

29: R Dickens, P Gregg, J Wadsworth, 'Non-Working Classes: Britain's Chronic New Unemployed', as above, p13.

30: As above.

31: J Hills and K Stewart, *A More Equal Society? New Labour, Poverty, Inequality and Exclusion* (Cambridge, 2004).

32: See A Walling, 'Workless Households: Results from the Spring 2004 Labour Force Survey', Office for National Statistics, p440. http://www.statistics.gov.uk/articles/labour_market_trends/workless_households.pdf

33: R Dickens, P Gregg, J Wadsworth, 'Non-working Classes: Britain's Chronic New Unemployed', as above, Figure 3, p15.

34: Figures in this paragraph are from J Wadsworth, 'The Labour Market Performance of Ethnic Minority Workers in the Recovery', in R Dickens, P Gregg, J Wadsworth (eds), *The Labour Market Under New Labour*, as above.

35: See G Gall, 'Trade Union Struggles Today: Back from the Brink or Still on the Margins?', in *International Socialism* 105 (Spring 2005).

36: *Labour Market Trends*, March 2004, Table 2, p100.

37: J Wadsworth, 'The Labour Market Performance of Ethnic Minority Workers in the Recovery', as above.

Blair's vision for education: business, business, business

Terry Wrigley

Capitalism has always had a problem with education. Since the Industrial Revolution, the ruling class's need to increase the skills of future workers has been contradicted by its fear of them becoming articulate, knowledgeable and independent-minded. Hannah Moore, religious philanthropist and founder of the Sunday School movement at the time of the Napoleonic Wars, justified her initiative on the grounds that she would teach children how to read but would certainly not allow them to write:

> They learn, on weekdays, such coarse works as may fit them for servants. I allow of no writing for the poor. My object is...to train up the lower classes in habits of industry and piety... Beautiful is the order of society when each, according to his place, pays willing honour to his superiors.

Policy documents throughout the Victorian period openly stated that working class children must not be educated beyond their station in life. In our own day, even when more forward-looking employers declare a need for creativity and communication, co-operation and thinking skills, there are unspoken limits on how many children will develop these abilities and what they are allowed to think creatively about.

New Labour's 'Five Year Strategy for Children and Learners'—the real manifesto for education—is another variation on this theme, in tune with our own times: it is fully in keeping with the Blairite version of neo-liberalism. This government has constantly argued that driving up test scores is a key way to attract foreign investment and revitalise the economy. It has pursued this single-mindedly, though at a cost of real learning and, probably, long-term economic development. The Five Year Strategy is riddled with contradictions, but behind the rhetoric lies a manifesto for increasing control of education by the employing class. Between the opening flourish: 'Children, and all those who learn, are our future... We need to think about that future—about the kind of world we want our children to grow up in,' and the final fanfare: 'We have a vision of the future,' we find a hundred pages of phoney arguments for subjecting education to the demands of the employer class.

Even a word count is revealing. 'Employer' appears 146 times, plus 'employment' 30 and 'business' 36. The words 'creative' and 'creativity' appear once each. 'Critical' features six times, but always means 'essential' rather than thinking critically or challenging the status quo: 'All young people should be equipped with the skills critical for success in employment.' The word 'choice' appears 99 times, but its meaning is slippery. What choice is offered and to whom? It serves both to give a positive spin to the document and to reinforce the consumerist ideology that making educational decisions is like choosing goods from a supermarket shelf. The consumerist language provides a shell for promoting a wider concept of educational 'market', namely schools and colleges run as businesses for private profit. In some places, it refers to the brave new world of computerised instruction or 'programmed learning'. Sometimes it means choosing between different schools. Sometimes it's about children being divided up into different classes—an odd kind of choice. Most often, it's about privatisation—a 'choice of providers'. Slimmed-down Local Authorities will no longer run schools themselves but contract some out to private businesses: 'Choice implies greater diversity of provision and providers.' (ch 1, para 36).

There is scarcely a hint that schooling might serve any purpose other than employability. It is, of course, an important role of education to prepare young people to make a productive contribution to the economy—whether as wage labourers in a capitalist enterprise or as thoughtful and innovative participants in a future socialist economy. But education has many goals besides. Schools and colleges should be a space where creativity is developed, where we learn to live together, where we learn empathy and sensitivity towards one another, where young people can reflect on their relationships. Schools for the young—and also, as learning centres serving the whole community—should be places where we can become acquainted with a cultural heritage and re-shape it for our own times, where we can engage in critical thinking about our society and world. Critically, in our own time, schools and universities must create opportunities to question and challenge injustice, racism, environmental destruction, militarism, consumerism, the media, political spin… None of this forms any part of New

Labour's 'vision'. The role of education is simply and solely to meet the immediate demands of the employing class.

Of course, New Labour's ideologues cannot divorce themselves entirely from Old Labour history. The introduction makes concessions to the ideals of comprehensive education, in a potted history which damns it with faint praise. This government talks incessantly about 'raising standards', but in truth the most dramatic rise in achievement came when comprehensive schools were established. For the first time, almost all 16 year olds, not just the 20 percent who got into grammar schools, were able to gain end-of-school qualifications. This is increasingly recognised by those whose vision is not entirely obscured by New Labour's blinkers. In fact, the latest OECD study (PISA 2003) explicitly blames Germany's poor performance on its selective system, and ascribes the sudden improvement in Poland to its recent adoption of comprehensive schools.

Perversely, the authors damn the post-war welfare state, and subsequently the comprehensive school reform, as 'monolithic' and unconcerned with 'standards'! This really is to rewrite history. It was not until Thatcher's National Curriculum, slavishly sustained under New Labour, that schooling became monolithic; and it shows poor judgement to equate the present obsession with test scores with genuine achievement for all.

So what does New Labour have to offer in place of the 'monolithic' system of 'traditional comprehensives'? 'Choice' and 'personalised learning' mean little more than privatisation and selection. These principles permeate the Five Year Strategy, from the 'Educare' edu-businesses for 0-5 year olds, to new degree courses 'led by employers'. Schools will be 'freed' from Local Authority control, so that they can enter into long-term deals with businesses and 'faith sponsors'. Local Authorities will be the 'commissioner', not the 'direct supplier'. At the most extreme, in an act of wanton asset-stripping, hundreds of secondary schools in the poorest urban areas will be privatised, as 'academies' (see below).

They have clearly moved on from privatising school buildings to direct capitalist control of the curriculum. Employers will be involved in reforming the curriculum for 11-14 year olds; there will be 'Young Apprenticeships' for 14-16 year olds; the core curriculum in communication, mathematics and Information and Communication Technology (ICT) for 14-19 year olds will be determined by employers; and the next expansion of degree-level education will be 'led by businesses' rather than universities. The Five Year Strategy represents a very serious threat to education as we understand it. The following sections can only summarise New Labour's plan, in some of its major areas.

Paulo Freire referred to neo-liberalism as a fatalistic ideology—and Blair constantly spins us the story that he is driven irrevocably by global forces, though in truth he often leads the way in a global attack on public services. We need to build a mass resistance, with our own sense of vision: since another world is possible, then another school is possible—and necessary.

Nurseries and primary school

Provision has been extended for the under-fives under New Labour, but dependence on the private sector has led to a patchwork. The 12.5 hours a week at nursery for three and four year olds usually mean five mornings or afternoons, which is difficult for working parents and unsettling for the children who have to be moved around. The proposal is to make early education and care more flexible (now called 'educare', an ugly word!)—which would have happened in the first place if the government had used public provision with proper consultation. The women (predominantly) who work in this sector continue to suffer low pay, which is a scandal for such an important role. We are promised a slow extension of 'Sure Start Children's Centres' to provide a unified service and advice centres, including early education and childcare, family support, ante- and post-natal health care in the most deprived neighbourhoods; nothing is offered for the many families in poverty elsewhere.

The section on primary schools is headed 'Excellence and enjoyment for every primary child', disguising the fact that government policies have made school a grind for many children. The literacy and numeracy hours have some good features, including an emphasis on collective learning, but they have also brought a high degree of regimentation and less pleasurable reading and activity. They have separated reading, writing and mathematics from real contexts and purposes, turning them into separate exercises and practice to raise test scores.

Driven by the pressure to meet targets, schools are neglecting history and geography, sport and creative arts. Some woolly proposals are made to remedy this: 'every child should have the chance to learn a musical instrument'; 'every child should have two hours a week of physical activity or sport'; 'every child should have a chance to learn a foreign language'. Most of these new opportunities are to be run by poorly trained assistants and volunteers from local clubs, rather than qualified teachers. There is no proposal to ease the pressure of testing. The authors seem to be sure it will work: in Orwellian tones, they inform us that by 2008 'OFSTED will show that standards of teaching have risen across all subjects'. How do they know? Perhaps inspectors should simply consult the government's spin doctors, and won't need to visit schools at all.

What do all the tests tell us about achievement?

The answer appears to be—the whole truth, twice the truth, maybe three times the truth. The government constantly uses rising SAT scores in claims that its policies are working, but recent research raises serious questions about whether they can be trusted.

The National Numeracy Strategy has enforced a particular way of teaching maths, with a big emphasis on whole-class practice of mental arithmetic. It cost £400 million but according to well-respected researchers it has brought about only two months progress—and may have led to a deterioration on mathematical skills other than calculation. Professor Margaret Brown and her colleagues at King's College, London (*British Educational Research Journal*, October 2003) point out that two thirds of schools showed progress, but in a third results went down. Results got worse for low-attaining pupils, probably because of insufficient individual attention during whole-class teaching. The gap got bigger between the lowest-attaining pupils and the rest. There was also very little improvement for the most advanced pupils in the class, who became frustrated. Government press releases claim a 14 percentage point improvement; the researchers question why 1998 was used as a baseline, rather than 1999, just before the strategy was introduced. This would have shown only a 4 point improvement. The researchers also argue that this might be due to careful coaching for the test.

Professor Peter Tymms (CEM, Durham—one of the most expert research units on assessment) casts similar doubt on literacy scores (*British Educational Research Journal*, August 2004). He compares SATs data with 11 other sources of evidence (other tests, etc). He concludes that the statistics are rising because the tests are easier, and because of intensive coaching by teachers. Official claims show a rise from 48 percent (1995) to 75 percent (2000). Tymms' estimate for real improvement is from 48 percent to 58 percent (little change happened after that). When the SATs were tried out on pupils in Northern Ireland, who have a different system of education and had not been coached for the SATs, the pupils also said they were getting much easier.

There was a switch from more subtle questions involving inference or deduction to simple questions of fact. The most dramatic year-on-year 'improvement' happened because of a shift from a novelist's thoughtful personal account of her childhood to a much simpler text about spiders (Mary Hilton, Cambridge, in *Reading* 2001, no 1).

All this trickery makes the government look good, but narrows down children's learning. They become less able to read critically. Inspectors have pointed to an increase in basic exercises where children just practise, rather than reading that has some meaning. They called these 'holding activities' which 'occupied pupils but did not develop or consolidate their literacy skills' and reduce interest and motivation (HMI 2001 'National Literacy Strategy: The Third Year', www.ofsted.gov.uk). Some schools had abandoned independent reading, which didn't fit into the prescribed Literacy Hour. Boys were responding badly to one lesson in eight (even when the inspectors were watching!) and the gap between boys and girls was not closing. Worry about the test scores was leading teachers to neglect other subjects. 'The development of enquiry skills in history and geography, and the refining of technical skills in practical subjects, is being neglected.' The inspectors suggested that teachers connect reading with real knowledge, in history and science for example—which is just what many primary teachers used to do before the government stopped it!

Secondary schools

New Labour's proposals for secondary education are perhaps the most dangerous. They have in mind a major shift towards a business agenda, starting at age 11, where employers will determine the English, maths and computing which will be taught. Many 14-16 year olds will be encouraged into 'Young Apprenticeships', spending two days a week in a factory or office and studying qualifications related to that job. The number of young people studying after age 16 will increase, but (in the words of the document) only into 'some sort of' education or training.

The National Curriculum introduced by Thatcher's government in the late 1980s was technologically advanced but socially reactionary. Half was devoted to maths, science, design and technology, and information technology. In the other half, great care was taken to prevent young people gaining a political understanding of the world (eg sociology and media studies didn't figure, and it was a very conservative view of history). There was at least a broad spread of subjects for *all*—English, history, geography, art, music, languages, PE. New Labour has eroded this breadth, making many subjects optional, especially for students from poorer families. Increasingly, it seems, secondary school will be about training for work.

The authors of the document are forced to admit that many young people are 'bored and frustrated'. There are many reasons for this: the high levels of poverty; the disciplinarian regime; too few opportunities to show initiative and independence in learning, or work co-operatively in groups; a standardised curriculum which doesn't allow teachers to take account of young people's interests. None of these is recognised by New Labour, whose only answer is—preparation for work.

When they talk about education being more 'personalised', they seem to mean teachers matching tasks more closely to the learner's National Curriculum level. This still assumes a standardised content, as determined by national government. Completely missing is any notion that teachers might listen to the learners' suggestions and negotiate specific topics in some subjects, as in Scandinavia.

Teaching and learning in secondary schools is in need of reform, because teachers have been encouraged to lecture at classes, drill them with facts for the test, rush to cover the syllabus. In-depth understanding has not been a priority, though many good teachers persist in this. Learning needs to be more engaged and more active. Learners should spend more of their time outside of the classroom, on community-based investigations, visiting interesting places, and so on. Schools could be much more engaged with their communities. In the Five Year Strategy, active and community-based learning only occurs in terms of preparation for work. It's not surprising that work skills and vocational courses are very attractive to students growing up in poverty, and at risk of unemployment and low wages, but it is not enough; a good education should also help young people to understand the causes of poverty and how to challenge the conditions they live in. All young people are entitled to understand science and history and the environment and to learn to paint and dance—though the content and styles of learning will need to be changed.

There's a scatter of feel-good promises: more clubs, more visits, less disruption, better attendance. The approach to poor attendance appears to be 'get them in then kick them out'! Special patrols will bring disaffected youngsters in from the streets, but groups of schools will set up Pupil Referral Units into which the same youngsters can be decanted.

The strategy says nothing about why so many teachers are quitting. It's better than three years ago, when half of those in their final year of training had left teaching within two years of qualifying, but even now half quit in the first four or five years. There is a serious problem of disaffection among teachers as well as learners. Tying pay more and more closely to performance (ie to test results) can only make things worse, especially for schools in deprived areas: few teachers will want to work in schools where it is harder to get high results and claim performance pay. No wonder the strategy tries to pull rabbits out of the hat—unqualified adults who will 'bring new skills', sending youngsters out to learn in offices and factories, finding 'undergraduate volunteers'.

Schools with high exam results are encouraged to become independent organisations, to own their own land and buildings, expand, run their own admissions policies, and so on. Although, for the present, the Local Authority will still hold the reins, there is plenty of evidence of schools manipulating admissions procedures, such as holding interviews to select 'suitable' pupils—and 'suitable' parents! And how can schools 'own' their own land and buildings when they belong to a bank or construction company under PFI/PPP?

Back to the future

GCSE results have been used for many years to make judgements about schools, and in many towns and cities have led to local pecking orders of popularity. To some, it appeared that the government was becoming more flexible, by giving increased status to practical studies, chiefly in the form of vocational certificates such as GNVQs. This requires closer examination.

Firstly, there are many other ways of giving the secondary curriculum greater relevance in addition to training for work. These should include gaining a better understanding of our society and wider world, including the gross inequalities. One German example is 'real problem-solving', whereby a town council or hospital or voluntary group approaches the school with a genuine problem, and invites pupils to research and present alternative solutions. A major reform in Queensland, Australia, culminates not in a written examination but in 'rich tasks'. For example, a group of students might investigate the health needs of their neighbourhood and present proposals. Such projects draw on skills and knowledge from different subjects—science, sociology, literacy, statistics, computing. There is no reason why a design and technology course could not involve redesigning and rebuilding a local playground.

New Labour sees practical learning entirely in terms of training for employment. It has gone overboard to give the appearance of equal status to GNVQ certificates, but is this a real equivalence or simply a statistical trick? Officially now, a GNVQ (Intermediate) in computing, for example, counts as the equivalent of four GCSEs at A*-C grades. This has enabled some schools to claim a massive 'improvement' (one school jumped from 25 percent to 75 percent of pupils hitting the five-subject target within a single year). The government can also appeal to disillusioned heartland voters, by claiming to be improving inner-city schools.

There was uproar in January when it emerged that a distinction in cake decorating now counts for more than an A grade in physics. A government minister called critics of the new regulation old-fashioned elitists. There is value in work-related courses, as part of a broad and balanced curriculum for all young people, but not when a vocational course simply replaces other important learning. We also have to ask about the 'exchange rate' of this new currency in the real world. How will employers and colleges judge them? When Jane, with her computing certificate, is in competition with Marie, who has five good GCSEs and computer skills as well? When Karen, with her new found self-esteem, concentration and delicacy of hand, and her certificates in cake decorating and computing, develops an ambition to become a brain surgeon, which university will take her on? In reality, this is another piece of New Labour spin—a phoney egalitarianism at the expense of the most disadvantaged young people.

The government's real intentions are far from egalitarian. Indeed, their response to the Tomlinson Report (October 2004) was an outright rejection of a proposal to give equal status to different types of study within a balanced curriculum. The report won widespread praise when it came out, and there has been outrage from many quarters at its rejection by the education secretary Ruth Kelly (February 2005). It wasn't without faults, but it was a genuine attempt to end snobbery over qualifications by setting up a unified diploma system for 16 to 18 year olds. The new diploma would include and give equal weight to academic and vocational studies.

It would reduce exams for 16 year olds, replacing GCSEs with courses which would largely be assessed by teachers (with suitable external checks). The proposal to encourage deeper student-centred learning instead of exam cramming won support from universities, including Cambridge (in Tomlinson's words, A-levels are 'strangling scholarship'). It would encourage more young people to stay on beyond 16. At present, a quarter of 17 year olds receive no full- or part-time education or training (according to the OECD, this makes Britain 25th out of 29 industrialised countries).

Kelly has scuppered the Tomlinson reforms. Instead of a unified system, she is keeping GCSE and A-levels as they are, and setting up vocational diplomas alongside them. As Steve Sinnott, General Secretary of the NUT, said, 'The White Paper uses the language of Tomlinson but has a fundamentally different meaning. The academic/vocational divide has been widened rather than narrowed.'

He points out that many universities will refuse to recognise the separate vocational diplomas, and that the government is creating two separate routes from age 14. This is at the heart of Blair's policies for education. The government originally claimed that specialist schools would enhance provision for particular subjects while maintaining a full curriculum. Now they are setting up separate 'vocationally led' schools and 'skills academies' from age 11, as well as separate vocational skills centres from age 14 upwards. In the poorest neighbourhoods, many 11 year olds will go to a specialist school for construction work or caring. The lucky few will attend a 'city academy' run by private business, which will provide higher-level vocational skills for business or engineering.

We are fast going down the road of lowering the school-leaving age to 14 for many young people. In Knowsley, 300 14-16 year olds are on a 'work-based programme' with up to five days a week in the workplace. At one of its schools, 21 pupils have full-time placements at garages, hairdressers and painting and decorating firms.

This is supposed to be the answer to disaffection, but there are many different ways to engaging young people, with fewer tests, less sense of failure, and active learning such as problem-solving projects across a broad curriculum. All young people need to learn about science and history as well as acquiring useful skills for work. We need to educate for democracy, including learning about the environment and the mass media and the causes of poverty. Now the very principle of a 'broad and balanced' curriculum has gone out the window.

Abandoning the Tomlinson report has created widespread anger—universities, the Chief Inspector, all the teacher unions. But it is just the tip of the iceberg of a wider project of dismantling comprehensive education. As in the system before comprehensive schools were introduced, there will be three kinds of people, following three different routes:

(1) Higher-grade GCSEs and A-levels;

(2) Vocational diploma plus functional literacy and numeracy;

(3) 'Young apprenticeships'.

Young apprenticeships are to be expanded to include a third of 14 year olds, who will spend large parts of their week out at work. This figure will be much higher in the poorest areas—maybe 60 to 80 percent. Blair is returning us to the Victorian principle of educating people 'to fit their station in life.'

The vocational diplomas are also likely to involve about a third of 14-18 year olds. They will be 'employer-designed', so altogether the education of two-thirds of young people will be determined by employers.

Under this reform, nobody is safe. Everything is geared towards employers' short-term demands. English will be focused on 'functional literacy'—no time for reading for pleasure or critical studies of the mass media. The Tomlinson report meant broadening education for pre-university students, by giving credit for 'wider activities' including voluntary work, outdoor pursuits and creative interests. Now, there will just be more exam pressure, with some extra 'stretch' questions for entry to elite universities.

This is far worse than anything the Tories did to education. Thatcher's government failed to break up the comprehensive system. Sir Keith Joseph introduced GCSEs, providing a school-leaving qualification for all 16 year olds. The National Curriculum, despite its conservative versions of English and history and its stranglehold on innovation, at least upheld the principle of a broad and balanced curriculum for all pupils.

Blair and his crowd always hated the idea of their own children going to comprehensive schools. Their project now is to end comprehensive schooling altogether.

The academies

The most daring plan is to establish 200 city academies, ie 50 percent of secondary schools serving the poorest urban communities. This is an escalation of Blair's privatisation agenda. We knew it wouldn't stop with privately owned buildings (PFI). This is asset-stripping on a massive scale.

But it is asset-stripping in another sense too—a bid to control minds. Nobody can be sure where it might lead. In the US, hundreds of thousands of teenagers are forced to watch a commercial TV channel for 20 minutes a day—not an educational programme but adverts and its version of the news—just because it provided the school with some equipment. Most of the academies here specialise in business and enterprise. Pupils at Bexley Business Academy spend their Fridays doing business and stock-exchange role plays and other training; a mini stock exchange dominates the foyer.

How would you like your local school to be run by a second hand car dealer? New Labour's latest plan is precisely that. Of course, it's not restricted to second hand car dealers. Any company executive with £2 million to spare can become the proud owner of your school.

And it's a bargain. We pay most of the cash for a new building—£20 to £30 million—from our taxes, and all the running costs, but, in this unique business arrangement, we don't have a single share in the 'business'. The business 'sponsors' appoint the head. They choose the teachers. They decide what your children will learn. They doubtless claim tax rebates on their £2 million, they can recoup money by selling off land, and one academy has already handed £300,000 to the sponsor and his relatives for 'services rendered'—over £100,000 for 'advertising and recruitment advice' (*File on 4*, 23 November 2004, transcript from BBC website).

As well as businesses, Christian fundamentalists have already shown massive interest. In some schools, children are taught creationist rather than evolutionary accounts of how the world began in their science lessons, and there will soon be many more. Five of the 17 academies already open are religious schools, four of them associated with right-wing Christian groups.

But do they work?

(1) The government claim it's a way of getting money to rebuild rundown inner city schools. That is a strange claim, since most of the money comes from our taxes. Couldn't the government spend that anyway on a new building? And even if it cost a bit more, it wouldn't be squandered on a 'mini Stock Exchange', as at Bexley.

(2) They claim the running costs are no higher—yet they are managing to pay teachers £1,000 more a year. Perhaps it's because they don't need to spend on computers or repairs while the school is quite new.

(3) They claim the results are better. In fact, of the first three academies (opened September 2002), comparing the 2004 GCSE results with those of the predecessor school in 2001, two schools' results went down, not up. One of the academies established a year later has the second worst GCSE results in the country.

(4) The academies are supposed to be about social inclusion, but some are expelling less successful pupils. The two Middlesbrough academies expelled 61 pupils in two years; the other seven Middlesbrough schools only expelled 15 pupils between them all.

> Headteacher: One of the things that our foundation believes very strongly in is that in running a school you should think like a parent. What do parents want?
> Interviewer: Well they don't throw their children out. They keep them in the family. (*File on 4*, 23 November 2004)

The academies are also, potentially, another attempt to reintroduce selection at 11. There's no way the surrounding schools can compete with the sparkling new academy and its high-tech facade. The academies are bound to attract parents, but at other schools' expense, leading to a two-tier system like the old grammar schools and secondary moderns. The government should be improving all schools, not using this as a lever for privatisation and selection.

Obviously these schools are not all bad. Some of them are showing creativity in rethinking the curriculum, and some heads are determined to be inclusive. It's not the individual cases that are the problem—it's the insanity of a government policy which invites injustice and abuse. It's great that some of the worst-off children have exciting and welcoming school buildings at last. But why, since almost all the costs are carried by the taxpayer, should this depend on handing over control to private business executives? We need greater democratic control of public services, not less.

Two planned academies have already been stopped by parents. In Conisbrough, South Yorkshire, parents forced fundamentalist Christian Sir Peter Vardy to withdraw his plan. Parents in this ex-mining area were determined to hold on to their one remaining asset. Protests included large notices in the school car park—'Used cars for sale!'

This is a massive project, dreamed up by New Labour spin-merchants with precious little evidence or research behind it. Education authorities are being bludgeoned into line with threats that they will get no other money for new buildings. We need to build up popular resistance. Already the National Union of Teachers are building a campaign, and we need to intensify this at grassroots level, to build an alliance of students, parents and staff.

Training and higher education

The strategy's authors are rightly concerned about the large number of young people who get no training or education beyond the age of 16. This has actually increased in the last ten years. 25 percent of 17 year olds do not receive any form of education or work-based training. The strategy shows little understanding of the widespread concern about the many poor quality 'apprenticeships' which give the young person minimal training, low pay and no security.

The strategy makes grand claims about the reputation of university education in England and Wales, but provides no evidence or sources. The proportion entering higher education has risen to 43 percent, but the chance of getting to university is as slim as ever for the most disadvantaged.

It is hard to see how the situation can improve when university education brings massive debts and insecurity. The prospect of a loan means something completely different to youngsters who've heard the bailiff or the moneylender's hardman knocking at the door. The authors of the strategy seem to think it's reassuring to promise that a graduate's outstanding debts will be cancelled if they haven't been paid back after 25 years!

Conservatives often claim that university standards are falling because more young people are getting in. This argument is reactionary myth, but there is some justification in suggestions of falling standards. Twenty years ago a university degree in England meant three years full-time study (one of the shortest but most intensive in the world). Students normally got temporary jobs in the holidays, but could focus on their studies in term time. Now an English university degree means three years of part-time study, juggling with one or more part-time jobs even in term time. It would be miraculous if standards were unaffected.

Again, the rhetoric of 'choice'. The Five Year Strategy argues that the recent decision to allow universities to charge students fees of up to £3,000 a year will enhance choice. It can only mean that students from poorer families will choose cheaper universities, with fewer staff and poorly resourced labs and libraries. The strategy announces that universities should become less reliant on public funds and more dependent on sponsorship and fundraising (which will benefit only the most prestigious and elite establishments).

Finally, while promising a further expansion of student numbers, they will do it by creating Foundation Degrees (one- or two-year courses) in work-related courses. They will be led not by universities but by employers, perhaps in conjunction with local colleges.

If this is New Labour's 'vision for the future', we should all be worried.

Urban landscapes

Alex Law and Gerry Mooney

Cities are at the centre of politics in Britain today. More than 80 percent of the UK population live in cities and their suburban hinterland.[1] New Labour has made the regeneration of urban spaces through an 'urban renaissance' a key plank of their mission to 'modernise' Britain. John Prescott, deputy prime minister, claims, 'Many of our larger urban areas have begun to show substantial progress. There's great new architecture, expressing a new confidence, and people are coming back to the city centres'.[2]

New Labour's Urban Task Force, set up under the architect Richard Rogers in 1997, declared that it would 'identify causes of urban decline' and 'establish a vision for urban regeneration founded on the principles of design excellence, social wellbeing and environmental responsibility *within a viable economic and legislative framework*'.[3] Such laudable aims are therefore made dependent on the right economic situation. New Labour's 'urban renaissance' is shot through with all the contradictions that mark their broader project—a historical contradiction between planning for social need and competitive accumulation. And it finds its most marked expression in the urban spaces where most of British society lives and works.

The state of UK cities

As they stand, UK cities are far from the utopian images of them. Capitalism faces the insurmountable contradiction that it is driven to destroy its own lifeblood in the city. Much of the urban fabric is dilapidated, with some 1.3 million buildings lying empty, and public spaces are turned into hostile surveillance zones. Capitalism also creates extreme uneven geographies of growth and decline.

London and its south east hinterland contrasts sharply with the rest of England in terms of changes in population, sectoral employment, labour productivity, inequalities and ethnicity.[4] It is one of three 'global' cities, along with New York and Tokyo.[5] Globalisation has not dispersed the need for the close physical proximity of economic activities. The control and command functions necessary for capitalism continue to gather around core areas like London. It has managed to sustain its base as the locus of economic and political power despite the loss of 250,000 jobs in the early 1990s. The logic of such spatial concentrations of corporate power brings in its wake a plethora of support functions not usually considered to be part of the so called knowledge economy. These include the routine and specialised tasks that produce, distribute, maintain, clean, equip and house corporate control capabilities.

Cities grow by sucking in new workers. While the number of 'white' people in London and the other urban areas fell by 1.17 million in the 1990s, cities were repopulated by 1.13 million people from ethnic minorities. London took nearly 50 percent of the national total of inward migration. Far from being a drain on local services or employment, the economic and social activity of ethnic minority groups often helps to rejuvenate urban spaces that would otherwise deteriorate even further.[6]

London has therefore continued to grow numerically in terms of in-migration and employment while cities in the north and west of England suffer from protracted decline. Financial services employment has grown by some 50 percent, faster than anywhere else. But London is also the most polarised city in terms of extremes of wealth and poverty. In terms of poverty indices, the highest proportions of adults claiming Income Support and Job Seekers Allowance benefits in 2003 were in Liverpool (18 percent), Hull (17 percent), and Birmingham, Hastings, Newcastle and Middlesbrough (13 percent). But London was not far behind at 10.3 percent. Its 19 percent growth in employment between 1991 and 2001 was mainly in part-time work, which grew by 47 percent, and, to a much lesser extent, self-employment. A skills audit of the Thames Gateway zone found that two-thirds of local workers did not have the qualifications to take up service-sector jobs.

Population change in UK core conurbations, 1995-2000

	Population in 1991	Change 1995-2000 (%)
Glasgow	631.7	-1.5
Liverpool	480.7	-0.8
Birmingham	1006.5	-0.7
Leeds	717.4	0.2
Sheffield	529.3	0.3
Manchester	438.5	1.6
London	6889.9	5.3

Pollution and congestion hit the urban poor hardest. Congestion charges displace vehicle traffic from the core of the city and increase walking, cycling and bus use. But the wealthiest car users can readily afford to pay a levy that gives them less congested city streets to drive through. The health impact of urban car use typically falls on the poorest parts of town rather than on the suburban commuters who congest them. In the case of industrial location, polluting factories are twice as likely to be situated in postcode areas where the average income is less than £15,000.

The political economy of housing

Housing is always a critical factor in the political economy of the city. In many northern cities, a vicious cycle has been under way for decades. Economic restructuring has cut the demand for housing for skilled workers in many neighbourhoods, resulting in hundreds of thousands of unoccupied homes and rock-bottom property values. As the population density of localities falls it becomes unprofitable for retail and services to operate there. By contrast the concentration of economic growth in other regions is creating acute shortages. Housing the working class in cities in the south, especially but not exclusively low-paid public sector workers, is creating huge tensions for servicing future rounds of accumulation. New Labour admits that another 200,000 homes are needed in London and the South East, over and above their previous estimates. The average price of housing in London is five times more expensive than Burnley. And the government estimates that an extra 3.8 million households will form between 1996 and 2021, an increase of a fifth, chiefly as a result of changes to household structure with more people living alone for longer. At the same time as around 730,000 dwellings, mostly privately-owned, are lying unoccupied, there are also more than 85,000 homeless households in temporary accommodation, most with children and disproportionately from ethnic minorities.[7]

State intervention in the housing market, albeit in the perverse form of 'public-private partnerships', has again become essential to the attempt to sustain the UK's world city of accumulation, London. New Labour wants the local state to step back even further from taking direct responsibility for housing and to give a more central role to private uses of public money. Local authorities are being forced to abandon their 'landlord function', that is to directly own and manage housing tenancies, while £11.3 billion of public money is spent on 'Arms Length Management Organisations', Private Finance Initiatives and Housing Stock Transfers. Far from disappearing, then, as a political issue housing has been reignited as a matter of deep contention, with tenants' groups initiating a succession of campaigns against such privatisation, most notably in Birmingham and Glasgow, but also in Camden, Kingston-upon-Thames and Wrexham.[8]

Planning for profit

Urban planners have often been cast in a heroic role, protecting the public from shoddy contractors and the short-term drive for profit by speculators.[9] But town planning has been skewed historically by deeply undemocratic practices. It emerged as a profession in Britain, consolidated by the 1947 Town Planning Act, precisely in order to mediate the contradiction between the social need for liveable spaces and capital's need for concentrations of labour power. It supported an ideology of spatial determinism, where antagonistic social relations could be tethered by how people are arranged in space. Democratic participation in planning for municipal socialism was always secondary to the technical expertise of the planners, architects and building contractors. Urban space was treated in an abstract, neutral way, with the overall goal to create an urban order divorced from class content. So, for instance, the dominant response to the inner city riots of the 1980s was for better 'design solutions' to control the social problems occurring within urban space.

The apparent class neutrality of planning has confronted a fundamental problem in recent decades. Landowners and developers actually need the legal, financial and political stability and predictability that planning provides, as the experience under the Tories shows.[10] But urban policies are based increasingly on destabilising forms of competition between cities for scarce investment from both the state and private capital. Planning is deregulated as an adjunct to smoothing the activities of private investment funds. As the Urban Task Force put it:

> The land use planning system is not attuned to the complexity and diversity of the urban condition. It often takes too long to reach decisions and there is too great an emphasis on controlling development. We want to see a more flexible approach to planning. Too many authorities adhere rigidly to employment and other non-residential zoning for sites with no demand.[11]

Local councils enter into partnership with developers and speculators to re-brand their city as a physically enticing place to do business and one that also, coincidentally, has pools of relatively cheap and skilled labour. Planning is made the subordinate partner to urban developers. It should 'enable' and 'facilitate' the market for socially desirable ends. As the Urban Task Force put it:

> One of the most efficient uses for public money in urban regeneration is to pave the way for investment of much larger sums by the private sector... Our principal concern in relation to private finance is the market's failure to provide the kind of medium and long-term risk capital that complex area regeneration projects require. Government can help to attract this kind of investment by enabling funders to spread their investment risk more effectively.[12]

This is a highly precarious way to plan the city, if it can be called planning at all. Not only is it a blatant form of using public money to subsidise private capital, but it also depends on a naive view, at best, on the part of politicians of how finance markets work. Take the much-celebrated 1980s London Docklands project. Its legacy is one of monumental folly. In less than a decade private speculation, constantly 'pump-primed' by the state, created luxury housing for the few but little in the way of new jobs. Instead, deregulated planning produced a mini-crisis of the overproduction of office space in huge glass-clad, white-collar warehouses.[13] More recently, the Thames Gateway project, which has been called 'the largest piece of urban regeneration and development ever proposed anywhere in the world', is similarly premised on using state finances to bankroll property regeneration.[14]

Appearance over content

A renewed emphasis on architectural design fits well with the marketing of cities as classless places providing a quality lifestyle for the new middle class. Physical appearance is elevated way above other priorities such as decent working class housing. Waterfront sites are developed with culture, heritage and conspicuous consumption in mind, as with Bristol's harbour, Leith's dock area, Glasgow harbour, Dundee Waterfront, London's Tate Modern, Liverpool's Tate galleries and the proposed £400 million public-private redevelopment of the King's Waterfront, or Newcastle's Baltic gallery and Millennium Bridge. Retail is being used to revive city centres like Leeds, Birmingham's notorious Bull Ring, and Glasgow, with its 'Golden Z' of lengthy, shop-lined city centre streets.

The appearance of city-centre building surfaces is now given heightened attention, perhaps unprecedented since the municipal civic pride of the Victorian bourgeoisie. It also parallels the development of 'gated communities' for the urban middle class. George Monbiot points to the Montevetro Tower built in the late 1990s by New Labour's Urban Task Force chairperson, Richard Rogers:

> The Montevetro Tower, on the banks of the Thames in Battersea, contains some of the most expensive apartments in Britain. The top penthouse suite costs £4.5 million. Residents enjoy one of the best views that any building in London affords. They can play tennis on the all-weather court, relax in the sauna and order theatre tickets, limousines and even maids through the porter's lodge. Best of all, they don't have to share any of these luxuries with their neighbours: a security barrier at the entrance to the grounds ensures that the hoi polloi in the council estates across the road will stay where they belong.[15]

Here, as Walter Benjamin recognised, the parading of 'cultural treasures' is only made possible by the labour of a working class which is kept concealed at all times.[16]

At the same time, the physical appearance of many UK city centres and public spaces belies the new metropolitan enthusiasm for architecture, design and heritage. Green public spaces like urban parks are being lost or left in a poor state of upkeep, where they are not being sold off to private speculators. The New Opportunities Fund, the main funding source for urban parks, play areas and civic squares, only managed to allocate £3.8 million out of a budget of £125 million between 1998 and 2002.[17] Between 50 and 60 percent of people in Scotland view urban green spaces like parks as unattractive, unsafe, and poor places for children to play.[18]

Identikit high street retail units are flattening out the distinctiveness of city centres. Ralph Lauren, DKNY, Starbucks and Gap stand at the expensive end of every city while at the bottom of the pile are found McDonald's, Ladbrokes and Blockbuster. As one architectural journalist put it, 'Tesco branches are breeding like shrink-wrapped rabbits. Where once we had a church in every village, town and city, now we have Tesco with its Extras, Metros and Expresses'.[19] This is leading to a shift from abandoned city centre 'ghost towns' to what some call 'clone town Britain'.[20]

This strategy of edge of town retailers re-entering the city centre takes advantage of the deeper concentrations of mainly white-collar workers gathered in city centres. Single-person and dual-worker households are doubly exhausted and harassed by the intensification of work and the foreshortened time economy of living and working in the 24-hour urban economy. The built environment becomes a blurred backdrop for such workers, and the creeping standardisation of cities often goes unnoticed.

Glasgow's widely acclaimed culture-led regeneration programme is the pre-eminent example of enticing back middle class consumers and service-sector jobs to restore the fortunes of a city beset by long-run industrial decline, unemployment and slum housing. Glasgow shed 197,000 manufacturing jobs and acquired 145,000 in services between 1971 and 2001, and now has a much lower proportion of manual workers than the UK as a whole. It has become the subject of an incessant marketing campaign, emphasising art, culture and architecture, designer shopping and luxury apartments in the restored bourgeois residential quarter, the Merchant City. Last year saw the risible promotion of the city as Scotland's fashion answer to Milan: 'Glasgow: The New Black' or 'Glasgow: Scotland with Style'.

Left behind are the working class of Glasgow's large peripheral housing estates, which are in an acute state of decay. As a recent study puts it, 'Working class residents of the core city have lost out from this shift in the composition of Glasgow's economy, while better qualified suburban commuters have prospered'.[21] The city has some of the worst poverty and the highest mortality rates in Europe. Seven out of the top ten UK constituencies for premature deaths are in Glasgow, with life expectancy actually declining in some districts like Shettleston, the UK's poorest constituency, where men have a life expectancy of 63 years, ten years less than the Scottish average and 14 less than the UK as a whole:

> 'The Glasgow model' has contributed to the worsening levels of poverty and deprivation and to the deepening inequalities that characterise the city today. It has done this primarily by constructing Glasgow's future as a low paid workforce, grateful for the breadcrumbs from the tables of the entrepreneurs and investors upon which so much effort is spent attracting and cosseting—and by marginalising and ruling out any alternative strategy based upon large-scale public sector investment in sustainable and socially necessary facilities and services.[22]

When Liverpool assumes the mantle of European City of Culture in 2008 it will find that, as in Glasgow, place marketing and flagship cultural boosterism offer no panaceas for the deep-seated class polarisation in that city.

Communities and capitalism

The physical proximity of different classes in the city often only reinforces their social distance. Urban planning is now virtually synonymous with security and control. 'We will put "planning out crime" at the heart of the planning process,' says New Labour's 'sustainable communities' policy.[23] This is part of a more general effort to 'design out' of the city potentially disorderly spaces. Hence the one way to do this is through designing of public space with a full range of the technologies of urban control, such as the ubiquitous CCTV apparatus. The Home Office hopes personal identity cards will blend seamlessly into these controlled spaces.

Urban design becomes another weapon in the arsenal of a middle class resentful that the utopian promise of 'gentrified' inner cities has to confront the dystopian realities on the ground nearby—vandalism, violence, drugs, homelessness, begging, and generalised impoverishment. Many categories of crime, especially street crime, are in slow but gradual decline. Yet the perception of dangerous crime-ridden streets persists, particularly among affluent groups. Meanwhile the state keeps in reserve a range of punitive measures like Anti-Social Behaviour Orders (ASBOs) as well as the regular forces of law and order. All this chimes nicely with New Labour's reconstitution of the idea of morally listless poor communities.

New Labour sees communities, based on local neighbourhoods, as the basic building blocks of social order and cohesion. The state and capital undertake to enter a 'partnership' with them as a pragmatic route to 'social justice'. 'Community' is narrowly conceived as a self-regulating organism overseen by volunteer 'community leaders', with no place for struggles from below or any sense of 'communities of resistance'.[24]

As the Urban Task Force put it:

> Persuading people and organisations to care for their urban environment is partly a matter of re-awakening civic pride. Community involvement needs to be supported by strong enforcement action to deal with vandalism, graffiti, intimidation, noise pollution and other anti-social behaviour.[25]

Individuals are supposed to overcome the atomisation of market relations by acquiring 'social capital' through developing a strong sense of cultural belonging, civic responsibility and mutual co-operation through localised networks.[26] There is a strong nostalgic appeal here to a lost golden age of 'respectable' working class communities—although in so far as these ever existed they tended to be organised around the routines of the local workplaces that have mostly disappeared.

Those sections of the working class worst hit by decades of capitalist restructuring are to somehow pull themselves out of the circumstances they find themselves mired in. A moralising rhetoric about community is invoked precisely for those communities most damaged by capital and reviled by the state.[27]

Even the term 'community' is suspect. Community has been made to bear all manner of ideological inflections from the 'community charge' to 'care in the community'. Community is a category usually reserved by policy-makers for the poorest neighbourhoods. Typically, these are cast in terms of 'social pathology', where the poor are blamed for their own predicament, allowing the structural inequalities intrinsic to capitalism to be neatly side-stepped. Working class activity is frozen in the form of classless 'community' action, subordinated to reform experts whose object is to bleed dry the class content of urban movements.[28]

Community-friendly urban design fills up a vacuum created by the absence of sustained urban regeneration and widespread prosperity. Good design in prestige projects is assumed to be a stamp of social progress and urban renewal—in a manner similar to Tory urban policy from a quarter of a century ago.[29] 'Quality' design solutions are provided by private consultants who have little territorial or social connection to the working class whose everyday space they aim to govern by managing the appearance of the urban environment.

There are those who see the 'urban renaissance' in terms of anti-modernist design values. Here the post-war reconstruction of British cities was a brutalist failure of architectural ideology: 'the root of all this was the dominance of modernist ideology among the architectural elite'.[30] It was less ideology, modernist or otherwise, that produced the crisis of mass housing for the working class, than the role of urban planning in different stages in the development of capitalism. The post-war creation of deracinated housing estates, tower blocks and New Towns was an orderly reformist response to the 'slash and burn' clearing of inner city slums. That reconstruction of the urban landscape was integral to the wider programme of national accumulation under direct state supervision and management. Today's urban planning has to fulfil the contradictory demands of neo-liberal capitalism by flexibly reconciling economic competitiveness and social cohesion.

Thus the launch in 1998 of the National Neighbourhood Renewal Programme (in England) was about combining area-specific programmes for 'zones' as in Education Action Zones, Health Action Zones, with New Deal programmes, which are about tackling 'worklessness' and increasing labour force participation. There is a constant emphasis in New Labour social policies and area-based programmes on the need to include disadvantaged areas in the drive to enhance national competitiveness. Social exclusion and a lack of social cohesion in run-down inner city areas and peripheral estates are regarded as a source of economic inefficiency, hindering economic competitiveness and flexibility.

Whose city?

Cities are permanent sites of struggle and potential places of emancipation. The uneven development of UK cities means that they are caught up in a contradictory bind. All the possibilities of communal life present themselves but only in highly distorted ways. Town planning does not plan the productive activities or consumption needs of the city. It simply rearranges the scraps left behind in capitalism's disruptive wake in narrowly specialised technical and legal ways. But planning need not mean uniform rows of boxes, varied only by some cheap ornamental quirk:

> Order and some degree of regulation do not mean turning London or Manchester into a vision dredged from the notebook of Albert Speer, the Nazi architect. London County Council housing estates from the turn of the century, designed by young socialist architects, still surprise with their gentle and civilised order. Here were not just so many soulless 'housing units' as we have learnt to call the homes for the poor, but a celebration of the ideals of John Ruskin, William Morris and the Arts & Crafts movement: formal, ordered, yet not without beauty, designed to be a decent home to the poorest Londoners, the cockneys of yesterday, the Bengalis of today, and a far cry from either Broadwater Farm or their free-market successors.[31]

We don't have to accept the wistful nostalgia for Victorian socialist-architects as a model, just as we have no need to accept modernist plans uncritically either. But at least they pose an alternative vision to the impoverished one offered by New Labour. And it is here that the communities of resistance need to be couterposed to the New Labour image of communities of competition and cohesion.

While the state strengthens its coercive arm over working class areas it retreats from the provision of basic services—public transport, council housing, health services and leisure facilities. The closure of local swimming pools, for example, can rouse local people into action—as evidenced in the intense protest movements in 2001 at Manchester's Neptune Kingdom, known locally as the Gorton Tub, and Glasgow's Govanhill pool—and help create an active community of resistance:

While New Labour is keen to celebrate certain types of active communities who engage in 'approved' forms of local action, it is also prepared to use the full coercive force of the state to deal with active communities who challenge the authority of local government. Indeed, the experience in Govanhill demonstrates the revanchism of New Labour's project for an urban renaissance based around active communities: an iron fist lurks with the velvet glove of New Labour's urban regeneration agenda.[32]

Unspectacular local resistance is an in-built feature of the urban environment. Much of this takes place at subterranean depths, around concrete issues (sometimes literally). At times, urban struggles burst beyond the banks of local issues and put into sharper relief the wider forces shaping British cities. This now hidden, now visible struggle therefore continually poses the question, 'Whose city?'

NOTES

1: Department of the Environment, Transport and the Regions, *Our Towns and Cities: Delivering an Urban Renaissance* (London, 2000).

2: J Prescott, Foreword, *State of the Cities: A Progress Report to the Delivering Sustainable Communities Summit* (London, 2005). Prescott, as New Labour's deputy prime minister, has responsibility for delivering the urban regeneration programme.

3: Urban Task Force, *Towards an Urban Renaissance: Report of the Urban Task Force—Executive Summary* (London, 1999), p2 (our emphasis).

4: See *State of the Cities*, as above.

5: S Sassen, *The Global City: New York, London, Tokyo* (Princeton, 2000).

6: New Economics Foundation, *Ghost Town Britain II* (London, 2003).

7: *Sustainable Communities: Building for the Future* (London, 2003), p11.

8: See the Defend Council Housing campaign website for campaign updates: http://www.defendcouncilhousing.org.uk/dch/

9: S Howieson, 'Out of the Dead Zone', *Socialist Worker*, 22 January 2005.

10: P Allmendinger and H Thomas (eds), *Urban Planning and the New Right* (London and New York, 1998).

11: Urban Task Force, as above, p17.

12: As above, p23.

13: A Coupland, 'Docklands: Dream or Disaster?', in A Thornley (ed), *The Crisis of London* (London and New York, 1992).

14: P Hall, *Cities of Tomorrow: An Intellectual History of Urban Planning and Design in the Twentieth Century* (Oxford, 1996).

15: G Monbiot, 'Drawbridge Society', *The Guardian*, 24 June 1999.

16: W Benjamin, 'Theses on the Philosophy of History', in *Illuminations* (London, 1992).

17: New Economics Foundation, *Ghost Town Britain* (London, 2002), p21.

18: R Edwards, 'Urban Green Spaces are "Wastelands"', *Sunday Herald*, 6 February 2005.

19: J Glancey, quoted by A Simms, 'The Gaudy Sameness of Clone Town', *New*

Statesman, 24 January 2004.

20: See *Ghost Town Britain*, as above; New Economics Foundation, *Clone Town Britain* (London, 2004); and *Ghost Town Britain II*, as above.

21: I Turok and N Bailey, 'Glasgow's Recent Trajectory: Partial Recovery and Its Consequences', in D Newlands, M Danson and J McCarthy (eds), *Divided Scotland: The Nature, Causes and Consequences of Economic Disparities within Scotland* (Aldershot, 2004), p54.

22: G Mooney, 'Cultural Policy as Urban Transformation? Critical Reflections on Glasgow, European City of Culture 1990', *Local Economy* 19.4, 2004, p337.

23: *Sustainable Communities: Building for the Future*, as above, p21.

24: A Sivanandan, *Communities of Resistance: Writings on Black Struggles for Socialism* (London, 1990).

25: Urban Task Force, as above, p11.

26: See the statement by John Prescott, *Sustainable Communities: Building for the Future*, as above.

27: A Cochrane, 'New Labour, New Urban Policy?', in H Dean, R Sykes and R Woods (eds), *Social Policy Review* 12, 2000; A Holden and K Iveson, 'Designs on the Urban: New Labour's Urban Renaissance and the Spaces of Citizenship', *City* 7.1, 2003.

28: See Sean Damer's critique of planning in Glasgow in *From Moorepark to 'Wine-Alley': The Rise and Fall of a Glasgow Housing Scheme* (Edinburgh, 1989), and Cynthia Cockburn on Lambeth in *The Local State: Management of Cities and People* (London, 1977).

29: Department of the Environment, *Urban Renaissance: A Better Life for Towns* (London, 1980).

30: S Howieson, as above.

31: J Glancey, 'Exit from the City of Destruction', *The Independent*, 23 May 1996, p20.

32: G Mooney and N Fyfe, 'Active Communities of Resistance: Contesting the Govanhill Pool Closure in Glasgow, 2001-2002', paper to Social Policy Association conference, 2004.

Labour's organic crisis

Charlie Kimber

Only a fool would attempt to make some comments about the health and future of the Labour Party just a few weeks before a general election provides a very useful snapshot of its popularity and makes the task much easier. So here goes.

What nobody can deny is that Labour faces a crisis on many fronts. Its membership is in virtual freefall. Its popular support is shrinking. Its hold on the trade unions is challenged in historically unprecedented ways. Its claim to stand for mainstream social democratic values is shattered. And I believe that this is happening in a way that is much more profoundly significant than has happened in previous periods when a Labour government has attacked its own supporters.

Two factors are very important here. The first is the war on Iraq. The government's unflinching support for conspiracy to murder alongside Bush has destroyed any hope Blair might have had to be remembered as a 'pretty straight guy'.[1] It has alienated millions of Labour voters and caused tens or hundreds of thousands of Labour members to walk away from the party. Blair's crucial role in the war will haunt him to his grave.

The second key factor is the appearance of alternatives to Labour from the left. It is stupid to make too precise a prediction about how Labour will do at the next election; it is even more dangerous to attempt to predict the performance of Respect or the Scottish Socialist Party or others. The British election system, a century of Labour voting, the massive imbalance of media coverage and other factors make it very difficult for small parties to establish themselves electorally. But they will certainly mount the most serious radical challenge that Labour has faced at a general election for decades.

This is extremely important in analysing Labour's decline. For as long as there is no credible force to the left, people who hate the war, who are revolted by the anti-immigrant tirades of the main parties, and who believe in public services not private profit will face invidious choices. They can grudgingly vote Labour because they sometimes sound less bloodcurdling than the Tories, vote for the opportunist Lib Dems, or not vote at all. Many have followed these roads before, and many will next time. None in the end really threaten Blair. But if there is an alternative to the left it becomes a material factor in the break-up of Labour's support.

People who are still firmly wedded to Labour can sense the crisis. So Mark Seddon, a member of the party's national executive committee, wrote recently:

> Half of Labour's membership has simply disappeared, given up, retired to their armchairs or thrown their energies into other campaigns as the great moving right show of the last decade gathered pace… Active participation in Labour politics is withering on the vine. In many 'traditional' Labour seats, it is not unusual to find that membership hovers around the 200 mark. It is also older as well as being less active and less political. Party branches have merged, or are frequently inquorate; the local trade union links are often atrophied. If the checks and balances, the democratic structures and the hard-fought debates and votes at conferences have been hollowed out, it follows that a Labour prime minister can take Britain into an illegal war and not fear

> the consequences. It also follows that the same prime minister can tell the *Times*, as he did on 5 November 2004, that 'the US neo-conservatives are not a world away from the progressive left', secure in the knowledge that the only response will be a shrugging of shoulders and a shuffling of feet. New Labour's command of the political void is so total, the opposition, from right and left, so feeble, that all of us are becoming helpless spectators.[2]

Strong stuff indeed, and it could be replicated in a thousand voices from top to bottom of the party. And a deeper look shows just how much Labour is in trouble.

Labour members

Membership was 265,000 when Tony Blair became leader in 1994. He said he wanted to produce a mass membership party with up to 1 million members. The early signs seemed positive and by 1997 membership had reached 407,000. This increase of over 140,000 occurred at the same time as Blair drove the party rightwards. He dumped Clause 4, the party's commitment to social ownership, declared that the class war was over and introduced the first of many waves of constitutional reforms designed to reduce the collective input of trade unionists and constituency parties in the formation of policy. This has led to a myth that the people who joined during this period were cappuccino-sipping, Tuscany-holidaying, Islington-dwelling Blair clones...or worse. Blair certainly celebrated the 40 percent increase between 1994 and 1997 as evidence of the 'newness' of the party and the sharp separation from 'Old Labour'. In 1995 he chose the News Corporation leadership conference on Hayman Island in the Pacific Ocean to announce:

> We have increased our individual membership by over 120,000. By the next election over one half of our members will have joined since the 1992 election. It is literally a new party.[3]

In fact, as an authoritative study by Patrick Seyd and Paul Whitleley[4] makes clear, the members who had joined after Blair became leader were in many respects more 'classically Labour' than those who had previously made up the party. They were younger (average 48 compared to 54!), blacker (6 percent non-white compared to 3 percent) and more likely to be manual workers (17 percent compared to 13 percent).[5]

Their views were also more 'Old Labour' than many would have expected: 'Throughout the 1990s members remained attached to certain basic social democratic principles centring on issues of redistribution, public service and equality'.[6] However, 'At the same time they had a strong interest in winning elections, given the experience of nearly 20 years of Conservative dominance. This meant that the members were willing to support modernisation in the interests of electoral success'.[7]

People joined Labour not so much as a positive affirmation of Blair but as a reflection of a deep desire to dump the Tories. If this picture is correct, we would expect Labour's membership to expand up until the moment that victory was achieved—and then for the numbers to slump. This is almost exactly what happened. Blair's dream of a mass membership party foundered on the rock of his electoral success.

Once New Labour actually achieved office and started implementing its programme, members began to leave almost immediately. The election day champagne bottles had only just been put in the bin when some people began hurling their Labour membership cards in with them. By 1998 the figure was 399,000, in 2001 it was 311,000, and it had fallen to 280,000 in 2002.[8] Since then people have been leaving in large numbers, with Labour losing 33,000 members during 2003 alone.

At the end of July 2004 the party's accounts, released by the Electoral Commission, revealed that membership was at its lowest since records began. They showed there were 214,952 individuals registered as members at the end of 2003. This was the smallest figure since Labour started compiling individual membership statistics in 1928.

There was worse to come. Hard on the heels of the Electoral Commission's revelations, the party's national executive committee was told that membership had dipped further—to 208,000. But when those who had let their membership lapse for the past six months were discounted as well (as the party's rules said they should be), the figure stood at 190,000, a drop of 25,000 in six months. Some of the biggest drops have been in Labour's inner-city heartlands. Party membership was far more likely to have remained stable in semi-rural seats such as Wrekin in Shropshire.[9]

New Labour has been systematically kicking away the props of mainstream social democratic politics—council housing, comprehensive education, opposition to further inroads for private medicine and so on. Of course Labour was appalling on all these issues in the past. But the declared mission was different and there was not the same zeal for capitalist policy. That explains why figures like Roy Hattersley, Frank Dobson and Peter Kilfoyle find themselves clashing so often with the party's leaders.

The classic Labour response to such disastrous falls in membership is to say that it has happened before and, in those cases, the party has recovered. Certainly the party has been in trouble before. In particular membership dropped drastically during the earlier Labour governments of 1964-70 and 1974-79. Fred Lindop, in a detailed study of a local Labour Party in south London, gives a revealing glimpse of how previous Labour betrayals gutted the party of activists:

> From the mid-1950s, the Greenwich Labour Party went into a long term decline in membership and levels of activity. Membership declined by over 75 percent between 1954 and the mid-1980s.The records show an almost continuous concern with the inactivity of wards and other party organisations, interspersed with very brief periods of resurgent confidence (early-mid 1960s, early 1970s). The decline was clearly part of a national trend... Reports in the late 1960s and early 1970s constantly refer to the Labour Party being 'remote in recent years from the people it should represent'. The catastrophic collapse of membership between 1965 and 1970 was identified as a direct consequence of the unpopularity of the Wilson government's economic policies (though the secretary in February 1968 attributed much of this to 'the fact that the electorate in general and party members are not aware of the positive achievements of the Labour government').[10]

Overall disillusion with the 1964-70 Labour government meant that nominal membership dropped from 817,000 (1965) to 680,000 (1970). Assessments of Labour membership in the 1960s and 1970s, which look much better than today, should be treated with caution. In particular, the rule between 1963 and 1980 that each constituency had to register at least 1,000 members, even if it had far fewer, caused vast over-counting: 'The method of counting members hid the scale of the decay. But when a more honest system was adopted in 1981, the supposed membership of 666,000 was shown to be only 348,000'.[11] Steven Fielding notes:

> Analysing a situation she thought 'deplorable', in 1965 Labour's national agent believed parties claiming 1,000 only had about 250 members. On that

basis membership that year was inflated by about one-third, a distortion that only increased with time.[12]

But there are powerful factors which underscore the particular depth of the present crisis. The decline from the 908,000 members of 1950 to the 190,000 today has not been seamless. But it means Labour now begins from a very low base. The second point is that probably the only way Labour could recover members would be to lose an election. If, as everyone expects, Labour wins again and implements the 'unremittingly New Labour' policies that Blair promises, then the decline is likely to deepen. And there are wider processes in the working class which are contributing to a structural crisis.

Labour votes

Labour has been lucky in the collapse of its traditional enemy, the Conservative Party. This has enabled Blair to rack up massive parliamentary majorities on many fewer votes than you might expect. In 1992 John Major's Tory victory was based on 14 million votes across Britain. Blair's landslide in 1997 rested on fewer votes, 13.5 million. By 2001 the Labour vote was down to 10.7 million. This is fewer than the 11.5 million won by Neil Kinnock when he lost to Major in 1992. (Indeed it is perilously close to the 10 million achieved by Neil Kinnock in the crushing electoral defeat of 1987.) It is worth watching at the next election to see if Labour exceeds the 1987 figure or slips towards the 8.5 million who voted for Michael Foot's Labour in 1983—when a further 7.8 million voted for the SDP-Liberal alliance. It was the humiliatingly low 1983 vote that was used as the excuse for the whole New Labour project.

Labour's huge majorities survive because, even though 20 percent fewer people voted Labour in 2001 than in 1997, the vote of the main opposition parties also fell. The Conservatives continued to lose votes. Some 1.3 million fewer people voted Tory in 2001 than their catastrophic return in 1997, and 5.7 million fewer than in 1992. The Tories' divisions over Europe have torn the party apart (and continue to do so). As for the Lib Dems, half a million fewer people voted for them in 2001 than had done in 1997, and 1.2 million less than in 1992. In fact, the Lib Dems' share of the electorate fell from nearly 12 percent in 1997 to less than 11 percent in 2001.

As Susan Watkins writes:

> In 2001 fewer than one voter in four (24 percent of the total electorate) actually marked a cross for Blair's government, while turnout fell from a (then) record low of 71 percent in 1997 to a mere 59 percent in 2001. Unrepresented in parliament are the 2.8 million Labour abstentions in Britain's former industrial heartlands—the metropolitan conurbations of Tyne and Wear, Manchester, Merseyside, the West Midlands, Clydeside and South Wales. It was the hard-core Labour vote that stayed at home: whites in the old colliery districts, Asians in the Lancashire inner cities, under-25s in particular. Turnout fell below 44 percent in the blighted constituencies round the Tyneside shipyards, the bleak Glaswegian council estates and the semi-derelict terraces of Salford and central Leeds; below 35 percent in the ruined zones of Liverpool's docklands. Measured in terms of working class disenfranchisement, the Americanisation of British politics has accelerated dramatically under New Labour, to abstention levels worthy of the US itself.[13]

It would be no surprise if the 2005 election saw a continuation in all these trends—low turnout, an historically low Labour vote, but still a comfortable majority for Blair because the Tories remain confined to their core voters and the Lib Dems make little headway. This should not be allowed to obscure the deep disenchantment with New Labour.

Trade union base withering

One factor demonstrates most clearly that the crisis of New Labour is deep-seated and organic, not some passing fad—the splintering of the party's trade union base. For almost a century it has been automatic for unions that wished to have a political voice to affiliate to Labour. It has hardly been questioned, even at times of deep anger with the party. Now that has changed.

At 12 noon on 7 February 2004 the RMT rail and maritime union, which had helped to found the Labour Party, was expelled because it refused to back down in the face of an ultimatum from the leadership. RMT members had voted to allow their union branches to affiliate to parties other than Labour. The party decided this had to be crushed in case the example spread—and so the RMT was thrown out. Labour was now overtly in alliance with Bush's warmongers, in confrontation with its trade union base.

In June 2004 the FBU firefighters' union passed a motion saying, 'The aims and objectives of the Labour Party no longer reflect those of the Fire Brigades Union. Therefore, this Conference demands that the FBU disaffiliates from the Labour Party nationally.' The vote, against the strong recommendation of the union's leaders, reflected total frustration and fury at the government's bitter assault on the union during its national strike. But it also represented something more. There have been many occasions when Labour governments have attacked groups of workers—think of the 18 times the 'golden age' government of 1945 used troops to break strikes, the slanders against the seafarers' strike in 1966, the confrontations of the Winter of Discontent in 1978-79.

None of these led to widespread calls for disaffiliation or branch support for other parties. But in 2004 the atmosphere created by the Iraq war—and the resistance to it—came together with anger at betrayal on the industrial front and against Labour's policies on privatisation, pay and other issues.

The RMT and FBU may have gone (or been pushed) further than any other unions. But they are part of a continuum. In the CWU post and telecom workers' union the leadership first had to propose cutting funds to the party and then accepted a conference motion which said that the union would break from the party if postal privatisation went ahead. These manoeuvres were necessary to head off powerful pressures to democratise the union's political fund or even disaffiliate from Labour. The GMB has cut its funding to Labour by £4 million over five years. The only reason that the PCS civil service workers' union is not discussing cutting money or disaffiliating from Labour in the wake of the mass job cuts is because it is not affiliated in the first place!

The damage to Labour is not primarily financial—although that matters. At least in the short term it is possible for the party to pay its bills by attracting the silken cheques of the very rich. Major donations in 2004 included £2.5 million from Lord Sainsbury, the billionaire trade minister, £1 million from Sir Christopher Ondaatje, the retired businessman, £200,000 from Sir David Garrard, the property magnate, and £50,000 from Patrick Stewart, the actor.[14]

But the rich don't go on the knocker at election time, they don't persuade their friends at work or in the housing estate or in the pub to vote Labour. They don't act as 'ambassadors in the community' in the way that almost 1 million members did 50 years ago.

If Labour continues to lose its base in the unions it will damage the party far more than its present leaders may believe. But it will also open a new era where the questions about trade unions, politics and Labour—which seemed decisively settled 80 years ago—will once more be opened. And attempts to 'reclaim' Labour by and for them have been singularly ineffective. The 'reclaimers' argument itself has become increasingly desperate as Blair has continued regardless. First the left rested its hopes on an influx of new members who would throw out the right and reinstall the policies pre-1994. When that didn't happen it was claimed the trade union members would force their delegates and representatives to shift Labour policy leftwards. And then it became a matter of hoping that a group of left union leaders would do it from above. It hasn't happened. Instead the great bulk of union leaders have allowed Blair to get away without having a proper debate on Iraq at the last two conferences, and have extracted only the most meagre promises in return for their continuing support.

Conclusion

Senior ministers are afraid that Labour may be mirroring the Conservatives in the 1990s, when there was a sudden deterioration in grassroots activism and membership. Whatever activity one focuses on, participation has been declining over the past ten years. The extent of the commitment of the average member is increasingly merely one of paying a yearly subscription and occasionally donating money to the party when asked to do so. In an organisational and political sense the fate of the Conservative Party is an object lesson for Labour. The Conservatives lost their grassroots party organisation in the long years of the Thatcher incumbency. This neglect went beyond the point of recovery, so that after the 1997 election defeat they were unable to rebuild it.

That will not happen overnight with Labour. Blairism has shallow roots, Labourism has deep roots. In 1993 I wrote an article on a similar theme to this one, partly to argue that Labour was in decline, partly to insist that it could win the next election! I wrote:

> Labour can win the next election, although the haemorrhage of membership and the distancing from the unions will make it more difficult. But even if Labour does win it won't be a party committed to workers' interests and it won't hesitate to turn on its own supporters once in government. Moreover there are more important considerations for revolutionaries than the prospects of Labour's electoral success. Whatever has happened at the polls, Labour

> remains the party that the overwhelming majority of advanced workers define as 'their' party. Reformist consciousness—the idea that the only way to change society is a little at a time through the mechanism of the existing state—remains strong. As long as capitalism exists this reformist consciousness will exist. Even large scale struggle has the effect of strengthening reformist ideas as well as revolutionary ones. Reformist notions can (and must) be overcome only when workers feel their own power and are given an alternative political leadership that is well enough rooted in the class to provide a viable alternative. Building such an alternative means both analysing Labour's failures and putting forward a different model.[15]

And that is essentially true today. Indeed the task is even more urgent because British politics is opening up and there is a danger of a growth of right wing forces if the left does not seize the time. At the European elections in June 2004 less than half the electorate voted for Labour and the Tories combined (Conservatives 26.7 percent, Labour 22.6 percent). The field is open in a way it has not been for a long time.

It is important to restate that the existence of a left alternative is a crucial factor in the future development of Labour. Seyd and Whiteley write:

> Capitalist society generates inequality, and if left unchecked this becomes severe inequality... Traditionally the losers in this process in the United Kingdom have looked to the Labour Party for protection, with polices such as the redistribution of income, support for the legal right to organise effective trade unions and the provision of high-quality public services free at the point of use. If the party looks very closely after the interests of the winners in the capitalist lottery, and favours low taxes, little or no redistribution, attacks on trade union rights and poorly funded or nonexistent public services, then it will rapidly lose its traditional supporters. Quite rationally they will look elsewhere for a party to represent their interests.[16]

In Respect and the Scottish Socialist Party we have to meet the challenge posed by the crisis of Labour.

NOTES

1: Blair's own description of himself, *On the Record,* BBC2, 16 November 1997.

2: Mark Seddon, *The Guardian,* 29 November 2004.

3: P Seyd and P Whiteley, *New Labour's Grass Roots: The Transformation of the Labour Party Membership* (Palgrave, 2002), p40.

4: As above.

5: As above, pp41-42.

6: As above, p168.

7: As above.

8: There are many technical arguments about exactly how many members the Labour Party has at any particular time. Much of the confusion is caused by whether you count as members people who have long ceased paying their subscriptions. These figures, taken from the BBC website, give a good picture of the trend even if they are not absolutely correct.

9: *The Guardian*, 27 July 2004.

10: F Lindop, Greenwich Labour Party 1920-87, www.microform.co.uk/guides/R97567.pdf

11: P Seyd and P Whiteley, *Labour's Grass Roots* (Oxford, 1992), p16.

12: S Fielding, *The Penny Farthing Machine Revisited: Labour Party Members and Participation in the 1950s and 1960s*, www.psa.ac.uk/cps/1999/fielding.pdf

13: S Watkins, 'A Weightless Hegemony', in *New Left Review* 25 (Jan-Feb 2004).

14: *The Guardian*, 27 July 2004.

15: C Kimber, 'The Labour Party in Decline', *International Socialism* 67 (Winter 1993).

16: P Seyd and P Whiteley (2002), as above, pp181-182.

Respect: the record so far

Respect was formed in January last year as a coalition of socialists, anti-war activists, Muslims and disillusioned Labour supporters, including the expelled MP George Galloway. Centrally it is opposed to Bush and Blair's war, to the neo-liberal attacks on workers and their rights, and to racism.

Its first challenge to New Labour was in June's elections to the European parliament and for the London Mayor and London Assembly—the only elections in England with a degree of proportional representation.

It got more Euro votes than any other party in the inner-London borough of Tower Hamlets, and came second in neighbouring Newham. It also did well in inner-city areas of Birmingham, Leicester, Preston and north east London, although its national Euro vote was damaged, as with the left elsewhere in Europe, by the huge, dispersed constituencies.

In the Assembly elections, across the whole of London (which includes big middle class areas) it got 4.57 percent of the vote—with 14.9 percent in east London and 8.3 percent in north east London.

It built on these results to get 6.3 and 12.7 percent of the votes in first past the post parliamentary by-elections in Birmingham and Leicester in July. It stunned New Labour by winning a council seat in a predominantly Bengali area of Tower Hamlets and then by beating New Labour to come second in one of the borough's ethnically mixed areas. More recently, it picked up 15 percent of the vote in a council by-election in nearby Hackney.

Respect entered the election campaign better placed to challenge Labour's stranglehold over working class votes than the left has been at any time since the Communist Party lost its last two MPs in 1950. But a general election—on the first past the post system—presents special difficulties, given a virtual blackout by the national media.

Respect has for this reason concentrated its forces on about 30 constituencies, expecting to do best in east London, where it has the possibility of emerging as a central political force.

Can we change the world without taking power?

A debate between John Holloway and Alex Callinicos World Social Forum, 27 January 2005

John Holloway: I don't know the answer. Perhaps we can change the world without taking power. Perhaps we cannot. The starting point—for all of us, I think—is uncertainty, not knowing, a common search for a way forward. Because it becomes more and more clear that capitalism is a catastrophe for humanity. A radical change in the organisation of society, that is, revolution, is more urgent than ever. And this revolution can only be world revolution if it is to be effective.

But it is unlikely that world revolution can be achieved in one single blow. This means that the only way in which we can conceive of revolution is as interstitial revolution, as a revolution that takes place in the interstices of capitalism, a revolution that occupies spaces in the world while capitalism still exists. The question is how we conceive of these interstices, whether we think of them as states or in other ways.

In thinking about this, we have to start from where we are, from the many rebellions and insubordinations that have brought us to Porto Alegre. The world is full of such rebellions, of people saying NO to capitalism: NO, we shall not live our lives according to the dictates of capitalism, we shall do what we consider necessary or desirable and not what capital tells us to do. Sometimes we just see capitalism as an all-encompassing system of domination and forget that such rebellions exist everywhere. At times they are so small that even those involved do not perceive them as refusals, but often they are collective projects searching for an alternative way forward and sometimes they are as big as the Lacandon Jungle or the Argentinazo of three years ago or the revolt in Bolivia just over a year ago. All of these insubordinations are characterised by a drive towards self-determination, an impulse that says, 'No, you will not tell us what to do, we shall decide for ourselves what we must do.'

These refusals can be seen as fissures, as cracks in the system of capitalist domination. Capitalism is not (in the first place) an economic system, but a system of command. Capitalists, through money, command us, telling us what to do. To refuse to obey is to break the command of capital. The question for us, then, is how do we multiply and expand these refusals, these cracks in the texture of domination?

There are two ways of thinking about this.

The first says that these movements, these many insubordinations, lack maturity and effectiveness unless they are focused, unless they are channelled towards a goal. For them to be effective, they must be channelled towards the conquest of state power—either through elections or through the overthrowing of the existing state and the establishment of a new, revolutionary state. The organisational form for channelling all these insubordinations towards that aim is the party.

The question of taking state power is not so much a question of future intentions as of present organisation. How should we organise ourselves in the present? Should we join a party, an organisational form that focuses our discontent on the winning of state power? Or should we organise in some other way?

The second way of thinking about the expansion and multiplication of insubordinations is to say, 'No, they should not be all harnessed together in the form of a party, they should flourish freely, go whatever way the struggle takes them.' This does not mean that there should be no coordination, but it should be a much looser coordination. Above all, the principal point of reference is not the state but the society that we want to create.

The principal argument against the first conception is that it leads us in the wrong direction. The state is not a thing, it is not a neutral object: it is a form of social relations, a form of organisation, a way of doing things which has been developed over several centuries for the purpose of maintaining or developing the rule of capital. If we focus our struggles on the state, or if we take the state as our principal point of reference, we have to understand that the state pulls us in a certain direction. Above all, it seeks to impose upon us a separation of our struggles from society, to convert our struggle into a struggle *on behalf of, in the name of.* It separates leaders from the masses, the representatives from the represented; it draws us into a different way of talking, a different way of thinking. It pulls us into a process of reconciliation with reality, and that reality is the reality of capitalism, a form of social organisation that is based on exploitation and injustice, on killing and destruction. It also draws us into a spatial definition of how we do things, a spatial definition which makes a clear distinction between the state's territory and the world outside, and a clear distinction between citizens and foreigners. It draws us into a spatial definition of struggle that has no hope of matching the global movement of capital.

There is one key concept in the history of the state-centred left, and that concept is betrayal. Time and time again the leaders have betrayed the movement, and not necessarily because they are bad people, but just because the state as a form of organisation separates the leaders from the movement and draws them into a process of reconciliation with capital. Betrayal is already given in the state as an organisational form.

Can we resist this? Yes, of course we can, and it is something that happens all the time. We can refuse to let the state identify leaders or permanent representatives of the movement, we can refuse to let delegates negotiate in secret with the representatives of the state. But this means understanding that our forms of organisation are very different from those of the state, that there is no symmetry between them. The state is an organisation *on behalf of*, what we want is the organisation of self-determination, a form of organisation that allows us to articulate what *we* want, what *we* decide, what *we* consider necessary or desirable. What we want, in other words, is a form of organisation that does not have the state as its principal point of reference.

The argument against taking the state as the principal point of reference is clear, but what of the other concept? The state-oriented argument can be seen as a pivoted conception of the development of struggle. Struggle is conceived as having a central pivot, the taking of state power. First we concentrate all our efforts on winning the state, we organise for that, then, once we have achieved that, we can think of other forms of organisation, we can think of revolutionising society. First we move in one direction, in order to be able to move in another: the problem is that the dynamic acquired during the first phase is difficult or impossible to dismantle in the second phase.

The other concept focuses directly on the sort of society we want to create, without passing through the state. There is no pivot: organisation is directly prefigurative, directly linked to the social relations we want to create. Where the first concept sees the radical transformation of society as taking place after the seizure of power, the second insists that it must begin now. Revolution not when the time is right but revolution here and now.

This prefiguration, this revolution here-and-now is above all the drive to self-determination. Self-determination cannot exist in a capitalist society. What can and does exist is the drive towards social self-determination: the moving against alien determination, determination by others. Such a moving against determination by others is necessarily experimental, but three things are clear:

(a) The drive towards self-determination is necessarily a drive against allowing others to decide on our behalf. It is therefore a movement against representative democracy and for the creation of some form of direct democracy.

(b) The drive towards self-determination is incompatible with the state, which is a form of organisation which decides on our behalf and thereby excludes us.

(c) The drive towards self-determination makes no sense unless it includes as its central point the self-determination of our work, our activity. It is necessarily directed against the capitalist organisation of work. We are talking, therefore, not just of democracy but of communism, not just of rebellion but of revolution.

For me, it is this second conception of revolution that we have to concentrate on. The fact that we reject the state-centred conception doesn't obviously mean that the non-state-centred conception does not have its problems. I see three principal problems, none of which is an argument for reverting to the idea of taking state power:

The first issue is how to deal with state repression. I do not think the answer is to arm ourselves so that we can defeat the state in open confrontation: we would be unlikely to win, and anyway it would involve reproducing precisely the authoritarian social relations we are fighting against. Nor do I think that the answer is to take control of the state so that we can control the army and the police forces: the use of the army and police on behalf of the people obviously comes into conflict with the struggles of those who do not want anyone to act on their behalf. This leaves us with trying to find other ways of dissuading the state from exercising violence against us: this may have to involve some degree of armed resistance (as in the case of the Zapatistas), but must surely rely above all on the strength of the integration of the rebellion into the community.

The second issue is whether we can develop alternative doings (alternative productive activity) within capitalism, and to what extent we can create an alternative social nexus between activities, other than value. There are many experiments that point in the direction of some sort of solution (the *fábricas recuperadas*, factories reopened by the workers, in Argentina, for example) and the possibilities will obviously depend on the scale of the movement itself, but this remains a major problem. How do we think of a social determination of production and distribution that moves from the bottom up (from the interstitial revolts) rather than from a central planning body?

The third issue is the organisation of social self-determination. How do we organise a system of direct democracy on a scale that goes beyond the local level in a complex society? The classic answer is the idea of councils linked by a council of councils to which the councils send instantly recallable delegates. This seems basically correct, but it is clear that even in small groups the operation of democracy is always problematic, so that the only way in which direct democracy can be conceived is as a constant process of experimentation and self-education.

Can we change the world without taking power? The only way to find out is to do it.

Alex Callinicos: Whatever our differences, John and I stand for changing the world through a process of self-emancipation, where there aren't leaders who tell people what to do but rather people who collectively liberate themselves. I admire the honesty, clarity and consistency of John's work, which is evident in his presentation today. But I also have to be honest and say that I find the ideal of changing the world without taking power ultimately self-refuting.

I agree with John about uncertainty. There are lots of things we cannot know. But one thing I am certain about. That is that it is impossible to change the world without addressing and solving the question of political power.

I absolutely sympathise with one of the impulses behind the slogan 'Change the world without taking power'. Among a lot of the traditions on the left worldwide there has been what has been called 'socialism from above'. Whether it is a Communist party with Stalinist traditions or a social democratic party like the Workers Party in Brazil today, it involves the idea that the party changes things for you and everyone else remains passive.

The political tradition I stand in is a very different one. It is that of socialism from below summed up in Marx's definition of socialism as the self-emancipation of the working class. Socialism is about the oppressed and exploited of the world effectively liberating themselves.

My fundamental difference with John is that I believe this process of self-emancipation requires us to confront and overthrow the existing state and replacing it with a radically different form of state power.

John invites us essentially to turn our backs on the state. He says that we should carry out what he calls an 'interstitial' revolution. It's been summed up by other thinkers sharing the same ideas as John as life despite capitalism. We should all try and cultivate our autonomous gardens despite the horrors of capitalism.

The trouble is that the state won't leave us alone and that is because capitalism itself, the system that different states sustain, won't leave us alone. Capitalism today is invading the gardens of the world to carve them up and turn them into branches of agribusiness or suburban speculation and won't leave us alone.

We cannot ignore the state, because the state is the most concentrated single form of capitalist power. This means strategically we have to be against the state, to pursue the revolution against the state.

Does this mean we ignore the existing state and do not ever put demands on the capitalist state? No. The existing capitalist states try to legitimise themselves to win the consent of those they oppress and exploit. This means that if we organise effectively, we can force reforms out of capitalism. Also, if we ignore the state, that means we will be indifferent to struggles over privatisation. For example, at the minute George Bush wants to privatise the pensions system in the US. Do we say we don't care about that because the social security system in the US is organised by the state? I think, no.

Finally, many workers these days are employed by the state. Part of the process of privatisation means those employees of private companies replace these workers. Often that means the service to the public is worse and the conditions and wages of those employed by those companies get worse.

But if we are not indifferent to the state, that does not mean we can rely on it. In the long run capitalism and the state which seeks to sustain it will seek to take back any reforms it concedes temporarily. That is what they are seeking to do at the present time.

Moreover, as John has highlighted, the state is a hierarchical organisation which organises violence to keep the mass of society subordinated.

This means we cannot simply try to seize the existing state. If we seize the existing state, in the end, at the worst we will get Stalin, at best we will get someone like Lula or Mbeki in South Africa who comes out of a mass movement which seeks to change the world but ends up administering things for capitalism.

What's the alternative then? It is to build up a movement that is powerful and focused enough to break the existing forms of state power and institute radically different and radically democratic forms of state power. In other words, there has to be a revolution which is not a party taking state power by seizing the existing state, but the oppressed and exploited—above all workers—who break the existing state and in the process of doing so create radically new and democratic forms of power in order to manage society for themselves.

This alternative is not just a fantasy that I've spun out of my head. If we look at the history of the working class movement over the last 150 years, again and again workers have created new ways of organising in order to wage mass struggles effectively. These have been much more democratic, much more subject to the control of the workers themselves. In order to wage their struggles, they have created delegate structures that break down the hierarchy that John talks about. And in doing so they have created new forms of political power, even if they don't know it.

There are many examples: the soviets in the Russian revolutions of 1905 and 1917 are the most famous examples; there were the workers' and soldiers' councils that were formed in the German Revolution of 1918-20; right up to the *cordones* that were formed in Chile in 1972-73 at the height of the struggles under the Popular Unity government of Allende. There are many other examples of mass popular organisation that represent a new sort of political power.

The important thing about these forms of organisation, whatever the intentions that led to their formation, is that they have the capacity to challenge and break the existing state and institute new forms of power.

We are not saying, as John was suggesting, 'Wait for the revolution.' But any struggles that begin to build towards self-organisation are pointing the way towards the way a future non-capitalist, socialist, society can be organised. The problem is that for any movement towards self-organisation to succeed in breaking the power of capital, there has to be a moment of concentration and centralisation. You can't deal with the concentrated power of capital—the state and the multinational corporations—without the movements themselves becoming focused to confront the power of those corporations directly.

John will say, 'When you talk about centralisation and concentration, you are returning to the old ways of organising, you are beginning to organise in a way that reproduces the centralised and hierarchical structures of the existing state.'

I agree it isn't easy. John was very honest and talked about the difficulties with his strategic conception, and I agree there are difficulties with the approach I am defending. Combining centralisation with self-organisation is not easy. But without a degree of centralisation we will be defeated.

If we simply have fragmented and decentralised and localised activity, all cultivating our autonomous gardens, capital can isolate us and destroy or incorporate us piece by piece. And we cannot address problems like climate change unless we have the capacity to coordinate and, to a degree, to centralise for global change. We cannot reduce CO_2 emissions to the necessary level without global coordination. We will not achieve the world we want to see if we simply rely on the fragment and the local.

This is related to the question of parties. John is critical of the party as a form of organisation. He says it reproduces the hierarchical structures of the existing state. But if we look at our movement, there are parties within the movement—that is, there are ideologically organised currents which have in their different ways a total strategic view of the transformation of society. In that sense of party, John and the people who think like him are as much a party within the different movements as are the Workers Party and the PSOL in Brazil,[1] or the Socialist Workers Party in Britain.

1: The new left wing party formed by those expelled from the Workers Party.

People who organise such a current can say they are not a party, but it is a form of self-deception. Recognising the role parties can play in the movements can lead to a more honest and open articulation of different strategies and visions for change. Parties can contribute to the development of a movement that is both self-organised and sufficiently coherent to take on the task of social transformation, of revolution.

My ideal in this respect is the one articulated by the great Italian revolutionary Antonio Gramsci. He talked about the dialectical interaction between the moment of centralisation represented by the parties and the self-organised impulse from the movement which is the fundamental driving force of revolution.

To sum up: First of all we cannot avoid the question of the state and political power. It is a delusion to believe we can avoid it. The critical question is who takes power and how. If it is simply a question of a party taking control of the existing state by whatever means, then it is absolutely true that will be a change that simply reproduces the existing relations of domination. But the conception of a self-organised working class seizing power to institute new forms of political organisation and state organisation along with all the other oppressed and exploited groups changes the question.

Revolution then becomes a process of self-emancipation which starts here and now, in the way we organise resistance to capitalism, and culminates when we create a self-organised society, and capitalism and all the oppression associated with it becomes simply a bad memory.

First contributor from the floor: I agree mainly with John's idea. This discussion is not new. The same discussion happened in the 19th century. The people who believed we should focus on taking power in the state won the debate, and they created movements in that direction. Stalin was one result, Lula another. Once the state becomes the focus of the fight we cannot avoid the change becoming just a mirror of the state. The revolution was not really a revolution for the people.

Second contributor: We haven't looked so far at Venezuela in this debate. There both sides of the question are being developed. They are looking at the state while making the internal transformation from below, beginning with the new constitution which embodies decentralisation and participation. Economically they are undertaking development, with agrarian reform, ending landlordism and redistributing land to the peasantry. Educationally they are ending illiteracy for 3 million people. By participatory democracy and social inclusion they are trying to bring about the self-emancipation talked about here. Venezuela represents a new and quite different way of resolving the questions we are discussing here. It is achieving levels of self-organisation that mean it is no longer dependent on the world system. It is five years since the IMF and World Bank determined what happened there.

Third contributor: All over the world we have people creating progressive parties based on a mishmash of neo-Keynesian policies, reform, reinstituting regulation and so on. If we advocate revolution here and now, simultaneously with an attempt to replace the state by the anti-state, we have to think about what the alternative is going to be. Capitalism is the indefinite accumulation of capital until the point where you have the obscenity of money in the hands of so few that it really amounts to mass destruction. We should add to the Chávez revolution the ideas put out by *Z* magazine that look back to Marx's idea of a federation of producers and turn it into a federation of producers and consumers.

Fourth contributor: I want to ask two questions. One, what is the significance of the concept of fissure or crack which John uses? The second is whether there is not some concept of power other than that of state power.

Fifth contributor (Chris Nineham, SWP): There is a sense in which this debate has been false. John made a very good critique of the tradition which says a small number of people should take power for everyone else. It is a critique of social democracy, of a whole tradition of trying to operate from above through getting a few individuals into the state. That is a failed strategy. Those people always get drawn into the system. They get bullied, bought off or simply compromise with capitalism.

But that is not an argument against the Marxist tradition of revolutionary politics which says that the capitalist society is our enemy. We have to get rid of the capitalist state and create a society that is based on a completely different, radically grassroots structure.

John's solution is effectively to say that we just ignore the state. The question of how we challenge state power has to be central to everything we discuss, since state power is so visibly shaping the world around us today.

One reason we cannot avoid confronting the state is that the state tries to divide us, it tries to separate off each struggle from every other, women from men, gays from straights, whites from blacks, and make us think of ourselves in the smallest possible way. We have to have an argument in the movement that unity is strength—and that argument has to be organised. Learning to act together and discussing it consciously is essential if we are to develop a strategy to take on the power of the state.

Sixth contributor: I would really like to know how John's theory of changing the world would apply to Iraq or Palestine, where people are being attacked daily and their lives turned into misery by the state. They cannot ignore the state. They have to fight it directly, head on.

My relatives live in Iran. I live in Britain. If the British state attacks Iran, do I simply ignore it?

Seventh contributor (from South Korea): We can change the world by taking power or by not taking power. The difference is one of time. Taking power will be quicker. We should not be afraid to take power, because we are the ones who will change the world.

John Holloway: A lot of people did not want to talk about revolution a few years ago. But today lots of people want to. Alex and myself are in agreement on this.

Secondly, someone said this is a false debate. But Alex and I were not saying the same thing. We have different perspectives. We have different conceptions of the state. For me it is a specific, capitalist form of social relations which excludes us, Alex talks about a workers' state and the possibility of a radical democratisation of the state. According to my conception that is absolutely absurd, since the state has a form of organisation that excludes us.

To talk about a radical movement, a soviet movement for instance, culminating in the creation of a new state, is nonsense because a really democratic organisation, a council organisation goes in one direction while the state is a form of organisation that goes in the opposite direction. To talk about a working class state introduces confusion that conceals the most horrific process of repression and violence that we have seen several times in the 20th century.

The questioner who spoke of us turning our backs on the state—I am not saying we should ignore the state. It would be lovely if we could. In a way that is what the Zapatistas are doing now. They are turning their backs on the state. But that is not something that most of us can do. I am an employee of the state. It is not about pretending the state does not exist. It is about understanding the state as a specific form of social relations which pushes us in certain directions, and trying to think about how we can struggle against those forms of social relations and push in a different direction, so that our relation is in and beyond and against the state. It would be lovely if we could pretend that the state does not exist. Unfortunately we can't. But we certainly don't have to fall into the state as a central reference point in terms of logic or of power or space.

The question of Venezuela is very important for all the Latin Americans here. I liked the way the question was presented. It was not as it is sometimes put in terms of 'Venezuela shows we must take power.' It was in terms of Venezuela shows there has to be a combination of the two approaches—the state-oriented approach and the non-state-oriented approach. This is what characterises the World Social Forum, this combination, a cooperation, between these two different approaches. But in that we have to see there is always a tension, a contradiction, between on the one hand saying, 'We ourselves shall decide how society will develop' and on the other hand saying, 'The state will decide for you or show you how to decide for yourselves.' It will be very important to see how that tension plays itself out in Venezuela.

On the question of fissures. We often feel helpless because capitalism weighs so heavily on us. But when we say No we start off with an appreciation of our own strength. When we rebel we are in fact tearing a little hole in capitalism. It is very contradictory. By rebelling we are already saying no to the command of capital. We are creating temporary spaces. Within that crack, that fissure, it is important that we fight for other social relations that don't point towards the state, but that they point towards the sort of society we want to create. At the core of these fissures is the drive to self-determination. And then it is a question of working out what does this mean, and how to be organised for self-determination. It means being against and beyond the society that exists. Of expanding the fissures, how to push these fissures forward structurally.

The people who say we should take control of the state are also talking about cracks. There is no choice but to start with interstices. The question is how we think of them, because the state is not the whole world. There are 200 states. If you seize control of one, it is still only a crack in capitalism. It is a question of how we think about those cracks, those fissures. And if we start off from ourselves, why on earth should we adopt capitalist, bourgeois forms for developing our struggle? Why should we accept the template of the concept of the state?

It is impossible to focus on the state without having a special definition of struggle. It means struggling within the space of the state, whereas at the World Social Forum we are in rebellion against that space. The space defines a concept of space and time.

Alex Callinicos: John said we have a transhistorical conception of the state which separates the state off from capitalist relations of production. So let me say clearly that the state under which we live is an irredeemably capitalist state. I don't want to be part of a movement whose aim is to take control of the existing capitalist state.

Nevertheless, this is not the only state that has existed in history. There have been many different forms of state in the history of class society. What they have all had in common is organised and institutionalised class violence, the violence of an exploiting minority over an exploited majority.

The question we are addressing now is, 'Can the working class as it organises itself collectively and socially to resist exploitation by capital turn this situation round?' In other words, can the working class create its own form of organised class violence, distinctively working class in the way it is organised but which makes the struggle against exploitation by capital more effective and also helps the working class build a new society? As John knows, the answer to that question in the classic tradition of Marxism, in the writing of Marx and Lenin, is yes. There is the idea of a workers' state, of workers' power, which is a temporary transitional form through which the working class organises itself to get rid of capitalism and as part of the same process democratically organises itself to create a new form of society.

I used the L word, I mentioned Lenin, and of course John will say this question was tried and proved to be definitely wrong during the Russian Revolution of 1917 and particularly with the Stalinist aftermath.

One of the contributions referred to the great debate between Marx and Bakunin at the time of the First International in the late 19th century. He said that the experience of Stalinism proved that Bakunin's anti-state position had been proved to be right.

But how did that happen? If the idea is that state thinking was deep in Marx or Lenin's head and that led to Stalinism, it is simply wrong. Marx said we need a revolution against the state in his critique of Bakunin. It was an idea Lenin enthusiastically took up during the 1917 revolution.

So how did it happen? John talked about fissures. The Russian Revolution of 1917 was a fissure. It tore a great hole in the capitalist system, the biggest fissure so far in world history. But just to break a hole in capitalism, even a hole as big as Russia, was not enough. There was a simple reason. The power of capital is global and it can concentrate its forces massively to destroy any fissure that threatens it. That is what they have been trying to do with Chávez in Venezuela. Whatever the problem is with his politics and so on, the US and its allies have been trying to break the experiment taking place in Venezuela because it threatens to open up a fissure.

The power of capital is so great that usually they can close the fissures. Usually they do so by overthrowing the revolutionary process and destroying its leaders and activists. There are many examples of that. In the Russian case there was a particularly horrible way in which capital won, by creating such pressures as to cause the revolutionary regime to transform itself into a barbarous replica of the global system.

The reason that happened was not that Marx liked the state, but that there was not a powerful enough global movement to break the power of capital globally. That doesn't have to be our fate. We are already in the process collectively of creating the greatest global movement against capitalism in world history. But we won't do that if we think that simply creating holes, fissures, in the existing system is enough to destroy it.

Eighth contributor (South Korean woman): If you say we can change the world without taking power, you are saying that the capitalist power that exists right now is acceptable. Holloway says that the state excludes us. But the state oppresses us at every level. Even our sexuality is oppressed by the state. I come from South Korea where we have a history of military dictatorship and they have crushed a beautiful resistance. It is not that the state excludes us but that at every level it oppresses us.

Alex is not saying we have to go into the state and use the power of the capitalist state. He is saying we have to create new forms of power where the working class will form an organisation capable of overthrowing the capitalist state.

Ninth contributor: Karl Marx said the state was the executive committee of the bourgeoisie, and that is exactly what it is. Its laws and its procedures protect profit at the expense of ordinary people and its won't give up those things lightly. That is why we have to deal with the question of state power.

Tenth contributor (Chris Harman, SWP): John Holloway said that the position which revolutionary socialists put forward means that we focus activity on the state. This is not true. Most of our activity consists in being involved in struggles of one sort or another—struggles against repression, struggles for women's liberation, struggles against racism, struggles over wages, above all at the moment the struggle against the horrific war waged against Iraq. But what we know from the experience of our movements is that every time those struggles reach a certain stage you come up against bodies of armed men—and these days mainly armed men and some armed women. And this is the core of the state. John, you use the word state in a wider sense—sometimes we all use it in a wider sense—but the key sector we are concerned with is these bodies of armed men.

You can then have two approaches. You can pretend that you can control them or ignore them. There is the approach of the social democrats. John says we have the same approach as Lula. We don't. Lula believes he controls the Brazilian state. In reality the Brazilian state and Brazilian capitalism control Lula. The hierarchies of armed forces officers, the generals, are the same as were there under the military dictatorship. All that is different is a different president and a different parliament.

The other approach is to say that you can ignore the state, leave it to later. That is all right until it starts breaking up your picket line or waging war. Every struggle reaches a moment where the question of force becomes decisive.

Gramsci made the point in his distinction between a war of position, a slow struggle to unify people, to fight back, to get some resistance. That is what we are involved in most of the time. But at some point you have to wage a war of manoeuvre. You have to move forward to challenge the state.

And if you don't do that, Latin America is full of histories of what happens. In 1964 the military coup in Brazil, in 1973 the coup in Uruguay, in 1973 in Chile, in 1976 in Argentina. On each occasion people said, 'We don't need to challenge the state, just build the movements from below with the parliamentarians and we will win.' On each occasion the state hit back.

And I say to the comrades who talk about Venezuela, unfortunately, the state in Venezuela is still essentially the same state as before. The country has transformed itself massively in the last six years. It is much more hopeful than six years ago. But the state remains the same. Many of the old officers are still there, the civil service works in the same way, the same hierarchies remain. And so at some point in Venezuela the point will come where either people will begin to form workers' and soldiers' councils to challenge that state or the state will crush them.

John Holloway's real misunderstanding of Marxism is not to understand that the central point of Marxism is that from below we can create new structures, structures that have to be democratic, have to be based on mass self-emancipation, self-activity, but have to be centralised and have at some decisive point to disarm the ruling class before they kill us.

Eleventh contributor: I want to use the experience of Argentina since the Argentinazo of 2001 to underline the points made by Alex. We had the biggest movement of the unemployed anywhere in the world in recent years. Factories were occupied and taken over by workers. They demonstrated that you did not need a capitalist class to keep production going. In the districts of the capital popular assemblies were extremely radical. In hundreds of places people got together and discussed and determined how they would act and what political direction they would take. And in the first few weeks after the Argentinazo several governments were overthrown. There was a brutal process in which many comrades died. It was an example of how we can develop our movements.

But what Argentina showed, brutally, was how the state still existed. We have all these examples of important and very radical organisations. But not only did the state exclude and marginalise us, it turned on us, it repressed us, it drove down our wages and repressed our movement. Today there are 30 political prisoners in Argentina and thousands more who are due for trial at some point soon, and we have in power a government under Kirchner which is not particularly different to Lula.

The state showed how real its existence was. On the other hand we had a huge popular mobilisation, created radical movements involving very large numbers of people which nevertheless had this weakness, which is they did not address the question of state power. So today we still have a capitalist government despite the movement's existence and its combativity, It's not enough for workers to develop a social movement, although its existence is indispensable. We also need a perspective of taking on the question of political power. Otherwise the state will show its existence with attacks on us.

Looking for an alternative

Mike Gonzalez

It had been a very hot summer in Porto Alegre. The grass was scorched all along the riverbank site where the 2005 World Social Forum was held. Only the converted gas plant which served as a communications centre offered any kind of shade. Unlike previous years, the meeting was divided by areas—environmental, indigenous struggles, social movements, culture, and so on—each with their own complex of different sized marquees to accommodate the meetings and debates.

Walking along through the ranks of tents and past the 2,500 or so talks, you could pick up snatches of the discussions going on inside—though it was over an hour's march from one end to the other. There were heated conversations about every aspect of the movement—global warming, land rights, sustainable development, the role of trade unions, the future of social movements, the political strategy to follow. It was as if you were listening to the soundtrack of a new, living movement.

The 155,000 gathered in Porto Alegre were the delegates and representatives of a huge and growing movement, multiple in language and background, wide and diverse in its range of concerns. It was extraordinary to think that it had not existed six years earlier—that this movement emerged in Seattle, weathered the post-9/11 demand that we declare ourselves for civilisation against the terrorists, and embraced the anti-war impulse without losing sight of the enemy. Far from being diverted from the critique of capitalism as a system, as some leading intellectuals had feared, a predominantly young mobilisation now rediscovered imperialism, its systematic use of violence in pursuit of economic ends, and linked them in a deceptively simple slogan—'No blood for oil.'

In January 2003 the third World Social Forum took place just weeks after the election to the Brazilian presidency of Lula, candidate of the Workers Party (the PT), which he had led since its creation in 1980. For the 60 percent of Brazil's electorate who supported him, Lula's election promised change. The civil servants who had been fighting for years over their pension rights, the landless workers whose organisation (the MST) had been involved in bitter struggles with private gunmen and government forces for nearly two decades, the poor families who were pressing for a democratised education system, all had invested their optimism in Lula. And it was optimism encouraged by many sections of the left, including one Trotskyist tendency, the DS, which joined his government—and remains there.

Yet when Lula visited the forum in 2003, and was rapturously received, he was already on his way to the World Economic Forum at Davos, where he would be photographed shaking hands with the luminaries of the world financial system. The World Social Forum began two years before precisely as an alternative, a counterweight to the meetings of the bankers whose decisions would directly affect the vast majority of the peoples of the world while giving them no access or involvement in reaching those decisions. So it was particularly ironic that Lula should go straight from Porto Alegre to Davos.

The WSF, after all, was not intended as a lobbying group but as an *alternative*, a place where the strategies of resistance against the programmes and projects of the WTO, the World Bank and the IMF could be discussed and coordinated. It was already obvious, however, that Lula was bent on renegotiating the terms of Brazil's engagement with the world economy, not on challenging or rejecting them. His first tests came early in 2003, with the confrontation with the civil service unions, new land occupations and the nomination of representatives of capital to key posts like the head of the national bank and the ministry of agriculture. Three PT deputies and a senator opposed to the government's pensions and tax policies were first disciplined and later expelled from the party.

Meeting two years later (the intervening WSF took place in January 2004 in Mumbai, India) the promise and the disillusionment could not help but shape the atmosphere and political direction of the forum. Lula's presence caused friction, anger and frustration. There was no sign of the euphoria of two years earlier, despite the attempts by the PT to recreate it at Lula's rally in the Gigantinho sports stadium on the first day. But it was a staged affair: the seats had been packed early with party loyalists, though there were a small number of critics who shouted from the benches. A demonstration outside by a number of left groups accused Lula of betrayal.

But in a sense the evidence of a wider disaffection was provided by the PT's recent loss of power in the city. And this was Porto Alegre, the symbol of a new kind of political arrangement embodied in the 'participatory budgets'. Some of the key figures in the WSF organising committee, people like Hilary Wainwright, had written passionately about the Porto Alegre experiment. It seemed to fit well into the framework of arguments about taking power without necessarily seizing the state.

In fact it was always open to serious question, as the popular assemblies could only discuss the allocation of a small proportion of the municipal budget, let alone address the overall priorities of the distribution of wealth on a national scale.

In any event, the loss of Porto Alegre was an enormous blow, and no amount of grandstanding could conceal that from a radical Brazilian audience. But the reality was that the implications of Lula's defeat set the whole political agenda. The national rally of PSOL (the Socialism and Freedom Party founded by the deputies expelled from the PT and others) drew some 1,800 mainly young people and announced the creation of a political space of great potential significance. On a wider panorama, the Lula experience called into question the very positive spin that sections of the movement had placed on the group of new Latin American presidents—Gutiérrez in Ecuador, Kirchner in Argentina, Parra in Paraguay, Chávez in Venezuela (and the recently elected president of Uruguay, Tabaré Vázquez). Kirchner still enjoyed some degree of popular credibility because he had moved against the perpetrators of the human rights abuses under previous military government and seemed to be acting with some independence in the face of international capital. Gutiérrez, on the other hand, had compromised and abandoned his commitments to the mass movement that carried him to power.

Just before the conference the death was announced of the venerable Brazilian economist Celso Furtado, the main architect of a theory of dependency and its attendant strategies of independent national economic development. Months before his death he had broken with Lula—and the new president did not attend his funeral. The symbolism was inescapable. The promise of a solution based on a single nation-state taking on a global capitalist system had foundered in Brazil as it had in Ecuador and elsewhere.

Yet the forum had always had at its heart a strong current of reformism led by ATTAC, the coalition opposed to international finance whose strongest section was in France, and the majority of NGOs. For them the focus was always on a moral case which could persuade social democratic governments to acknowledge a responsibility to aid and debt relief programmes. Blair and Brown's much-vaunted Africa initiatives, for example, seemed to encourage that kind of approach. On the other hand the recent failure of most of the governments of the wealthy nations to deliver aid in any quantities to the victims of the tsunami called that perspective into question. And recent Latin American experience, with Lula at its heart, did not augur well for any serious challenge to global capital and its priorities—despite the defiance displayed at the WTO conference in Cancun last year.

Against this background, strategic questions were again on the unwritten but acknowledged agenda of many of those present at Porto Alegre.

It had always been a rule of the social forums that political organisations should not take part directly. The rationale was that the problems should be addressed in terms of practical solutions and in a wide-ranging debate. The rule was always honoured in the breach—but it did have the advantage of limiting the intervention of political parties with little or no involvement in the movement. In some ways, the physical organisation of the forum—this year in particular—encouraged the view of its work as a series of parallel and specific debates, with strategic thinking informed by 'regional' considerations alone. This year, as opposed to all previous years (and very particularly to Mumbai), there was no central event or space which could bring together all the components and create a sense of the whole movement—with all its tensions and contradictory pressures.

This undoubtedly did present a problem at this key conjuncture. Faced with the failure of the Lula alternative, the central question for all of us was how to develop a central and united strategy to confront the highly centralised and coordinated project of global capital. In 2003 the decision to back the worldwide protest against the Iraq war on 15 February brought 20 million people into activity worldwide and vindicated our common purpose. This year, while the Assembly of Social Movements did emerge ultimately with a clear anti-war position and a call for global action on 19 March, it was harder to achieve than two years earlier, precisely because there was an emphasis on diversity and fragmentation rather than unity of action.

Yet at the same time there was clearly a counter-impulse within the forum. If fragmentation encouraged a lobbying view of the political role of the forums (world, regional, social) there was a different, although not fully formed, political understanding present as well. The questions that were being debated showed the openness of many delegates to discussions about socialism, alternative ways of organising society and explorations of how a different world might look and feel.

And in some ways the alternative was summarised—in a rather contradictory way—by the reception given to Hugo Chávez. He appeared at the end of the forum—in effect his visit to the Gigantinho stadium was the closing act of the forum. And it was clear that the reception he was given was spontaneous and authentic—unlike Lula's in the same place a few days earlier. For three and a half hours he addressed a crowd inside the arena, and outside it, with the kind of populist rhetoric he is so good at. He spoke with real instinct to the audience he had before him, insisting on his anti-imperialism, arguing for the arming of the people and for the first time ever describing his political objective as a socialist revolution.

Chávez symbolised a more radical alternative with its emphasis on organisation from below, on popular power and on a vision of a socialist future. And in that sense, he spoke for and to the anxieties and concerns of the majority of the delegates to the forum, particularly the young, for whom the issue now was a way forward moving from protest and resistance towards a purposive struggle.

The problem, of course, was that what Chávez *said* at Porto Alegre was not at all the same thing as what his government is *doing*. Within Venezuela, the movement for change is also facing a crossroads. It is the upsurge from below that has saved Chávez three times in the last three years from the attempts by the right to overthrow him. But on each occasion he had pulled back from the demands of the movement, seeking compromise with the US and even with sections of the bourgeoisie. The government itself includes people who are bitterly hostile to the project of popular power and democracy from below to which Chávez committed himself in Porto Alegre.

Thus, while Chávez could symbolise the alternative the movement was seeking, he could not claim to be implementing it. If there was a model of a different kind of power, it came not from Venezuela but from Bolivia, where a mass popular movement had twice defeated capitalist economic strategies imposed by the international financial agencies.

For the left, the challenge of Porto Alegre and the period to come is twofold: to build the movement in all its breadth and diversity, as activists and organisers on the one hand, and to raise within that movement the larger political questions on which the revolutionary socialist tradition can offer a body of understanding, experience and ideas. But in fulfilling that double task, there are habits that have to be abandoned—habits of sectarianism and isolation, of a refusal (or perhaps an inability) to engage with those sections of workers, for example, whose daily resistance will bring them into a closer engagement with those ideas—but whose starting point may well be distant from that of the left.

The successful experiences of recent times, the anti-war movement, for example, have built a united front around shared objectives; that has then become the space in which the politics of revolutionary transformation, whose starting point is exactly that self-activity of the class, can begin to take root and make sense. The openness of PSOL's first congress was an encouraging sign of the possibilities to come. For if the World Social Forum has taught us anything it is that in the absence of revolutionary ideas as a living force within the movement other ideas will fill the void, ideas which cannot offer the prospect of a socialist democracy or a transfer of power out of the hands of that minority that today seems so ready to place the future of the planet in jeopardy.

Venezuela: inside the Bolivarian revolution

Roland Denis is a leading revolutionary in Venezuela. He was briefly a member of the Chávez government (in 2002-2003) as vice-minister of planning, but resigned after ten months, together with the minister, in protest at the lack of grass roots involvement in the planning process. An organiser and activist since the 1980s, he was a founder-member of the 13 April Movement, which expresses some of the contradictions and tensions at the heart of the Bolivarian Revolution. Mike Gonzalez interviewed Roland in the youth camp at the World Social Forum in Porto Alegre, Brazil. Coincidentally, the conversation took place while Hugo Chávez was still addressing a crowd of some 18,000 at a local sports stadium. His rapturous reception was very different from the more hostile and critical way in which Lula, Brazil's president, had been received in the same stadium four days earlier. For some of those attending the forum, indeed, Chávez appeared to represent the more radical alternative to Lula's compromises with the world market. With his long experience in the movement, Roland was in an unrivalled position to discuss the truth or otherwise of that view.

Tell us about yourself and your own experience of the process in Venezuela.

I first became involved in the student movement in Venezuela. It was a very important moment, when the student movement was really in the vanguard of the social movement. It marked a break with the traditional left and began to produce its own forms of organisation that were new and different—more democratic, more horizontal, and bringing in new ideas. Those ideas began to spread and influenced activists all over the country. These new methods and ideas produced a new kind of self-organisation of the class that distanced itself from the old political practices, particularly the reformist parties with their old electoral practices. And it was also very different from the revolutionary parties, which were were still marked by the guerrilla tradition of the 1960s and 1970s. They had no influence any more.

In those circumstances, the student movement played a key role. The 1987 student movement lasted the whole of that year and more than 60 students were killed, and yet it was a struggle for very elementary things. Students, for example, who were very poor, won cheap student fares; it seems such a small thing but I like to remind the young comrades that 60 people died for them to have free travel.

This 1987 rebellion was in many way the prelude to the popular rebellion of 1989, the *Caracazo*.[1] Later the student movement declined but the popular movement and its local organisations survived in some working class areas.

The general situation was one of industrial decline and a massive export of capital that began in the early 1980s. Between then and the mid-1990s, 300 billion dollars left the country—it was virtually the whole national income that went, leaving behind dead industries and disinvestment, and of course the social desert of poverty and exclusion that that creates. The big capitalists took over financial institutions and the banks, but they didn't invest the capital, just reproduced it through financial operations, currency devaluation and so on.

That reaction to all this was a kind of primitive popular rage. No one could understand why prices kept going up or why the retail prices (the PVP) that used to be marked on all goods suddenly disappeared. In the end there was a kind of spontaneous rebellion and looting. It was massive and thousands died in the repression that followed. I was part of this rebellion; I went to jail, and had some disagreeable experiences—torture and that sort of thing. But within the prisons we began discussions with a number of people, some of them old guerrilla fighters like Carlos Lanz. Lanz was in prison for eight years, and it became a kind of Marxist graduate school. In there people would often break with their previous groups and begin to think in new ways. The question we were addressing was how to become part of the popular movement again.

This new current was a synthesis of a range of different ideologies—critical Marxism, liberation theology, the black movement, the indigenous movement, revolutionary Bolivarianism, social currents and so on. And it produced very interesting new spaces—in education, mass media, community work—but above all it was preparing a more subversive and obviously underground political activity. So we had to work at two levels. It's quite common in Latin America that activists have to work in that way and that is how we operated for ten years.

1: For more information on the *Caracazo* and the political process in Venezuela see M Gonzalez, 'Venezuela: Many Steps to Come', in *International Socialism* 104 (Winter 2004).

Did the Bolivarian tendency have real roots in popular movements too?
It was born out of Chávez's military group and his failed 1992 coup. The coup failed but it had a huge impact. People couldn't believe that the military had acted not as fascists but with a whole new nationalist rhetoric. It was a very Messianic movement, but it evoked that idea of a different kind of army embedded in the myth of Bolivar. As you know our nations are quite recent; it was Bolivar's armies that created Venezuela, so in a sense the army predated the nation. That's something deeply rooted in our collective consciousness and Chávez reawakens all those legends and myths.

As soon as Chávez came out of jail in 1994 he proposed that his group in the army should now transform itself into a revolutionary, anti-system but popular movement. A lot of people joined the structure that Chávez set up (MR 200) in a pretty spontaneous way. But it was vertical in structure and he was its undisputed leader. The tendency I was part of worked with Chávez, but we didn't join his movement. I certainly felt that the military movement completely lacked any basis for developing a political programme—a revolutionary democratic programme. Its *language and style* were completely Messianic.

But at that time we were beginning to work with a different idea, of building for what we called, a People's Constituent Assembly, which was radical but also democratic. We didn't want to set up a formal constituent assembly though. We understood it as a way of constructing a different kind of power, a power that that could not be delegated to anyone. Chávez still sometimes talks about this 'poder constituyente'—a process of creating a new kind of power, new organs and institutions and a new political culture that should be built from below.

So there were two ideas in contention—one from above and the other of building a movement from below?
That's right. There was a major contradiction there and that's why we couldn't join the Chávez organisation—because we couldn't accept his idea of political culture. We saw it as crucial that we change the political culture. That's why we concentrated on all the other levels of work—popular education, alternative media. Obviously the military found this idea of the horizontal integration of these different areas of work very difficult to accept. But Chávez learned from it and began to use a language that was more concrete and offered some clear idea of what he might do when he

came to power. But the reality was that Chávez had far more people than we did, and Venezuelan political culture was focused on an idea of the leader—the *caudillo*—it was centralised and personalised. That meant and it still means that our ideas were sidelined to an extent. Our weakness was really the political weakness of the whole society, because we insisted on the need for a new culture and for a new society that would be built in the course of the struggle itself.

That can develop through working units but it can't always grow up on a mass scale. In countries like ours that happens through a *monstruo politico* (a 'political giant') like Chávez. This evening there are 15,000 people still listening to him in the stadium—and he's been speaking for over three hours. Now that's a real political giant. There's nothing we can do about that; you can't change that situation. And in any case we wouldn't want to—we're quite happy with what he does, because he has been in a position to socialise and generalise some ideas and communicate them to a mass audience in a way we could never have done. You've got to recognise that.

How did things change when Chávez was elected president in 2000?

When Chávez came into government we had to look again at what we would do. In 2000 we called a meeting in a working class district in Caracas of all the historic political currents in the country. People came from all over Venezuela, leaders of Christian organisations, black groups, indigenous movements. It was a defining moment. And Chávez was part of it too. We had worked with him, but we represented what you might call the dark side of the moon. If he hadn't come to power then, there were political alternatives in place. But he was elected and it was electoral issues that dominated everything. We weren't in agreement with that shift; for us the movement around Chávez had reached a point in 2000 where the alternative of a mass popular insurrection was a real possibility in our view. We felt that the electoral solution had forced Chávez to create the electoral machinery that was later transformed into the perverted, counter-revolutionary organisation that is the MBR (the Bolivarian Revolutionary Movement).

Chávez became the reference point for all political life without ever having first had to define the kind of society we were fighting for beyond the general issues of sovereignty, nationalisation and so on. No one knew what he stood for apart from that.

There were members of the bourgeoisie, of the old oligarchy, who approached Chávez around this time; and there were also members of the old, opportunist and discredited left organisations—people like Luis Michelena—who managed to convince Chávez to take the electoral road. They gave him money for his campaign, all to ensure that he would present himself as a candidate for the elections within the traditional electoral framework of our country. And when Chávez moved in that direction it was a defeat for us. I wrote a book about all this because I felt that we had to understand what happened then if we were to make any sense of what came later.

Anyway, we held this meeting in October 2000 to determine our attitude to Chávez in power. There were people there like Douglas Bravo, the leading guerrilla commander, whose position was absolutely and completely hostile to Chávez—though there was obviously some element of rivalry and jealousy here. On the other hand there were people attending who were prepared to submit completely to Chávez and his movement. We argued that we should work with the new government and try to introduce political ideas and strategies that would enable us to push the process further and faster.

So we began to work, always from below, and we had an early success which was the Education Congress. It was organised through the ministry of education but its framework was that idea of a constituent power (poder constituyente) in education. More than 200,000 people took part in the process—teachers, students, communities. What came out of it, in the conclusions that emerged in 2001, was a whole new model of education which won official approval and began to be implemented.

It was a model of self-organised education, a pedagogy based on an exchange of knowledge; the schools would become the centre of community activity and the role of the teachers wouldn't be the classical graduate of the Teachers Training College only, but the midwife, the carpenter, the community would bring their knowledge into the school as well and the students themselves would elaborate a syllabus based on their own experience and needs rather than following one worked out by so called education experts.

Unfortunately the project was frozen—not cancelled but frozen with the entry of a new minister, a minister from another discredited party, the PPT, who reimposed the old model of state education from above. At least it wasn't a privatising policy he introduced, but from an educational point of view it created nothing new. So as you can see, we were accumulating very interesting experiences but also losing several battles.

For a while I worked as vice-minister of planning. There too we worked on the basis of seeking ways to change the institutional framework. This was in 2002, a very tough time when the oil executives were trying to sabotage things and the government was really just running on the spot. We were just beginning to have some influence but the pressure from the military and the bureaucrats drove me out. I was in government for just eight months.

By 2003 I had reached the conclusion that we couldn't go on working in this fragmented way within the institutions of a supposedly revolutionary government. It was time for us to develop our own forces and create an organisation that could carry things forward. So we created the 13 April Movement. It's just in process of formation—it doesn't have its own printshop or its own paper or organisation yet, for example. It's a completely autonomous organisation.

And would you describe the organisation as critical of the Bolivarian Revolution?
We are within the revolution; after all we were among the creators of the movement. We were outside and then joined in and have taken positions of leadership in the Bolivarian Revolution; in that sense we are inside it and part of it. But the government is a very different thing—that is not the Bolivarian Revolution. We are addressing those areas in which the government is failing to hold to the principles of the Bolivarian Revolution. We're talking about concrete things, about bureaucracy, about its plans like the Coal Plan which will wreck indigenous communities. Chávez is saying here in Porto Alegre that if we continue with the dominant model of capitalism we are living under now there will be no life left on the planet a hundred years from now. So that means it is absolutely imperative that we win the struggle against imperialism. But that's what Chávez says here in Porto Alegre—what he says in Venezuela is very different: there his government's plans contradict what he's saying.

But it's important to say that we're not going to get involved in elections. Today elections are the point at which a political decomposition is taking place that's hard to describe. Movements that used to be healthy and growing and to have developed their own leadership seem to fall apart when they operate in the electoral field. We're convinced that the Bolivarian Revolution is not going to be determined by what happens in elections. We wouldn't regard it as a tragedy if the right won the election, because the Bolivarian Revolution has another much more advanced expression.

It's an expression that emerged after the attempted coup of April 2002, and it reflects the self-organisation of the people and their capacity for independent organisation; it's a movement that didn't need a vanguard or parties but made an insurrection there and then. We have to think in terms of a long term resistance.

The reality is that Chávez's response to the attempted coup was terrible. It's almost as if he was embarrassed, ashamed at having surrendered. He didn't seem to realise how democracy had been won back. On the contrary, he seemed at that point to accept the arguments of the media that he had been too aggressive to the rich and that he was creating a polarisation in society. The people had started calling the rich 'los escuálidos' (the disgusting ones)—but Chávez never used the term. He fell into their trap and began to pursue a deeply conservative policy of dialogue.

For a while we were all taken in. Even I was stupid enough to take part in one of these dialogue sessions in the presidential palace. There were media moguls and trade unions and social movements there, the representatives of almost every section of society. I was there representing a social movement; I'd brought a letter insulting practically everyone. But then one of the media owners at the meeting stood up and insulted Chávez in the most humiliating way. Chávez had set up commissions to try and create a consensus, so he proposed that community radio stations should take part as well as the media moguls. And this guy stood up and said, 'If you think I'm going to sit at the same table as that rabble, you're wrong. I'm out of here.'

The truth is the right felt strong at that moment—they were organised, they controlled the military—so they were still strong even though they'd lost the attempted coup. And in fact they were preparing another assault that came with the general strike in December that year. We felt we needed time to accumulate our own forces for a future confrontation, but the confrontation came very quickly. The reality was that all of us, the whole mass movement, was in defensive mode throughout that time—we were just preparing plans to defend the minimal gains we had made. That's what we were doing for three years. That's all that was possible at that stage. To build a different kind of movement demands a high level of class consciousness and organisation; and in any case at that stage no one dared to take to the streets or build mobilisations that could be interpreted as attacking the government. At the same time everyone knew that the process is being corrupted and turned back from its original purposes; people talked about it all the time.

So what you're seeing is a combination of a determination to defend the government together with a growing disappointment?

I don't think there was disappointment. People still were and are full of hope, and believe that the present situation is a transition to something else. So they're saying there is a first priority which is to defeat the class enemy: after that we take the road you're suggesting. People have this simple tactical view—first the main enemy, then the secondary. That blackmail still works today, and it has allowed corrupt bureaucratic sectors to grow as well as sections of the conservative right, both within the government.

My impression was that during the referendum campaign, which was defensive, something else was happening too—a kind of questioning of the process. Would you agree?

There began to be criticism, critical analyses of the way the popular movement was becoming institutionalised from 2002 onwards, the way it was being incorporated through the national plans and so on. But that was at the level of articles and written argument—and it hasn't really moved on from there yet. Turning that critique into a political strategy is the point we are at now. The lid is off; for the moment the main enemy is in retreat. Now we can go for the conservative pro-capitalist wing of the government, which is very deeply embedded.

What are the new proposals you're suggesting?

We've seized the opportunity to speak about Chávez, because he's the great communicator and there's no point in trying to create a parallel discourse—that would be a stupid and sectarian response. On the other hand the language that Chávez used was born out of the popular movement; he didn't create it. Recently Chávez has launched four key ideas: first, that we are entering an anti-imperialist phase; secondly the development of people's power, fulfilling the promise of a participatory democracy embedded in the 1999 Constitution; thirdly, he speaks about the people under arms, the replacement of the army by a people's army; fourthly, he disusses the revolution within the revolution, deepening the revolution and not just going into the political institutions but breaking them, because they are of no use to us. And now Chávez has added a fifth element, in his closing speech to the World Social Forum—anti-capitalism.

It was we who launched the slogan of a 'people under arms' and he must have read it and taken it up. That's his great skill, because he didn't come out of the revolutionary movement—he just grabs what he sees as useful and makes it his own.

One of the good things about Venezuela today is that there is no single party—there are electoral parties, but there is no single party of the movement. What has emerged is a whole range of forms of organisation—health committees, co-operatives, local movements, Bolivarian circles and so on. Some are more linked to government than others, but the important thing is that there is no hierarchy among them. All these organisations are becoming part of a highly political movement and they all have to be the revolutionary vanguard. There is no internal division between the social and the political on the ground. It's a different matter at the level of electoral organisations. The MBR has not put out a single leaflet criticising the war in Iraq, for example; it has had nothing to say about the genocide in Colombia, despite everything that Chávez has said, because the people around him are the worst kind of bureaucrats.

What we have to do now is take those five points and build a political strategy on them—not for the government, but for a popular revolutionary movement that can drive the movement forward until those five promises are realised. But we have to accumulate our forces for that to happen. And we need to build that movement together with the rank and file of the Chavista movement, who are using the same language as us. That is what we are doing now.

Che and the socialist tradition: a reply to Mike Gonzalez

Fernando Lizárraga

Mike Gonzalez's latest book, *Che Guevara and the Cuban Revolution* (Bookmarks, 2004), is published at an opportune moment, constituting a formidable challenge to all those who see in Che's symbolism a guiding star for their political actions. When saying that the timing of this publication is the right one, I am thinking of the development of the anti-capitalist movement, which, in spite of its deep-seated tensions and uncertainties, provides a real framework for revolutionary endeavours. Given the obvious fact that Che Guevara still appears as an icon and source of inspiration for many in that movement, this book deserves to be read and debated with passion and honesty. Gonzalez is well aware of this context: he seeks to trigger a fresh debate on Che Guevara and it is quite clear that he avoids the easy and laudatory tone so often found in writings on Che's life. Certainly, Gonzalez does not intend to adjust his arguments to mainstream feelings on Guevara. On the contrary, his book seems at first glance to be a harsh attack on Guevara and, above all, a scathing critique of the Argentinian's conception of Marxism and revolutionary strategy.

I must state, right from the start, that I find myself in disagreement with Gonzalez's interpretation of many aspects of Guevara's thought. At the same time, however, I must admit that his arguments are powerful, founded on strong textual evidence and persuasively structured. It is not easy to rebut Gonzalez's contribution to this ongoing and necessary debate on one of the key figures of the worldwide revolutionary tradition. Therefore, in what follows I intend to identify some topics on which my disagreements with Gonzalez are most visible, and I will try to offer some evidence for an alternative reading of these matters. Far from expecting to bring the debate to a close, I want simply to add to it, fraternally. To be precise, there are two points on which I would like to focus: first, Che's understanding of class struggle and the role of the working class in the revolutionary transformation of capitalist society; and second, his idea that moral incentives were superior and more efficient than material incentives for the construction of socialism.

As for the issue concerning Che's revolutionary theory and strategy, Gonzalez essentially thinks that Guevara never came to understand one very basic and fundamental principle of the socialist revolutionary tradition: that the emancipation of the working class is to be attained by the working class itself and for itself. Even though Gonzalez presents us with some textual evidence on the matter, he dwells too much on only a couple of Che's writings at the expense of the bulk of his work. Gonzalez overemphasises Che's commitment to guerrilla war methods because he pays too much attention to Che's military writings: *Guerrilla Warfare*, *Reminiscences of the Cuban Revolutionary War*, and 'Guerrilla Warfare: A Method'. Gonzalez rightly remarks that these texts were both military and political, but for some reason chooses to ignore the fact, well known to Che and Lenin for example, that war represented the continuation of politics by other means, a line of thought coined by Clausewitz. Far from being a warlord who chose fighting for its own sake, Che subordinated this strategy to a wider political understanding of the Cuban and Latin American situation. In saying that Che's works were both political *and* military, Gonzalez presupposes a separation of these fields, a view which runs counter to the revolutionary tradition. In short, guerrilla warfare was the instrument of anti-imperialist struggle in the Third World and was meant to ignite the fight of the masses against pro-American regimes.

Our author holds in the early stages of this argument that Che's interpretation of the revolutionary tradition 'crucially left out the working class as the agent for social transformation'.[1] Then he contends that Fidel Castro and his brother Raúl did not endorse a true Marxist conception of workers' democracy and thought that 'change could be the result of the armed actions of a minority'.[2] To reinforce this train of thought, Gonzalez adds that in Che's 'vision of the revolutionary war—a war conducted by revolutionaries *on behalf of* the masses—the state of the workers' movement or the mass urban resistance was not an essential issue'.[3] In Gonzalez's view, Che preferred to wage guerrilla war in the remote areas of the Sierra Maestra where no alternative social base for the mass movement could be found. Guerrilla warfare in the mountains, then, constituted not just a tactical move in a wider revolutionary movement but the one and only way to make the revolution. Then, Gonzalez puts forward his understanding of the socialist tradition, the one that serves him to measure Che's distance from the true path to revolution. He says:

> For revolutionary socialists, a revolutionary process is one in which people become involved directly in shaping their own destiny, and it is the experience of becoming an active agent that will shape the new—socialist—society that emerges. Socialism is not a matter of changing leaders, but of building a society based in different values (production for need not profit, for example). It involves a completely different view of what democracy means—direct day-to-day involvement in shaping society rather than the occasional vote for one or other self-selected politician.[4]

The paragraph quoted above is correct and impeccably attuned to the most sober and orthodox reading of the Marxist tradition. I am not conceding this for the sake of my argument; I genuinely believe it to be an accurate presentation of the tradition in question. However, I will argue that Che's thoughts are not contradictory. Of course, this is not Gonzalez's view. He asserts that 'in identifying the poor peasantry as the key social group in the revolution, Che was specifically rejecting Marxism's central idea—that it is the power of the organised working class alone that can bring about a social revolution'.[5] The consequences of this conception of the social forces involved in the struggle would bear a pervasive mark on the society that emerged from that struggle. In the absence of a wider social basis for the revolutionary actions and given the overwhelming weight ascribed to military factors, the result could not be other than a society shaped by the logic of this strategy. Democracy and transparency, as Gonzalez holds, were features destined to be neglected in the new society. Here is an expanded version of Gonzalez's core argument:

> In Che's description of the revolutionary process there is a fundamental and

> glaring omission. Where are the masses? Where is the working class, whose liberation is the very definition of socialism?... This notion that revolution comprises the *self-emancipation* of the working class is absolutely central to Marx's thought. From being the objects of the interests of others, the majority become the governors of their own lives by transforming society through their own actions. It is a core principle in revolutionary Marxism. Yet the guerrilla war theory replaces this idea with another—that the revolutionaries will make the revolution on behalf of the wider class... The guerrilla theory makes a virtue of the separation between revolutionaries and workers.[6]

Gonzalez is right in his theoretical proposition, but too severe when judging Che's point of view. It is true that Che's appeals to the centrality of the working class are obscured in his military writings, but if we look at the bulk of this work, we find plenty of references which satisfy Gonzalez's demands.

In the 'Preface' to the book *The Marxist-Leninist Party*, written by Che in 1963, he says, in the first place, that the vanguard party is the 'vanguard of the working class, the leader of that class, which knows how to show the road to victory and accelerate the pace towards new social situations'. The 'fundamental goal of the party in the first stage of revolution is seizing power' and it is 'logical that this party be a class party. A Marxist-Leninist party could not be otherwise; its mission is to find the shortest way to the dictatorship of the proletariat, and its most valuable militants, its leading cadres and its tactics come from the working class'.[7] In this same 'Preface', Che makes a forceful statement which highlights the differences between the Mountains and the Plains. Che thinks that existing contradictions between the two areas are not merely matters of tactics. 'The Rebel Army already is ideologically proletarian and thinks with the dispossessed class in mind; the Plains are still petty bourgeois, there are future traitors in its leadership and it is heavily influenced by the environment in which it moves'.[8] In his 'Notes for an Ideology of the Cuban Revolution', published in 1960, Che writes:

> Parallel to the successive qualitative changes which occurred in the battle fronts, there run the changes in the social composition of the guerrilla, as well as the ideological transformations in its leadership... The peasant puts in

> his vigour, his capacity to withstand suffering, his knowledge of the terrain, his love for the land, his thirst for agrarian reform. The intellectual, any kind of intellectual, adds his little grain of sand by beginning to draft a sketch of theory. The worker brings his sense of organisation, his innate tendency to reunion and unification.

Che adds, 'Never before has the concept of interaction been so clear to us. We could sense how this interaction was ripening'.[9] So, there is no such separation between the guerrillas and the working class. Che talks explicitly about interaction involving the fighters in the mountains, the peasants and the workers. Clearly, Che thinks that peasants comprise the military core of the guerrilla, but in no way are the peasants the social core of the revolutionary process. The peasantry is necessary to win the revolutionary war against the dictatorship, but they are not the main social actor in the construction of socialism.[10]

If the evidence offered above were not enough, let us look at another fragment in which Che touches again upon the same topic. He says, 'The basis of our Socialist Revolution is in the working class. The working class is the engine of this Revolution, its reason for being, and as our people make their fundamental decision to build socialism, there it is also established, in parallel, the dictatorship of the proletariat, that is, the democratic dictatorship of the working class in all the levels'.[11] Similar statements are found in his more private talks with his staff in the Ministry of Industry.[12] In a nutshell: Che does not see the working class as an auxiliary to the guerrillas, nor does he ignore that it is the working class itself and for itself that will make the revolution happen.

It is a pity that Gonzalez devotes so little space to the Cuban Economic Debate. As he admits in a footnote, what he does is 'a simple and schematic attempt to sum up a very complex debate'.[13] However, he pays great attention to the issue of the new consciousness and the controversy on moral and material incentives. Gonzalez contends:

> Why did [Che] lay such emphasis on the question of a new consciousness? It was certainly not for economic reasons, or because committed people are more efficient producers—although the debates about moral incentives did reflect what he saw as the urgent need to transform Cuba's economy at speed. It went to the very heart of Che's political ideas, for it emphasised the

subjective over the objective, the effort of will that could overcome unpromising material conditions... For Che, the new society is born of a spiritual transformation.[14]

As Gonzalez reminds us, men make history but in circumstances not chosen by them, but circumstances can be changed in struggle, and that was Che's point. There is a dialectical relationship between circumstances and human agency. Men are shaped by history and vice versa. Organisation needs not to be completed before struggle begins, it can be achieved in struggle itself. Moreover, classes are not simply defined by their position in the productive system; classes are defined and shaped in class struggle. That is what Marx notoriously says in his writings on France. The objective conditions are not separate from the subjective conditions. The latter can change the former and the other way around. So, the question is: were there in Cuba both the objective and subjective conditions for a socialist revolution? This leads to the formulation of another pressing issue, in fact the very issue that sparked a deep and furious debate in Cuba in the mid-1960s: whether revolution could be made in a country where the forces of production had not reached their full development, in other words, whether the objective conditions were ripe for the proletariat to take power and begin its self-emancipation. Che thought that even though Cuba was not an industrial country and some pockets in the economy reflected pre-capitalist relations of production, it was also true that Cuba, like every other country on the periphery of the developed world, was connected to the world market and so belonged to the capitalist world system. Sugar refineries and mining plants run by US capitalists in Cuba were evidence of the extent to which Cuba was indeed part of the capitalist world.

Che was sure that socialism could be achieved even if the productive forces were not completely developed. This stance received, during the highlighted debate, the support of the leading Trotskyist economist, Ernest Mandel, and other leading Cuban figures such as Luis Alvarez Rom. The group which opposed Che's vision was led by the pro-Soviet French intellectual Charles Bettelheim and the former PSP (Cuban Communists) leader Carlos Rafael Rodríguez. Gonzalez does not pause to look into this debate but makes a comment which, in my view, puts things in the right perspective. He writes, 'What had appeared to be highly technical debates about the economy conducted in the second half of 1963 were in fact extremely political. The moral/material incentives controversy was really about whether the economy would be organised around ideas of profitability and efficiency or around social need. In later official accounts this dispute has been described as a difference of degree—for Che it was a difference of politics and principle'.[15] The politics and principles at stake in that debate highlighted the problems facing most revolutionary processes in the underdeveloped world. The Stalinist state had not been able to go beyond the experience of the New Economic Policy (NEP) and therefore advocated a centralised bureaucratic planning accompanied by a scheme of competition between firms. Each firm was allowed to save its profits in a separate bank account. The rationale underlying this system resembled that of capitalism, save for the fact that private property over means of production had been abolished. In order to meet the production quotas and increase their savings for investment, firms would not only cheat the plan but also seek to augment output by offering monetary prizes to the workers. The bottom line of this policy, according to Che, revealed that capitalism had not been totally superseded and the whole system ran the risk of collapsing again into the filthy business of capitalism.

For Che, socialism was not only a matter of building an affluent society but also a matter of conscience. Devoting all social efforts to obtaining abundance could not guarantee socialism as an outcome. If so, capitalist countries would automatically become socialist at some point. In my view, Che was addressing a crucial point which Marx had omitted in the *Critique of the Gotha Programme*. For Marx, distribution in the first stage of communist society would be made according to the individual quantum of production. This is known as the 'contribution principle'. Marx was not happy with this, but thought that this defect would be inevitable. For him, only when the productive forces had reached the highest stage could distribution according to needs be realised. For Che, this was somewhat fatalistic and he thought that moral incentives could play a significant part in this process. He did not think that material incentives should be eliminated wholesale; in fact, he put forward a system labelled the 'Budgetary Financing System', in which moral and material incentives were mixed. He did think, however, that moral incentives were more efficient than material ones. The socialist society he envisaged was superior to capitalism, among other things, because it was based on a different set of values, and values should be part of the process of building that society. Gonzalez quotes Che saying, 'I'm not interested in an economic transformation unless it's accompanied by a socialist morality'.[16] The full quotation comes from an interview with French journalist Jean Daniels and runs as follows:

> Economic socialism without a communist morality is of no interest to me. We fight against misery but at the same time we fight against alienation. One of Marxism's fundamental goals consists in eliminating interest, the 'individual interest factor' and benefit from the 'psychological motivations'. Marx was concerned about economic facts as well as about their translation into the mind. He called this 'a fact of consciousness'. If communism neglects the consciousness facts it will amount to a distribution method, but it ceases to be a revolutionary morality.[17]

This paragraph is known as Che's 'general conception' of socialism. As we can easily see, he does not disregard economic factors altogether. What he says is that economic factors themselves should be taken into account as much as the ideological factors. He believes, rightly I contend, that sheer distribution of wealth and income could only give rise to something he calls 'economic socialism'. In other words, if moral factors are relegated to a secondary role or ignored altogether, society will stagnate at the first stage of communism where individual interests and natural privileges (such as physical strength) are allowed to determine distribution. In order to reach the goal of communism, understood as a society ruled by the 'needs principle', Che stresses the need for a new morality, detached both from alienation and the pursuit of selfish interests. Here the 'new man' comes in.

This hotly debated issue of the new man relates to one key feature of the future society as it was outlined by Marx: that communist society encompasses both an optimal development of productive forces and well rounded individuals. If socialism and communism are to be realised there is a need for a change in what is nowadays called a moral psychology of the individual. A new society shapes new individuals who at the same time, dialectically, make that very society a feasible project. If human nature were fixed to the patterns of capitalism, socialism would be impossible. Marx stressed the fact that socialism would be burdened by the 'birthmarks' of the old society, capitalism, but these traits would eventually disappear. The scant remarks Marx makes on this issue have motivated an array of interpretations.

Some think that abundance, that is to say, the full development of productive forces, would suffice to bring about the desired change in motivations. Others, like Che, thought that the surviving features should be erased by education, formal and informal. This, and not another, was the goal behind voluntary work. It was intended to reshape the motivation of the workers, to bring about a new scheme of preferences. This has direct bearing on the conditions required to achieve communist distribution according to needs. In other words, the subjective factors made this type of distribution possible given a moderate abundance. To think otherwise, to affirm the unlimited expansion of needs, would make communism a truly utopian project. This is one of the important points made by Mandel during his contribution to the debate in support of Che's positions.[18] So, moral incentives were seen as taking precedence over material incentives because, in the first place, they could eventually prove to be more efficient and, second, because a change in the systems of needs was necessary in order to reach the stage of communist distribution. That is the reason why Che laid so much emphasis on the construction of a revolutionary morality. But, as we said above, Che admitted that material incentives were necessary at some point, and this must be underlined in order to reject all charges of utopianism pressed against him. I will offer some evidence to support this view.

As early as 1962, in one of the bimonthly meetings with his staff at the Ministry of Industries he said, 'We are not excluding the material incentives, we simply state that we must fight for moral incentives to be—for as long as possible—the determining factor in the performance of workers. We propose a mixed formula: not to obstruct the material incentive but to turn it from something quantitative to something qualitative'.[19] Later that year, during a public appearance, he stressed, '[Socialism] is based on social distribution of all goods, it is based on a new acquired consciousness, but also, in order for the construction of socialism to be possible, a sufficient amount of goods is needed to be distributed among the people'.[20] In 1963, the year when the Economic Debate begins, he makes an even more bold statement on this issue:

> Moral incentives are necessary because we are coming out from a society which thought of nothing but material incentives, and we are building a new society on the basis of that old one...and because we do not have enough as yet to give to each one according to their needs. That is why

> material interests will be present for a time in the process of building socialism... Material incentives are a vestige from the past, they are something to be taken into account, but it is necessary to diminish their pre-eminence in the consciousness of the people as the process goes on... The material incentives will not be a part of the new society that is being created, they will vanish on the way.[21]

These remarks should shed some light into Che's real conception about the role of material and moral incentives. It is important to note that he does not move, as Gonzalez contends, in a world of 'moral certainties'. Che is keen to distinguish what is normatively right, and what is really possible. Normative thinking sets the goals, reality draws the limits for the realisation of the normative model. Che knows that material incentives will be demanded by the workers and is ready to understand these demands in the light of what Marx said about distribution under the contribution principle. But this explanatory approach can exist along with a normative view. So he judges material incentives as a 'necessary evil' and is ready—albeit unhappily—to let it operate within his scheme for promoting the industrial development of Cuba. In 1964, in his famous article entitled 'On the Budgetary Financing System', he makes another categorical statement on this matter. Che writes:

> We do not deny the objective need for material incentives, we are instead reluctant to use it as the fundamental lever. We consider that, in economics, this type of lever rapidly acquires life of its own and then imposes its force on the relationships between people. We should not forget that it comes from capitalism and is destined to die in socialism.[22]

Last but not least, the same argument can be found in Che's remarkable 'Socialism and Man in Cuba'. For some reason, Gonzalez prefers not to quote the following remark by Che: '[To] build communism, simultaneous to the material basis, the new man must be made. Hence the importance of correctly choosing the right tools for mass mobilisation. These tools should be fundamentally moral in nature, without forgetting a proper use of the material incentives', particularly those which are assigned on social and not on individual criteria.[23] In short, it is not totally true, as Gonzalez holds, that for Che, 'the new society is born of a spiritual transformation'.[24] Spiritual transformation was indeed necessary but not sufficient, the same qualification applied to material abundance. Both are essential and Che knew it.

To summarise, Gonzalez reaches a disputable conclusion out of a correct diagnosis. In truth, the Cuban Economic Debate was not only technical, it was political, and to be precise, it was a debate on the political economy of the transition to socialism. It involved more than arguing about concrete policies, it was about the nature of socialist and communist societies. Gonzalez has a strong point when he says that Che favoured an economic scheme based on social need instead of a model oriented to attain economic efficiency and profitability. As Carlos Tablada Pérez, one of the most subtle of Cuban scholars, has noted, Che cared for social efficiency over cold economic and instrumental efficiency. Che defined socialism as a combination of high productivity and a new consciousness, without one being more important than the other. If he was committed to social need in the first place, in spite of dire scarcity, it was because he set out to build a communist society having in mind the distributive principle meant to rule that society, that is, distribution according to needs. This is not mere utopianism, but utopian imagination, an extremely useful mechanism to outline the desirable state of affairs and to choose the right policies to reach that goal.

Gonzalez misses the mark when he affirms that Che was convinced that an 'effort of will' could overcome 'unpromising material conditions'. This is not Che's position, at least not his more mature vision on the construction of socialism. It could be read as such in his military writings, Gonzalez's dominant source; but Che's economic works allow for a more balanced interpretation according to which moral factors alone, though necessary, are not sufficient in the face of scarcity. That is the reason why Che argues that the 'new man' is created simultaneously to an appropriate material basis. The bottom line of this argument consists in advocating a revolutionary morality built upon a reasonable material development. It could sound almost obvious, but it was not so obvious in Che's times.

In those days, Soviet ideologues and economists defended a line of thought based on a mechanical and deterministic interpretation of Marxism. For them, communism was the offspring of the growth of productive forces alone, and any means to achieve the development of those forces was acceptable. Che was far from endorsing the Jesuits' morality of any means justified by the right ends. For him, the ends were in the means, and so condemned the use of capitalist fetishes to build socialism, as he explicitly states in a letter to Ramón Medero Mestre.[25] So, as Gonzalez says, 'socialism is not a matter of changing leaders, but of building a society based in different values (production for need not profit, for example)'. This is precisely Che's vision, one that makes him a true member of the socialist revolutionary tradition.

NOTES

1: M Gonzalez, *Che Guevara and the Cuban Revolution* (Bookmarks, 2004), p18.

2: As above, pp47-48.

3: As above, p62.

4: As above, p77.

5: As above, p79.

6: As above, pp101-2.

7: E Guevara, *Escritos y Discursos* (Editorial de Ciencias Sociales, 1985), vol VII, pp4-5. My translation of all quotations from Che's writings.

8: As above, p8.

9: As above, vol IV, pp210-11.

10: E Guevara, *El Che en la Revolución Cubana* (Ministerio del Azúcar, 1966), vol VI, pp580-581.

11: E Guevara, *Escritos y Discursos*, as above, vol VI, p130.

12: E Guevara, *El Che en la Revolución Cubana*, as above, p276.

13: M Gonzalez, as above, p185.

14: As above, p149.

15: As above, p145.

16: As above, p139.

17: In T Pérez, *Ernesto Che Guevara. Hombre y Sociedad. El pensamiento económico del Che* (Antarca, 1987), p45.

18: E Mandel, 'Las categorías mercantiles en el período de transición', in E Guevara, *El gran debate sobre la economía en Cuba 1963-1964* (Ocean Press, 2003), p267. First published in *Nuestra Industria Económica*, June 1964.

19: E Guevara, *El Che en la Revolución Cubana*, as above, p146.

20: E Guevara, *Escritos y Discursos*, as above, vol VI, pp86-87.

21: As above, vol VII, p44.

22: As above, vol VIII, p14.

23: As above, p259.

24: M Gonzalez, as above, p150.

25: E Guevara, *Escritos y Discursos*, as above, vol IX, p384.

Cities in revolt

Esme Choonara

A review of Meena Menon and Neera Adarkar, ***One Hundred Years, One Hundred Voices*** *(Seagull Books, 2004), £19.95*

This book is an inspiring testimony to what can be achieved by the working class of a developing country in the face of repression from capitalists, right wing thugs and the state. It is a remarkable oral history and political narrative of over 150 years of labour history in Mumbai.

Mumbai, formerly known as Bombay, remains today the industrial heartland of India. It is a city undergoing rapid transformation. The organisers of the 2004 World Social Forum in Mumbai describe it as 'a megapolis of more than 13 million people of diverse socio-economic, cultural and political backgrounds. It is a city where skyscrapers and slums jostle for space along the sea; where great wealth and stark want exist side by side. The city has been witness to both extremes in exploitation and militant protests and trade union action in reaction. It has been the birthplace of many progressive social movements and yet, paradoxically, is today the power centre of right wing political parties like the Shiv Sena'.[1]

It was these contradictions that inspired Meena Menon and Neera Adarkar, both political activists in Mumbai for many years, to write this book. In particular they wanted to understand the social transformations that had taken place in a city with a history of strong trade unions, secular and left traditions for it to become the centre of anti-Muslim pogroms in December 1992 and January 1993 in which over 550 Muslims were murdered.

The book consists largely of interviews with activists from the Girangaon area of Mumbai, which has been the centre of India's textile industry since the first mills were built there in the middle of the 19th century. Today there are still over 1.3 million working class residents in the area despite the closure of many of the mills and the intrusions of wealthy land developers. The authors have added a commentary to the interviews to create a narrative that is both huge in scope and very detailed.

The book is organised chronologically, looking at five key episodes in the history of the city: the early growth of mills, the struggle for independence, the movement for a linguistic state of Maharashtra with Bombay as its capital, the growth of the Shiv Sena and the two year long strike of 1982-84. What emerges from each of these episodes is both the courage and combativity of the workers and a sense of some of the arguments over organisation and strategy that raged throughout the struggles.

The first mill was opened in Bombay in 1851. By 1892 there were over 100,000 mill workers, mostly migrants to the city. The average age of the workers at this time was 17 years old and they worked up to

14-hour shifts. There was a constant battle over working hours and conditions. The first recorded charter of workers' demands was presented in 1890 and called for a weekly holiday, a 30-minute lunch break and rest after sundown.

Mill workers staged their first general strike in January 1919. Despite only loose welfare support groups and no real trade union organisation, 150,000 workers joined the strike and stayed out for 18 days. The beginnings of formal organisation in the mills grew out of this and subsequent strikes.

A number of different unions and political groups have organised in Girangaon over the years, but the most interesting is probably the growth of the Communists. The Communist Party of India (CPI) established themselves at the heart of the mill workers' struggle in Bombay during a general strike in 1928 against increases in workloads and 'rationalisation' measures. A worker was killed very early in the strike and at his funeral thousands vowed to stay out until they won. The strike lasted for six months. Those active in the strike recall the international solidarity that they received and the impressive role of women in the strike, especially the thousands of women wielding broom handles who defended the picket lines. CPI activists also distributed grain among the strikers to boost morale. The Communists proved themselves during this strike and established a base at the heart of the struggle in Girangaon that would last for many years. When the CPI launched the GKU textile union (also known as Lal Batwa or 'Red Flag') in the year following the strike, over 100,000 mill workers lined up to join immediately.

The Communists faced huge repression from the mill owners and the British. Two GKU activists were hanged in 1929 for the killing of a British manager in a clash at one of the mills. In the same year 33 Communist Party leaders were charged with conspiracy to overthrow the king in a four-year trial known as the Meerut conspiracy case. The heavy sentences passed against the Communists drew protests from Albert Einstein and H G Wells among others. The CPI and the GKU were banned in 1934 though this didn't halt the activities of the Communists and trade union activists in the mills of Bombay.

The chapter on the struggle for independence is a fascinating account of the different forces involved in the fight against British rule. There were clear class differences in the movement. Many of the Indian mill owners supported independence, though not mass movements and agitation that might affect their profits. Gandhi had close links with many of the mill owners and opposed the use of strikes as a political weapon. His strategy of non-violence fitted the needs of a new rising nationalist class who wanted to exert enough pressure to get rid of the British but not to spill over into class conflict or revolution.[2]

The authors point out that 'mainstream history largely ignores the role of the Communists, terrorist groups, terrorist actions, the contributions of peasants' and workers' fronts in the struggle for independence'. As several of those interviewed make clear, the period running up to independence in 1947 was marked not just by Gandhi's campaigns of non-violence but by huge strike waves, riots, and attacks on police stations and transport links. Dr Shanti Patel, president of the Dock Labour Union, was a student during the independence struggle. He recalls both being inspired by Gandhi's speeches and also getting involved in an underground group blowing up train tracks. Others talk of the impact of hearing about the setting up by

Subhash Chandra Bose of an Indian National Army to fight alongside the Japanese against the British, and Dinanath Kamath, a Communist at the time, recalls attacking police stations, cutting electric cables and concealing bombs in shopping bags to throw at post offices.

Communist Party members were very much involved in fighting for independence but the Second World War threw them into confusion. When the British viceroy declared India would join the war, the CPI opposed the war as imperialist with the slogan of 'Na ek pai, na ek bai': 'Not one coin, not one brother.' After Hitler invaded Russia in 1941, the CPI, under direction from Moscow, changed its position on the war, rebranding it a 'people's war'. In 1942, just as Gandhi was launching the Quit India campaign, the Communists issued a thesis calling for support for the war effort. This included supporting calls for increased productivity and playing down industrial disputes. The British released many of the jailed Communists and legalised the CPI.

This support for the war effort was seen by the majority of Indian workers as a betrayal of the struggle and isolated the CPI from many former supporters. As one mill worker explains, 'Ordinary people could not understand this concern about fascism. All they knew was that the Communists were supporting the British.'

The Communists regained some credibility in 1946 when they supported the mutiny of the naval ratings in Bombay. On 18 February ratings on the RIN Talwar went on hunger strike against bad food and racial humiliation. The strike spread and 22 ships in Bombay harbour joined the mutiny, raising the national flag, the Muslim crescent and the red flag jointly over the ships. The strike spread across India to 20,000 ratings on 78 ships. The people of Bombay joined the struggle, fighting their way through police to gather at the harbour in solidarity. In Girangaon workers came out of the mills in their thousands, set up barricades and fought the police and armed forces. Over 300 were killed and official figures put the injured at 1,046. While the Communists supported the mutiny, the Congress and the Muslim League were much more wary and advised the ratings to surrender, aware no doubt that they would need the army to keep order when the British left India.

Independence itself was a mixed experience. Many of those interviewed in the book express their joy and sense of victory that the British were forced to leave India, though many talk also of the betrayal and confusion of partition. According to the authors, there was less communal violence in Bombay than elsewhere, but still 162 Hindus and 158 Muslims were killed in communal riots.

Following independence the new government of India was faced with the problem of the organisation of the Indian nation. In a number of areas, including Bombay, mass movements grew up calling for a linguistic state. In Bombay this took the form of the Samyutka Maharashtra movement, which fought for a Marathi-speaking linguistic state with Bombay as the capital. One of the Communist activists interviewed pointed out that the mainly Marathi-speaking workers identified the mill owners and industrialists as Gujaratis. He argues that workers of all religions and castes supported the movement as they thought that it would give workers more opportunities and more of a voice in the new state.

The movement was successful in the creation of a new state, but it left unsolved many of the problems of inequality and unemployment those involved in the mobilisations had been led to believe would be resolved. As one interviewee put it, the movement 'succeeded in winning Maharashtra for Bombay, but jobs and opportunities did not follow'.

It was in this context that cartoonist Bal Thackeray launched a magazine which, in 1965, began publishing lists of the Marathi speaking and non Marathi speaking populations and giving breakdowns of the background of business leaders and city bureaucrats of Bombay. When Thackeray launched Shiv Sena at a huge public meeting in 1966, many young people signed up immediately to join. The Sena appealed to the young and the unemployed and to a layer of the middle class who felt their ambitions were frustrated by 'outsiders'.

At its foundation Thackeray claimed that Shiv Sena was a social, not a political, organisation. In 1968 however they turned to elections, winning 42 seats in a house of 140. Shiv Sena had an uneasy relationship with the ruling Congress Party. The authors suggest that in the beginning, at least, Congress saw the left as a greater threat and gave support and encouragement to Shiv Sena's attacks on the Communists.

If Shiv Sena were going to build a base, they would have to deal with the Communists. They vilified CPI members in public, also encouraging children of CPI activists to publicly denounce their parents. In 1967 Shiv Sena attacked the CPI offices, sending shockwaves throughout society. The conflict between Shiv Sena and the left escalated into more violence. In 1970 Thackeray formed the 'Saffron Guard', a group of young activists that travelled with his motorcade. Meanwhile, Krishna Desai, a Communist Party activist, organised a militant left wing youth movement. Several people in the book suggest that Desai was the only Communist leader capable of preventing Shiv Sena from building a base among Marathi-speaking youth in the mill area. In June 1970 Krishna Desai was murdered by thugs associated with Shiv Sena. Despite a wave of anger, the demoralised CPI didn't respond.

Several interviews in the book give insights into the attraction of Shiv Sena. One former Shiv Sena member says, 'Look at me, I am neither strong, nor big. But I felt strong in such an organisation.' Several people, including the son of a Communist Party leader, mention the way in which the Communists focused only on the industrial struggle, while Shiv Sena made huge inroads into local culture.

The Communists should have been the best placed to oppose the growth of communalism and the rise of Shiv Sena. However, the twists and turns that they had made under instruction from Stalinist Russia had left them isolated. The lack of response to Desai's murder further demoralised their members. The enthusiastic participation of the Communists and other political groups in the Samyutka Maharashtra movement also made it harder for them to politically challenge or confront Shiv Sena. The Sena were building on the logic of linguistic nationalism and taking it to its extreme.

The authors argue that, despite establishing themselves in Bombay, Shiv Sena were never able to build a mass base among the mill workers. They attribute this to the aggressive violence of the Shiv Sena, which alienated many people including some of the former members of the Sena who they interviewed, and to Shiv Sena's cosiness with the industrialists and with Congress. They also point out the hesitation and uncertainty with which the Sena approached industrial disputes, including their prevarications in the historic strike of 1982.

Shiv Sena have continued as a major force in political life in Mumbai despite various ebbs and flows in their ability to build a base. As Dr Rajnaryan Chandavarkar points out in an introductory essay to the book, the focus of Shiv Sena's attacks has shifted since the 1970s from targeting non-Marathi speakers to targeting Muslims.

The chapter of the book dealing with the 1982 strike is a story of mass militancy. One woman active in the strike summed up the mood of the strikers when she explained that they felt like they were 'fighting for the wages of our blood'. 250,000 workers from 60 mills were on all-out strike for up to two years. During this time there was also a brief police strike and several riots. The government was determined to break the mill workers and the strike ultimately ended in disarray and defeat with up to 100,000 workers losing their jobs. The first-hand accounts of organisation, courage and solidarity in the face of huge deprivation remain hugely inspiring.

The book is packed with interesting details such as the many accounts of the importance of cultural expression to the growth of the mill workers' struggles—the plays and songs, stories and sculptures. There are interviews with Jewish activists and those in mixed Hindu-Muslim marriages that give some insight into the mixture of people living together in Mumbai. There are other accounts of little known struggles and organisations such as the Dalit Panthers, an organisation of dalits, the lower caste 'untouchables' who continue to suffer discrimination in Indian society, inspired into direct action by the Black Panthers in the US.

One of the great strengths of the book is that it draws out at every stage the contribution of women mill workers and activists to the struggles. It is a great rebuttal of every stereotype of Asian women as passive or submissive. The authors mention that as early as 1894 women were recorded holding stoppages in the mills and pelting their managers with stones and dirt. Several women interviewed talk about organising while in prison. One woman talks about prisoners pooling together different coloured saris to make a tricolour national flag and flying it from the roof of the jail. Another CPI activist talks about how women smuggled leaflets and pamphlets into the mills. She also recalls how she knew that the CPI's literacy classes for women were working when she found the slogan 'Crush the mill owners into chutney' written in the mill where she worked.

Both the authors and many of those interviewed in the book are still involved in campaigns over the future of Girangaon and over the rights of current and former mill workers. Mike Davis has recently pointed out that in the very near future the majority of the world's population will live in cities, largely huge cities of slums such as Mumbai.[3] The accounts of the mill workers and activists of Mumbai are an impressive reminder that the working class and poor of the developing world and the growing slum cities are not just victims but agents of change and resistance.

NOTES

1: www.wsfindia.org

2: For more on independence, the Congress Party and the rise of the right in other parts of India, see C Harman, 'India After the Elections: A Rough Guide', *International Socialism* 103 (Summer 2004).

3: M Davis, 'Planet of Slums: Urban Involution and the Informal Proletariat', *New Left Review* (March-April 2004)

Militant Dubliners

Kieran Allen

A review of John Newsinger, ***Rebel City*** *(Merlin Press, 2004), £14.95*

Many cities in the developing world had become gigantic slums with a huge informal proletariat, argued Mike Davis in a recent influential article, 'Planet of the Slums', in *New Left Review*. He suggested that their social base laid the basis for political formations often influenced by Islam or Christian Pentecostalism. Undoubtedly, religious-based networks which offer social support play a huge role. However, the central issue is politics, not sociology. The comparison which Mike drew with 19th century Dublin—a city that suffered from de-industrialisation rather than industrialisation—bears this out.

At one time the second largest city of the British Empire, Dublin at the end of the 19th century was a city of slums. The employers' spokesperson Arnold Wright noted that if you ascended Nelson's pillar in the centre you could count the factories on the fingers of one hand. The Dublin working class were concentrated in transport, ferrying out agricultural produce to the metropolis. The majority of workers were employed as casual labourers, fearful that the huge pools of poverty created many rivals for their jobs.

Yet this city became the focal point of an intense class struggle led by Marxists like James Connolly and Jim Larkin. True, they were not 'pure' Marxists, with Connolly occasionally swerving into a 'romantic Fenianism' and Larkin surging towards great feats of rhetoric that combined an appeal to Jesus Christ with demands for class solidarity. But, boy, did they bring about a real political movement of their class.

Between 1911 and 1913 the most militant form of class war was fought in the city. The story of those struggles is told in a succinct, sharp fashion in John Newsinger's excellent *Rebel City*. Newsinger quotes Lord Askwith, the government's chief conciliator, to sum up the situation: 'While the disputes in the ports and inland cities of great Britain had been chiefly based on economic causes, the serious riots in Dublin, although founded on poverty, low wages and bad conditions, included a determination to establish..."one big union" and put into practice the doctrines of syndicalism. The influences [for] the overthrow of capitalism and revolution against existing authorities were all present.'

For once this upper class spokesperson was correct. The industrial weakness of workers was compensated by an intense militancy that was informed by anti-capitalist politics. The 'solidarity strike' lay at the heart of the strategy of the Irish Transport and General Workers Union. As Connolly put it, 'No consideration of any contract with a section of the capitalist class absolved any section of us from taking instant action to protect other sections when said sections were in danger from the capitalist enemy.'

This anti-capitalist message was promoted on a weekly basis by the *Irish Worker*, a newspaper with a mass sale of 18,000 a week. The paper targeted scabs by name, roared and jeered at the employers, and educated vast numbers of workers on the tradition of class struggle and opposition to this system. Faced with a brutal police force, workers formed their own Irish Citizen Army—drilled, got hold of guns, and fought.

This amazing tradition is often honoured in a nostalgic sort of way but then undermined. There is, firstly, sometimes a generalised pessimism that casual workers in the informal economy cannot be organised. One sometimes gets the impression that if workers do not have stable jobs and come from tight knit mining communities, they cannot organise mass revolutionary unions. Yet in working class history there has always been an important dialectic between communities of politicised militants and the development of strategies to overcome the 'objective' difficulties thrown up by the system.

The tradition of Larkinism—as militant syndicalism came to be known—is also dismissed by Irish union leaders today. They claim that Larkin had to use 'brawn' while their modern strategy of social partnership uses 'brains'. A recent biography of Larkin by one of Ireland's foremost labour historians, Emmet O'Connor, goes even further and denounces Larkin as an 'inferior trade unionist'. O'Connor's method—a common one with modern academics—is to pick out random quotations to debunk labour heroes of the past. Fortunately, Newsinger's book puts paid to this nonsense. Even though Larkinism was eventually defeated in the great lockout of 1913, he shows how it took the full weight of the British state, a united employers' front and the Catholic church to crush it.

Yet if Newsinger is strong in his defence of Larkinism, he is weak on the connection between this militant syndicalist tradition and the fight against empire. The main reason is that he adopts an uncritical position on the arguments raised by the playwright Sean O'Casey. O'Casey was originally an active member of the Irish Republican Brotherhood, but when the republicans regarded the class war of 1913 as a mere 'sectional struggle' and refused to back the workers, he broke with them.

Trotsky once argued that the Irish working class vacillated between republicanism and syndicalism. If this was true of the class as a whole, the contradictions were more acute in the head of O'Casey. The former 'Irish Irelander' swung over to rhetorical denunciations of the 'foolishness' of workers who joined the republicans. All connections with republicans were seen as a source of contamination and so Connolly's involvement in the 1916 rising could only mean that 'the high creed of Irish Nationalism became his daily rosary'.

There is little doubt that Connolly's involvement in the 1916 rising was surrounded with all sorts of problems: he issued no independent socialist propaganda; his political moorings were unhinged by the betrayals of the wider socialist movement during the First World War; he adopted a purely military concept of revolution. But while modern Marxists are right to be critical, it would be wrong to pose a variation of syndicalism as the alternative to republicanism.

The real problem with the period is that no force emerged which was capable of overcoming the two dialectical opposites. Instead of simply denouncing those who wanted to fight the empire, socialists needed a strategy to work with them—while politically challenging every compromise their leaders made with the wider system. The failure to do precisely this meant that the same workers who embraced syndicalism on a mass scale in 1913 slid over to republicanism a decade later.

Newsinger's account of these great battles is informed by a real engagement with the Marxist tradition—but he does not always draw the right conclusions.

Barcelona class war

Andy Durgan

A review of Chris Ealham, ***Class, Culture and Conflict in Barcelona 1898-1937*** *(Routledge, 2004), £70*

A plethora of books have appeared over the years on the nature and roots of anarchism in Spain, including in relation to its Barcelona stronghold. Chris Ealham's fascinating new book is one of the most original and important. It also challenges the left-liberal consensus that underpins many historians' work on the period. The view has become increasingly popular that workers are basically passive, manipulated by or indifferent to revolutionary groups, or that even the idea of 'class' as such has lost validity. In the Spanish case this is extended to a general dismissal of the revolution of 1936 as at best a utopian distraction from the need to win the war or at worst an orgy of bloodletting.

Ealham locates the city's anarchist movement within the context of Barcelona's working class communities, showing how shared hardship and poverty interrelated with the collective experience of struggle in both the factory and the streets. This shared 'culture of resistance' engendered a conscious rejection of the priorities of capitalism, be it respect for private property, police or religion, and a profound sense of solidarity. Many workers had little time for the promises of reform of the middle class republic. Established in 1931 it often treated them with contempt, and strikers were soon faced with increasing repression. 'The Republican utopia', as Ealham succinctly puts it, 'thus dissolved under the acid of working class struggle' (p100).

The anarchist-led union, the CNT, did not, like its socialist rival the UGT, just concern itself with the workplace, but intervened directly in the community, with its district committees playing a pivotal role in local protest. During the great rent strike of 1931 union members reconnected electricity to strikers' flats or participated in avoiding evictions. Anarchist-led strikes involved whole communities in acts of solidarity such as providing for strikers' families. The sale of anarchist newspapers further strengthened the network of activists in any locality (p42). Anarchists also played a pivotal role in proletarian sports clubs, and in the cultural and educational centres, the ateneus.

The author details the overlap between 'illegality' and anarchist activism. The growing numbers of unemployed developed a whole series of strategies to draw attention to their plight. Protest marches by the jobless often ended in mass expropriation from shops or the invasion of hotels and restaurants in order to eat. There were protests outside factories demanding the employment, or in some cases reinstatement, of CNT members. Recalcitrant bosses were faced with invasions of their workplaces or threats of physical violence. Parallel to these activities, the CNT's defence committees and members of anarchist 'affinity groups' carried out bank raids and other forms of fundraising in order to finance the unions, which were under increasing attack from the Republican authorities. Experience of daily life in working class Barcelona 'provided ample justification for law breaking in order to make ends meet'.

'Moral panics' have been a recurring reaction of the middle classes from the 19th century onwards when confronted with the rebellion of the poor. Such moral outrage was not just the preserve of bourgeois circles or the right in the 1930s, but also became common among members of the new Catalan Republican authorities and their petty bourgeois supporters. The Catalan Republicans spoke of the poorest neighbourhoods of the city as dens of vice and depravity, of crime and disease, whose inhabitants were, implicitly at least, somehow an inferior species. The more extreme commentators did not balk at using pseudo-scientific racist explanations to explain the perverse nature of much of Barcelona's proletariat. The fact that by 1930 migrants from elsewhere in Spain formed 35 percent of the city's population, and that workers of non-Catalan origin were prominent in the CNT, added to petty bourgeois prejudice and the authorities tried, unsuccessfully, to organise the repatriation of these 'undesirable' elements.

Ealham concludes that 'having depicted this "underclass" as criminal and incapable of accepting its social responsibilities the implication was clear: the small welfare budget could be cut, for the provision of relief would merely aggravate the dependent and deviant condition of the "undeserving poor"' (p152).

Barcelona's poorest neighbourhoods produced the backbone of the CNT and the often-heroic affinity groups. The members of the most famous group, Nosotros, involving Durruti and others, were the instigators of the movement's insurrectionary wing during the pre-war years and at the head of the militias when the civil war began. The CNT, in general, had few activists but 'they had a mobilising power hugely disproportionate to [their] number'.

However, heroism and activism were not enough and Ealham shows clearly how the activities of radical anarchists, far from leading to the overthrow of capitalism, led to the destruction of union organisation and demoralisation. Between 1931 and 1936 the Barcelona CNT lost half its membership, and often-violent sectarianism towards other workers' organisations perpetuated the highly damaging division that plagued the Spanish labour movement.

The radical anarchist groups saw revolution as a military problem, a question of force. Only a spark was necessary to start the revolutionary conflagration—a conception of revolution, of course, familiar in later guerrilla-based movements. As Ealham puts it, 'The radicals substituted their own violence for mass union struggles' (p131). Thus only about 50 militants took the decision of the CNT National Defence Committee to launch the abortive armed insurrection of January 1933, and they began it on a Sunday, indicative of the lack of importance given to mass mobilisation in the workplace. Despite the myths about anarchist assembly-based democracy, the influential 200 or so activists who were the mainstay of anarchist insurrectionism were 'relatively aloof from the bulk of the working class' and rather contemptuous of formal union structures.

Along with the elitism of the radical groups went a short-sighted rejection of politics by the majority of anarchists. This apoliticism meant in practice unstinting hostility to the workers' parties, but an ambivalent attitude towards certain petty bourgeois leaders, such as Companys. So while most anarchists rejected any collaboration with the anti-fascist and decidedly class-based Workers Alliance, they effectively supported the Popular Front in the 1936 elections in order to secure the release of their prisoners and the restoration of legality for their unions. The same combination of sectarianism and political naivety led the CNT leadership to refuse to contemplate the creation of a new revolutionary state when civil war erupted and not to differentiate between the politics of the POUM and the counter-revolutionary politics of Stalinism. The majority of anarchist cadre accepted collaboration with the remains of the Republican state.

By centring on the relationship between anarchism and the poorest working class communities, Ealham appears to point to community rather than workplace as the basis of anarchist strength. However, the real substance of his analysis takes us beyond what at first sight appears to be an 'autonomist' understanding of class and social transformation. The primacy of the CNT's powerful workplace organisation contrasted with the limitations of creating 'liberated spaces', in this case the working class community. The 'men of order' certainly regarded the organised trade union movement as the biggest threat, and police raids into poor districts were 'directed heavily at union offices'. 'The factory remained the key organising force' in many working class neighbourhoods, Ealham points out. The failure of anarchist activists to generalise from this reality was at the centre of their eventual defeat. They were 'largely concerned with power at street level and not with the creation of new structures' (p179).

Power had to be taken, not 'ignored' as many anarchists, in effect, did in 1936. The consequence of this was both the eventual destruction of the world's most important anarchist movement and the defeat of the Spanish Revolution itself.

The only problem with this book, and no fault of the author, is its price. It deserves a far wider audience than just academia, so we must hope that a cheaper edition will be forthcoming in the not too distant future. For Spanish readers a more accessible edition will be published by Alianza Editorial in April 2005.

Emin matters

John Molyneux

Tracey Emin is the most famous contemporary artist in Britain. This is the first time a woman has occupied this position and that is, in itself, worthy of note. Moreover her fame is connected to what makes her a serious and important artist.

Media treat her as a celebrity because they have picked up on the fact that she is independently popular, she has a 'fan base'. Who are these 'fans'? Mainly, though not exclusively, they are younger women. They are part of the new expanded audience for modern art, but they are not art world insiders. They relate to Emin because Emin's work relates to their experiences in a way that no other artist's does.

Most of her work is autobiographical. Its main subject matter is her traumas and triumphs growing up in Margate, and becoming the person she is today. It is often criticised for being 'self-centred'. This criticism completely misses the point so eagerly seized on by her 'fans'. The experiences re-presented in Emin's art are not just personal experiences, but are common to a wide layer of young women growing up in this time, in this society. Normally these experiences remain private, confided perhaps to 'best friends' but otherwise hidden from public view and therefore shameful. By making these experiences into art, Emin actually engages in a process of 'democratic sharing' with her audience. The work is not didactic and does not preach. It does not seek to impose a specific response. It simply says, 'This is what happened to me; this is how I felt about it,' and perhaps, 'This is how I dealt with it.' If it strikes a chord, as it evidently often does, then so be it.

Emin's first work to make a public impact, her tent, or *Everyone I Ever Slept With, 1963-95*, was a good example of this. The tent sat on the gallery floor. On the inside Emin had sewn the names of her bedmates of the previous 30 years. To see or experience the work the viewer has to crawl into the tent. Thus Emin has created a 'private' space, a den with private information about her life which the public is invited to share. The fact, which she stresses, that the names included not just lovers but also others she had shared 'the intimacy of sleep' with (such as her twin brothers and aborted foetuses) is important. It does not negate the sexual interpretation of the title, but it modifies it, ensuring that the sexual is not separated from the emotional. What we are offered to share is not gossip or titillation but feelings, including painful feelings.

Emin's most famous work, *My Bed*, is a complex piece, which has appeared in different forms, but essentially it works on the same principle. According to the stereotype, women are the homemakers and responsible for housework. A messed-up house shames a woman, makes her a 'slut', much more than it does a man. The bedroom and above all the bed itself represent a place of privacy, intimacy and sex, pain and illness. The stained sheets are a visible trace of all this and thus taboo: 'You don't wash your dirty linen in public.' *My Bed* takes all this as its starting point and confronts it, knowing that for some of us all the time and many of us some of the time it is a lie. It is a spectacular coming out. And out there thousands, perhaps millions, of people say, openly or privately, 'Yes! I've been there, I know what that's about!' That is why *My Bed* is one of those few works of contemporary art that captures people's imagination and stays in the public memory.

Much of the media coverage of *My Bed* seemed to assume that she had simply transplanted her actual bed or bedroom into the Tate. This, as a moment's thought would have made clear, was nonsense. *My Bed*, which had already appeared in Tokyo, was a consciously constructed work, as much a made work of art as Van Gogh's painting of his bedroom. In so far as it was a sufficiently convincing representation of a disordered bedroom to persuade journalists that it was the real thing, this is testimony to Emin's skill. *My Bed* is also visually powerful in its own right.

Emin is a skilled practitioner in a range of media. Her drawing is superb. She is able, with great economy, to achieve very accurate and telling representations. Her line combines strength and vulnerability, confidence and pain in exactly the right proportions, and matching visual form to intellectual/ emotional content is precisely the key skill of the visual artist.

Three of the themes in Emin's work—class, sex and art—are more or less omnipresent and make for its distinctiveness and power.

Class: The most immediately striking and unusual thing about both Emin's persona and her work is the way in which she positions herself as a working class artist.

Clearly Emin is not currently working class. She is probably a millionaire and she functions, as all successful visual artists do, as boss of her own small business. Her class background was complex. Until Emin was seven her mother had a hotel in Margate, but bankruptcy and poverty ensued when she broke up with Emin's father, and Emin's youth, whether or not strictly proletarian, was plebeian. Nor is she an artist who sees or presents herself as associated with or representative of the working class *movement*.

What she does do is present herself as *culturally* working class. This is evident in the way in which she conducts herself: in her accent, of course, but more importantly in what she says and how she says it. She makes no attempt to engage in 'intellectual art speak' but sticks to unaffected everyday language. This is highly unusual in the art world, the ethos of which is very upper class. The language used in her many appliquéd blankets, films and monoprint drawings is the language of the street, including the swear words, the grammatical errors and the misspellings. But, above all, the experiences her art deals with are, by and large, the experiences of working class girls.

The short film *Why I Never Became A Dancer* is one of her most important and powerful works. It tells of Emin's aspiration to be a dancer and her participation in a dance competition in Margate, the prize for which meant going to London. Just as she feels things are going well she finds herself surrounded by a circle of local lads (many of whom she has had sex with). At first she thinks they are clapping her, and then she realises that in fact they are chanting in unison 'Slag, Slag, Slag', and she runs from the ballroom in dismay. The film ends with her dancing, alone and just for herself, and saying to the camera, 'Shane, Eddie, Tony, Doug, Richard...this one's for you.' Of her recent film on teenage suicide, *Top Spot*, Amy Lane wrote in *Socialist Review*, 'There is nothing that does not reflect the reality of

Britain's working class estates. It is a painfully accurate portrayal of modern adolescent experience'.[1]

There is an element of class prejudice as well as misogyny in the media and critical hostility to Emin. Middle class critics often miss the point of her work because the kind of experiences she deals with are not part of the world they inhabit.

Emin's consciousness of this relationship with her audience was evident in her fury at *Top Spot* being given an 18 certificate by the censors, preventing it from reaching the very people it was intended for.

It is often said that Emin is not political. If this were true I would not find it a problem for, as Trotsky insisted, art cannot simply be judged on its politics. As it happens it is not true. Emin does not see herself as an artistic representative of a working class political movement but she does have a political consciousness and outlook, and this is clear from many of her public statements and appearances. She is anti-racist, anti-homophobic, and anti-war. A colleague, who knows the London art scene, says that in that world Emin is known as 'a committed socialist'.

I set this down for the record, but I do not believe that either her leftish views or her affluent lifestyle constitute major grounds for the evaluation of her art.

Sex: That sex should be a major theme in Emin's work is hardly surprising. Sex has been a central theme in European art from the Renaissance to Picasso and beyond (not to speak of Ancient Greece and Rome, Japan and so on). But it should be said at the outset, there is no element of eroticism or titillation here, unlike in Botticelli, Renoir or Klimt. Nor is it sexual fantasy or dreams, as we might find in surrealism, or the sex of the brothel featured so heavily in late 19th century French art. It is real, everyday sex—as experienced by her, of course, but also by millions of other people. This, in itself, is remarkable. I do not think there is a precedent for it in the whole of European visual art.

The history of art develops dialectically with each new generation, movement or individual artist usually defining themselves in opposition to the immediately preceding dominant trend. Part of this process is the discovery of new material, both physically and in terms of subject matter, to make art out of, which was often previously thought of as 'unartistic' (or vulgar, ugly, etc). This is one of the reasons why new art so often meets with the reaction that it is 'not art'. Thus, mid 19th century French art painted 'the heroism of modern life' as opposed to the heroes of classical mythology; and the Futurists and Constructivists aestheticised the machine and technology, previously anathema to classicists and romantics alike. Picasso spoke of the difficulty of finding a new subject and cited Van Gogh's *Boots* as an example. Tracey Emin has found a new subject.

A key feature of Emin's treatment of sex is her disclosure of an early teenage phase of promiscuity in Margate. In the voiceover on *Why I Never Became a Dancer* she describes it as follows:

'And then there was sex. It was something you could just do, and it was for free. Sex was something simple. It didn't matter that I was young, 13 or 14. It didn't matter that they were men…19, 20, 25, 26. It never crossed my mind to ask them what the attraction was. I knew…sex was what it was…'

I suspect that even if it is not a majority experience, such a phase among working class girls is quite common, driven by a complex mixture of low self-esteem, the search for love, intimacy, pleasure, excitement, desire to grow up, ambivalent yearnings for a baby, and so on. Usually the experience remains hidden, for obvious reasons, from parents, or school and the authorities. It therefore remains largely unrecorded and unrepresented. Films and novels have occasionally visited the territory, but not, until now, the elevated world of fine art.

Emin's treatment of this experience appears simple—a plain rendering of the facts—but it is in fact quite complex and nuanced. In *Dancer* she defends herself against the charge of being a 'slag' and records her conviction at the time that she was 'better than all those boys'. But in *Masculinity* she writes that she 'developed the ridiculous habit of sleeping with men much older than me'. She also claims that her promiscuous phase was very 'educational' in an interview for *The South Bank Show*. This 'ambivalence' towards her sexual experiences runs throughout her work.

Emin records many bad sexual experiences in her art but she does not 'aestheticise' them. She deals with childhood abuse, humiliation, abandonment, rape and abortion in the way these things actually happen to women (never as her own or others' fantasy material) and with the severe emotional trauma and pain they caused. There is no romanticisation of abjection.

This central theme is held in tension with two others. The first is that her experiences, though often bad, have not proved insuperable. Yes, they were deeply painful but they were not, including the rape, 'unspeakable' or 'the worst thing imaginable'. She does not revel in her suffering, only in her ability to have overcome it. *Why I Never Became A Dancer* ends with a seagull soaring up and away from the shores of Margate.

The second is the retention, despite the traumas of the past, of an open, affirmative attitude to sex and sexuality:

'You don't fuck me over/You gently lift me out of bed/Lay me on the floor/And make love to me'[2]

Holding these three elements, each of them a humane and progressive response, in tension with each other but without allowing any of them to be compromised, is a very considerable artistic and emotional achievement.

Emin does not present herself as a feminist artist and is not generally thought of as one. But, in dealing with sex Emin deals also with sexism. *Why I Never Became A Dancer* confronts the—very crude—sexism rampant among certain teenage boys and young men. *My Bed* challenges the sexist attitude that makes a disordered bedroom much more shameful for a woman than a man. Indeed there is a sense in which the totality of her art practice and persona challenge the double standards about sex.

The question of class interacts with the question of sexism here. Emin is not seen as a 'feminist' artist because feminism and, especially, feminism in the art world has been a largely middle class phenomenon, focusing mainly on the issues that concern middle class and professional women: especially how women are represented in the media, literature, art, etc. The issues Emin deals with—how teenage girls get 'slagged off' and 'broken into'—are not recognised as feminist because they come from a different world. But the fact is that Emin tackles sexism at the sharp end.

Art: 'I Need Art Like I Need God', is the title and content of one of Emin's pieces in neon lighting, and 'art', in particular Emin's relationship to art, is a central theme in her work.

One of the ways 'art' features in Emin's work is through her references to other artists. Of course many artists do this, but Emin's range of reference is broad and impressive (which gives the lie to another of the myths about her, namely that she is some kind of 'primitive' or 'naif').

Most obviously she is indebted to her hero Edvard Munch, and to Egon Schiele. The use of language in both the monoprints and the blankets nods to Basquiat; the neon lighting pieces are influenced by Don Flavin and Bruce Naumann; *My Bed* recalls Rauschenberg's *Bed* and, more subtly, the bed of Manet's *Olympia*; The *Helter Skelter* construction references the Tatlin tower; the blanket work in general builds on the use of sewing and textiles by feminist artists of the 1970s and 1980s.

Of course if quoting other artists was the main point of these works it would make them banal, but with Emin's pieces this is not the case. Her principal tribute to Munch is *Homage to Edvard Munch and All my Dead Children* and is accompanied by her verbal scream which is truly disturbing and terrible. Her drawings may owe something to Schiele but are in no way imitations or similar in content. In the case of the blanket work Emin has transformed the genre, freeing it of its craft and genteel associations, and making it into vibrant new form in its own right.

As we know from Marx, in class societies the ruling class invariably (if not completely) dominates the culture. However the domination in the field of visual art has been more complete, more extreme than in other art forms. This is because whereas the poet or novelist needs only pen and paper, visual art must be embodied in materials (which are very expensive), stored, and exhibited, either in museums and galleries or in public places (which of course are never controlled by the public). And because in the capitalist epoch the art market has focused on the buying and selling of 'unique' and 'original' works, in contrast to music and literature, which centre on either the large-scale selling of mechanical reproductions—books, CDs, etc—or live performances to collective audiences.

As a result, from Tutankhamun to Lorenzo de Medici and Henry VIII to Rockefeller and Saatchi, visual art has been dominated by the very rich and very powerful. This in turn has meant that the exclusion and marginalisation of working class people, women and black people has been even more marked in visual art than in other art forms. There is no female painter whose standing compares with Jane Austen or George Eliot and not a single painting by a black artist in the National Gallery. In this context the work of Tracey Emin is both an example of limited change that has occurred and a challenge to the present and the future.[3]

Marx also tells us that art, like religion, philosophy and politics, is part of the superstructure of society, which arises from and is conditioned by the economic base. I would add that the economic base, that is, the forces and relations of production, gives rise to and shapes a developing ensemble of social relations which range from how people dress, to family and sexual relations, to how people look at a king or a beggar and how a king or a beggar looks at the people, to how we experience the sea, the countryside and the city.

What major art does is express and comment upon these changing social relations in a visually powerful way. Giotto and Brueghel, Hals and Rembrandt, Hogarth and Goya, Courbet, Picasso and Warhol all do this in their differing ways. And so does Emin.

The changing social relations that Emin addresses are those shaping the relative positions in society of women and men, especially young working class women and men. The changes in this sphere in the course the last half century or so have been spectacular: the huge rise in the number of women (especially married women) in paid labour, the Equal Pay Act, the Sex Discrimination Act, the pill, legalised abortion, freer divorce and lip service to equality all over the place.

In other ways they remain strictly limited: no fundamental change in the division of labour in the home, no equal pay in reality, women still hugely underrepresented in top jobs, sexist images all over the media. Of course the change is not evenly spread across society. In my judgement the least has been at the very top among those who own the wealth and control the state. There, bourgeois male power remains firmly entrenched. The biggest change has been among the professional middle classes—academics, intellectuals, media people, etc—where the success of girls in education and higher education has had its effect and equal opportunities policies abound.

Many working class women have also benefited from the changes, from the shift in general attitudes and the increased educational and job opportunities. But for the majority, especially in the manual as opposed to white collar working class, where money for child care is scarce or nonexistent and the struggle for survival dominates, the change has been minimal. Some working class men, in the main the politically more progressive, have changed their attitudes, but many have not and the old sexism remains rampant. The problems are particularly acute among teenagers and young men anxious to establish their virility, and this is what working class girls and young women have to cope with.

These are the contradictions which Emin has lived and which her art expresses and responds to with clarity and passion. Politically there is an obvious problem in that while Emin's work ultimately carries a message of hope, it is hope for an individual not a collective or social solution, and this can only be possible for a small minority. Unfortunately we don't get our art to political order and given the historical period of Emin's artistic formation, the 1980s and early 1990s, it is hardly surprising that collective working class emancipation through political action was not high on her agenda. What matters more than the correct politics is whether the problems addressed are real, whether the art has integrity and whether it is visually imaginative and powerful. Emin's work succeeds on all these counts with the extra factor that it really speaks to people, and people beyond the normal range of 'art lovers', in a way that is achieved by no other contemporary artist.

NOTES

Thanks are due to my students with whom many of these ideas about Emin have been discussed, in particular to Lucy Sanders, Roxanne Chappell, Jessica Masterman, Danielle Wright and Kim Heal for their stimulating presentation on My Bed.

1: Socialist Review, December 2004, p34. This short piece by Amy Lane is the best published article on Emin I have read anywhere.

2: Words appliquéd to Garden of Horror M (1998).

3: It perhaps needs emphasising that while capitalism remains, the ruling class's cultural hegemony in general, and its domination of the art world in particular, can be challenged and partially eroded—but not abolished.

More than Culloden

Angus Calder

*A review of Neil Davidson, **Discovering the Scottish Revolution, 1682-1746** (Pluto Press, 2003), £19.99*

To use the term 'Scottish Revolution' is provocative. Most people, including some very good scholars, have assumed that 'bourgeois revolution' in Scotland is somehow accounted for by what happened in England in the middle decades of the 17th century—as if after the Union of Parliaments in 1707 Scotland was simply assimilated with the successful 'English Revolution'. Neil Davidson shows that Scotland's escape from feudalism into capitalism was the result of a different, separate process, crystallised after, and because of, the defeat of Prince Charles Edward Stuart's Jacobite army at Culloden in 1746.

This was not because, as further lazy assumptions have had it, Highland Scotland with its Gaelic-speaking clansmen was the last redoubt of feudalism in Britain. Certainly, the area was distinctive in dress as well as in language. But the absolute authority of landowners over tenants was as strong in Lowland Scotland. While revenues from the sale of cattle on the hoof southward were important to landowners on Skye just as they were in Galloway, Lowland lords like clan chiefs had seen their estates not as sites for investment and development, but as arenas from which they could extract cash as well as services to support ostentatious lifestyles. Coalmines (where labourers were legally enserfed in the 17th century) were driven no deeper than was required to support a new mansion or pay gambling debts. The merchants and craftsmen who dominated the burghs in self-perpetuating oligarchies were for the most part unadventurously committed to familiar patterns of trade. In the unicameral Scottish parliament, until it voted its own dissolution in 1707, the dominance of great territorial magnates over lesser lairds and burgesses was represented by the layout of seating. The element of popular representation which, however skewed and thwarted, marked the English parliament, was wholly absent. So was the capitalistic afflatus which the English Revolution of the 1640s, triggered by commoners in parliament, either confirmed or released (depending on a historian's emphasis). The 'Commercial Revolution' of Restoration England was echoed in Scotland only in a one-off desperate gamble, the Darien debacle.

More of this, and of the crucial matter of landownership, later. Meanwhile Davidson, with prodigious reading in primary as well as secondary sources, with scrupulously exact definition of such treacherous terms as 'class' and 'revolution', and with eloquent, entertaining style, has surveyed the explosion of Scottish historiography in the last 40 years from a sturdily classical Marxist standpoint to produce a masterly account of the process which transformed Scotland quite suddenly into the most bourgeois of nations. As he justly observes in a 'Bibliographical Essay', the best of Walter Scott's fiction, dealing with Scotland from the 1640s through to the 1760s, presented a splendid analysis of 'the unfolding of the bourgeois revolution'. Yet Scott has been denounced by many left wingers as a Tory 'tartaniser', a creator of far-fetched 'romances' which mystified his beloved nation's history. And it is indeed true that the way in which Scott's novels, published from 1814 onwards, were misread, enfeebled historical writing for a century and a half.

Of course, Scott told stories about vividly presented characters, many of them versions of actual historical personages. And he projected vigorously the antagonisms of Calvinist Presbyterian Whig and Episcopalian, 'Cavalier' Tory, of high-tempered Highlanders and sober-sided Lowlanders, of canny businessmen and cranky lairds. Rather than paying attention to Scott's subtle analysis, rooted in the best thought of the Enlightenment, of the dialectics which generated transformation, readers were content with a simple dichotomy in which Scotland pre-Culloden was incessantly violent, heroic and 'romantic' as contrasted with succeeding peaceful prosperity. So the tendency set in to discuss olden Scotland in terms of personalities and dramatically opposed creeds.

A few excellent scholars, into the 20th century, stood against the current—William Law Matheson and George Pratt Insh are two to whom Davidson accords due respect. But most writing about Scottish history determined a common view in which the main question to be asked was not, 'Why did the Scottish Reformation occur and thereafter take a Calvinistic turn?' but, 'Did Mary Queen of Scots connive in the murder of her husband?'

As for the 1640s, attention was distracted from the conditions in which Presbyterian zealots briefly took over direction of the country to romanticised portraits of their bugbear, the Cavalier Marquis of Montrose, who made himself Charles I's champion in Scotland. And evocations of the pathos and excitement of the wanderings after Culloden of 'Bonnie' Prince 'Charlie' effectually concealed the fact that most Scots resented the efforts of this Roman Catholic foreigner to restore Stuart rule in London as a client of France, and that only a minority of Highlanders could be dragged forth by their chiefs to fight for him.

Yet Scotland over four centuries between Bruce's assertion of independence in 1314 and the Treaty of Union in 1707 had not been an unsophisticated country or even a particularly violent one. In the early 16th century poetic activity in the Stewart ('Stuart' was a later spelling) court was more impressive than in the Tudors'. The reputation of Scottish philosophers rode high through Europe. Arguably, the most important element in Scotland's espousal of Reformation in 1560 and thereafter was the spread of literacy among its middling people. The 18th century Enlightenment and the related efflorescence of Scottish literature had old roots in a distinctive culture. During the troubled 17th century Scottish architects produced work which was both imposing and distinctive. It was from circles interested practically and theoretically in architecture that Freemasonry developed in Scotland around 1600, eventually to become an enigmatically influential force in Europe and North America. Calvinism was one factor ensuring close links between Scotland and the Netherlands and the origins of Scottish pre-eminence in medicine, so marked by the late 18th century, can be traced to Dutch influence before the union.

The point about what may seem a digression into 'culture'—a matter in which Neil Davidson himself is extremely well versed—is to emphasise that Scotland's failure to keep pace with England economically before the 1640s, and especially after 1660, cannot be attributed to stagnant mindlessness. Paradoxically, even men whose violent activities might seem to justify the myth of a 'backward' nation—the multitudinous mercenary soldiers who roamed Europe as far as Moscow—tended to be rather well read chaps, and alongside the rustic literacy which formed the Bible-dominated mentality of lower class Covenanting rebels can be found erudite Calvinist theology. Scots were as well equipped as any people to understand new worlds of colonisation, commerce and finance, while the empathy between Calvinism and capitalism has long been a historians' cliche. So the familiar assertion that the Union precipitated revolutionary change in Scotland can be overturned by questions—why did Scotland, so much involved with England (on the same smallish island, damn it, after all...) politically, economically and in religious debate not 'catch up' until the mid-18th century, and how was it that this small country came thereafter to dominate the mentality of the rising European bourgeoisie?

To amplify the last point: by the early 19th century Scotland was respected throughout the western world. Agricultural 'improvement' had purged the land of the spectre of famine. English capital had helped make Scotland a centre of transformed or completely novel industrial activity. Scots were prominent and often dominant as soldiers, traders and administrators in every part of the British Empire—from the new convict metropolis of Sydney, New South Wales, to the British North American fur trade and the expanding territories of British India. Economic afflatus had transformed the filthy Scottish capital, Edinburgh, creating a spacious, and relatively hygienic new town in neo-classical style to house a rapidly expanding bourgeoisie, most of whom rejoiced in the recent triumphs of Scottish 'Enlightened' thought, and revelled in the writing of Burns, Scott and Byron which had conquered Europe and America.

One might say that as well as experiencing a bourgeois revolution Scotland had invented a complex of innovations which, in amalgams and permutations, would *constitute* the 19th century bourgeoisie. While her husband wrestled in his factory with the new social order created by the application of Watt's steam engine, before meeting his friendlier counterparts in the 'business community' to argue over whether Adam Smith's free trade was *always* the right idea, or talking to his pastor about Thomas Reid's 'common sense' rebuttal of the atheistical Hume, his proud wife would see her son poring, with the great treatise on geology by Hutton to hand, over specimens collected on earnest walks with his tutor, while her daughter sat enraptured with a novel by Scott or verse narrative by Byron. She herself would practise at her piano settings of Scottish songs by Beethoven, and if the illness of a child distracted her from this, she would at once consult Buchan's invaluable *Domestic Medicine*. Elsewhere in Europe young Karl Marx would soon be digesting the ideas of Smith and Millar. The controlling conceptions of the bourgeoisie, and those of master critiques of it, could both be tracked back (as it were) to conversations between Hume and Smith, over claret, in still-reeking Edinburgh...

Such future glory was far beyond the thoughts of the Scots who struggled, between the 'Glorious Revolution' of 1688 and the Union of 1707, with economic crisis and catastrophe, and even of those who came to terms with the shock of the final Jacobite Rebellion of 1745-1746.

In the 1690s the Anglo-Dutch merger represented by the arrival of William of Orange on the throne was accompanied by the climax of England's 'Commercial Revolution', symbolised by the initiation of the Bank of England in 1694, and by the beginning of the long war with France for supremacy which would continue till 1815. Both were critical for Scotland.

To compound Scotland's abject economic underperformance compared with its southern neighbour the country endured, from 1696 to 1699, four appalling years of famine, in which as many as 15 percent of the population—that is, 150,000 people—may have died. A general 'global cooling' at this time is not enough to account for Scotland's exceptional misery. Neil Davidson points to 'still dominant forms of feudal tenure which had prevented the commercialisation and increased productivity of agriculture... In some areas the collection of rents from tenants who had barely enough on which to survive went on throughout the famine.' Yet it was at precisely this juncture that such classes in Scotland as had any money were inspired to attempt, with one bold leap, to compete in the new world of intercontinental commerce where England and France had begun to contest for supremacy.

In 1695 the Scottish parliament passed an Act for a Company Trading to Africa and the Indies. Two forces conspired in the company's foundation—desire in Scotland to find new markets overseas, and the wish of certain London merchants to circumvent the monopoly of the English East India Company. Opposition in the English parliament extinguished London interest, and Scottish investors went ahead alone. Enthusiasm, in so poor a country, was astonishing. The nation's hopes were committed to the idea of establishing a colony in Panama as an entrepot for world trade. The first expedition of would-be colonists sailed in July 1698. In March 1700, after 2,000 lives had been squandered, the remaining colonists submitted to the Spaniards whose monarch had long claimed the territory on which 'Darien' stood. Spanish hostility was one factor in the experiment's failure, diplomatic opposition by King William was another. But Davidson argues that both these problems 'could have been coped with had either the Scottish state or civil society been resilient enough to sustain the venture'.

William was succeeded by Queen Anne, 'last of the Stuart monarchs', whose inability to produce an heir provoked a crisis of dynastic succession. James, 'the Old Pretender', in exile in France, was the favourite of the 'Jacobite' tendency which was fairly strong in Scotland. But he was a Catholic, and would surely be a puppet of France. The continuing existence of an independent Scottish polity which might ally with France was unacceptable to the Westminster parliament which favoured handing the throne to a son of the Electress Sophia of Hanover, related to the Stuarts. English pressure was such that in 1707, after huffing and puffing through stormy debates, the Scottish parliament voted itself out of existence. As Davidson's careful analysis shows, most Scottish opinion was dismayed by this. But opposition was chaotically divided—Jacobites yearning for a Catholic king were hardly natural allies for Calvinist ex-Covenanters and those fearful for the future of the national Presbyterian church. The economic penalty entailed in holding out—loss of trade with England—was a factor reinforced by the potential benefits arising from free and lawful access to England's overseas empire.

Davidson accepts the received wisdom that for four decades after Union, its vaunted economic advantages were not apparent, and explores with great erudition the fascinating rise of pro-Jacobite feeling to a high point in the 1715 rebellion, then its ultimate collapse in 1745-1746 when the 'Young Pretender', Prince Charles Edward Stuart, arrived to assert his father James's right to the *British* crown. It is worth stressing that 'Charlie' did not want to become king of an independent Scotland. He, and his sponsors in the French government, wanted his installation as monarch in London over a United Kingdom. He was, in that way, a 'Unionist'.

Discussing 'the '45', Davidson reinforces his basic point that landlordism in Scotland was much the same in the Lowlands as in the Gaelic-speaking Highland areas. On both sides, landowners could and did apply pressure on their tenants to fight, whether for Charlie or George. But Jacobitism had withered in the Lowlands, and it was the Highlands which were punished after Culloden—both by immediate, indiscriminate slaughter by occupying Hanoverian troops, and by such specific measures as the notorious banning of tartan dress. However—and this is crucial—Culloden precipitated the Heritable Jurisdictions Act of 1747 which applied to the whole of Scotland and abolished, suddenly, the most malignant features of surviving Scottish feudalism.

In Scotland the crown had never been strong enough to assert direct control of the countryside. Landlords had exercised powers of 'justice', even of life and death, through their own courts, and this had abetted extortionate economic tyranny over their tenants. Now, along with the pretence of 'paternalism' (clan chief as father of his 'family'), this anti-capitalistic anachronism was extinguished. A 'revolution' in the countryside, led by capitalistic 'improving' landlords, could now proceed unchecked. Ironically, the most familiar images of tyrannical landlordism in Scotland come from the second phase of the 'industrial revolution' which followed.

The 'Highland Clearances' have been a source of misunderstandings as fertile as the Nile Valley itself. The salient, undisputed fact is that large areas of the Highlands were depopulated by mass migration, largely to North America—but the notion that all migrants were cruelly expelled by landlords seeking to profit from sheep-farming, in an exceptional process of virtual genocide, does not bear cool inspection. Over the same period certain Lowland rural areas lost population equally, and in England John Clare produced his classic lamenting response in poetry to 'enclosure' in his beloved Northamptonshire. Scottish Gaels like English 'peasants' were sucked into the cities and into manufacturing industry. It is true that the Duke of Sutherland (an Englishman married to a clever Highland heiress) decanted rural people from the interior of his vast domain to 'model' villages on the coast where they could conduct fishing and other industries. This was 'improvement'. It is true that in Sutherland and elsewhere sheep supplanted Gaelic-speaking people: Bradford needed wool. In some cases, as in various other parts of industrialising Europe, evictions were heartlessly carried out. That the songs and tales uttered against the Clearances still sound so strongly in the 21st century bespeaks, paradoxically, the tenacity of Gaelic tradition in Scotland and counters the myth of 'genocide'. It would be good if Scots could come to see them as an exceptionally hardy protest against the widespread destruction of rural communities by triumphant capitalism, such as Cobbett's countrymen did not provide.

One strength of Neil Davidson's excellent book is that it coolly displays documentary support for the fact that cruel and exploitative landlordism was at least as common before 1747 as afterwards. My chief reservation about his compact and tightly argued survey is that he underestimates the portents of change in Scotland between 1707 and 1746. He notes the activities of improving, enclosing landlords—and the 'Leveller' uprising against such in the south west in 1724 which would provide the only notable example of widespread organised resistance to agrarian change in the Lowlands. But one should add to the picture a tremendous surge of Scottish activity within the British Empire. In the Caribbean, Scots rapidly, after the Union, came to dominate whole islands. More crucially, as George McGilvary demonstrated two decades ago, Walpole and his Whigs in the 1720s, seeking to appease and control Scots within the new British state, saw the potential of patronage through the East India Company, and the great Eastward Ho! phase of Scottish history was launched, more than half a century before Henry Dundas, as minister in the Younger Pitt's government who dealt with India, is usually supposed to have started it. The relationship between Scottish industralisation and Glasgow's astonishing rise through the Virginia tobacco trade has been well explored—the importance of profits (and later loot) from India should not be underestimated.Chris

Caught in a trap

John Game

A review of Vivek Chibber, ***Locked in Place: State-Building and Late Industrialisation in India*** *(Princeton University Press, 2003), £26.95*

Indian nationalists argued as early as the 1880s that British rule had transformed a pre-capitalist economy based on the export of luxury goods and the import of bullion into an economy based on the export of raw materials and the import of manufactured goods. The first result, they argued, was the deindustrialisation of the country and the throwing of millions into underemployment and poverty in a rural economy characterised by land shortages and recurring bouts of famine. Second, the export of economic surplus out of the country combined with competition from British manufactured goods to deprive Indian capitalists of the ability to develop modern industry, seen as the solution to the first set of problems.

Indian economic nationalists, like economists in Germany and the US, developed a critique of the empire of free trade as representing the interests of the British state and British capitalists rather creating the natural harmony envisaged by Adam Smith in his *Wealth of Nations*.

But Indian nationalists did not have a state of their own to carry out their programme. Instead they had a colonial state run by the British in the interests not of Indian but of British capitalism. By the first decade of the 20th century there was growing impatience with endlessly petitioning the colonial authorities to adopt policies which would lead to industrialisation rather then the further impoverishment of a predominantly rural economy. The widely held view was that behind the colonial state stood the capitalists of Manchester and Lancashire, with no interest in creating modern industrial capitalism in India and only concerned to increase the volume of trade. This, empirically detailed in pamphlets, petitions and speeches and argued repeatedly, was hardly the same as industrialisation. All that it led to was a healthy balance of payments for the British economy—with Britain having the balance and India making the payments, according to what became known as the 'drain theory' of colonial exploitation.

The development of Indian nationalism as a mass movement therefore crystallised around an ideologically-charged argument about Indian poverty, its nature, causes and solutions. This made more or less radical programmes for economic transformation logical to the burgeoning movement against British rule around which competing social forces organised themselves politically. By the 1930s nobody believed that independence would not inevitably bring with it radical changes in social and economic arrangements, even if the exact shape of these changes was unclear. This generated revolutionary hopes and panicked manoeuvring in equal measure. Even the grisly denouement of partition at independence, with its terrible communal mass slaughter, has to be understood as part of the vast social churning unleashed by the hopes and fears generated by the prospect of a transformation of the grotesque parody of capitalist property relations instituted by colonialism.

These competing radical programmes of social transformation did not simply reflect meaningless noises of narrowly self-interested sections of unrepresentative elites, as the British argued. Nor were they the uncritical acceptance of alien and inappropriate ideological transplants from Fabians in the London School of Economics or Marxists in the Soviet Union, as contemporary liberals argued. Sympathy for these ideas was motivated by already existing programmes of social transformation with real historical depth in a society where distorted economic relations, continuously analysed and lobbied against in the 50 years before independence, had produced the actually existing form of retarded colonial capitalism. Economic nationalism was not an unfortunate lapse of judgement. It constituted the ideological core around which nationalism had developed during the protracted night of colonial rule.

Vivek Chibber's important new book notes the historical depth behind the kind of policies adopted by Nehru, the leader of the Indian National Congress (which came to power in India after the British were finally driven out in 1947), and that this was reflected by support for economic planning within important sections of the capitalist class. The main representatives of Indian capital had come together by the 1940s and, in collaboration with Congress, generated a set of proposals about the future development of the Indian economy which came to be known as the Bombay Plan.

This was on the face of it not really very surprising. A programme of state aid to promote industrialisation might be expected to benefit industrial capitalists as well as transform the lives of the majority of the population. From this was born what Chibber refers to as the 'myth of the developmental bourgeoisie'. Its character was to be hotly debated by Marxists over the ensuing decades. There were at least three splits in the Indian Communist movement as the ability of what came to be called 'Nehruvian socialism' to reverse the economic legacy of colonialism came increasingly into question, creating political crisis and tumult that eventually issued in the suspension of democracy and the declaration of a state of emergency by Indira Gandhi in 1975.

This myth was also to inform analyses of this failure by the liberal economists who increasingly gained influence inside the state as the economic project of the developmental state put in place by Nehru began to unravel. After all, the new state had the support and goodwill of the vast bulk of the population, the services of perhaps the most sophisticated generation of economic planners seen in the post-war world, and the co-operation of a far-sighted capitalist class which identified with its goals of conducting planned capitalist development on a democratic basis. Instead of producing rapid industrialisation the result was a rate of growth too slow to change the conditions of the bulk of the population. There was corruption and inefficiency at all levels, economic plans which seemed to bear no relationship to reality, and above all continuing and crushing poverty for the majority of people, who remained dependent on employment in the rural sector. The liberal reformers were in the ascendant by the late 1980s, arguing that Indian capitalism had to be set free from a planning regime which had in any case fallen to pieces.

Vivek Chibber's attack on the 'myth of the developmental bourgeoisie' seeks to shift discussion away from questions related to the inadequate performance of the developmental state towards discussion of the failure of their installation. Crucial to this shift is Chibber's insight that the capacity to subsidise industry was not enough for the strategy of 'late, late developers'. This had to be combined with the ability to discipline capital. In return for subsidies capitalists had to relinquish control over what had hitherto been their sacred prerogative: investment decisions. This was necessary to overcome co-ordination problems which exist universally under capitalism but which underdeveloped capitalisms of this kind were peculiarly vulnerable to. Chibber presents persuasive evidence that there never emerged in India such a state, capable not only of providing subsidies for industry, but also of disciplining capital.

Chibber argues that the key to achieving such capacities revolves around questions of class power and not, as he puts it, hundreds of clerks obediently shuffling bits of paper from department to department in line with regulations. It is here that he parts company not simply with neo-liberal orthodoxy but many of those he designates as 'statists'. They argued against neo-liberals that the only successes in the developing world were states like South Korea, and they focused exclusively on policies pursued within the state at the expense of the relationship between state and capital. The question of how the state managed to subordinate the interests of capital to the developmental agenda did not seem particularly problematic to such theorists. They assumed that the weakness of indigenous capital in developing countries gave the state the ability to discipline capital if it only developed appropriate repressive mechanisms and strategies. Will and determination here stood in for any structural account of how such a state actually came to successfully impose its policies.

This, according to Chibber, fails to explain why the construction of a developmental state was so unusual. It assumes either stupidity on the part of planners or some natural proclivity to corruption for which the only solution could be liberalisation, given that most attempts to construct a developmental state ended in failure. In order to explain these failures, Chibber engages in a species of historical revisionism in the case of South Korea.

He argues that the key to South Korea's success was not the emergence of a developmental state but an alliance between South Korean and Japanese capital to set up joint enterprises in Korea, with the Japanese prepared to play a subordinate role in order to escape US tariffs. What Chibber, following neo-classical models, refers to as the incentive structure of export promotion (as opposed to import substitution) could only be put in place because Korean capital was prepared to take risks to follow through opportunities created by the alliance with Japanese capital. This opened up the historically unprecedented prospect of a 'late, late developer' gaining access to the US domestic market. There is little evidence prior to this, Chibber implies, that the Korean dictator of the 1960s, Park, had the capacity to discipline capital, however muscular his regime was. Its famous arrests of top businessmen, 'the illicit accumulators', simply provoked a recession. Nor is there evidence that a shift from import-substituting industrialisation to export-led industrialisation would have stood the faintest chance of success against what would have been determined resistance from the capitalist class as a whole, if an alliance with Japanese capital had not been present.

The analytical tools Chibber develops in his revisionist account of the South Korean state enable him to cast new light on the apparently paradoxical behaviour of the Indian capitalist class which has generated so much historical controversy and political confusion.

Utilising previously unexamined archive material, he demonstrates that while important sections of the capitalist class had drawn up proposals for planning when the social turmoil associated with the struggle against the British was at its height, attempts by the new Congress regime to actually implement them met with fierce and determined resistance. There were investment strikes and appeals to British investors to join in and teach the new state a lesson. The demobilisation and incorporation of labour, as well as peasant struggles for land reform by a Congress increasingly dominated by landlords (given insufficient weight in my view in Chibber's account), took away the threat to capitalist property relations which had previously made the more intelligent sections of the capitalist class cautious in their opposition.

This argument is not perhaps entirely novel (at least amongst Indian Marxists). What is novel, as well as being potentially politically illuminating, is the distinction Chibber draws between the measures necessary to accrue revenue to subsidise industry and the measures necessary to discipline investment decisions to ensure that this revenue leads to capitalist development of the country as a whole, rather than simply the development of fortunes of particular capitalists. They turn out on Chibber's account to be more interested in their profits than in the historical responsibilities imputed to them by some Marxists and most nationalists.

This allows him to open up questions about the trajectory of the post-colonial state and explain why the failure to impose the disciplinary component of a developmental strategy led even those previously committed to a planning regime to see liberalisation as the only way out, something which was evident as early as the mid-1960s. Caught between the reality that liberalisation would not lead to economic transformation of the country, but with no means of controlling investment decisions of capitalists, the state was locked into a trap which eventually exploded in the 1970s.

The ideology of the developmental state was dead, and by the late 1990s an Indian finance minister could make an inaugural speech praising the legacy of the British East India Company and asking for hundreds of more East India Companies to come to India to repeat the happy experience of the 19th century in an era of globalisation.

The fate of the Indian developmental state is important for socialists as it parallels the failure and crisis of most existing states in the world, producing similar patterns of ideological crisis on the left almost everywhere outside of the handful of developed capitalisms in the imperialist core. It is vital that socialists develop some kind of theoretical explanation of the current impasse, as the old reformist ideologies of development disintegrate, leading to protests on the one hand ('The East India Company is back: except this time it's the Americans,' chanted workers striking against liberalisation) and the growth of communal and ethnic nationalisms on the other. Vivek Chibber's book is an important, and in the academic market, unusual, attempt to do so and deserves to be read and widely.

Forgotten subversives

Chris Harman

A review of Jonathan I Israel, ***Radical Enlightenment*** *(Oxford, 2002), £20.99*

Occasionally a book comes out which challenges established ideas about some important historical event. This is one.

The Enlightenment was the great intellectual challenge in the century and a half between the English Revolution and the French Revolution to the role of superstition, magic and religion in justifying existing society. But there are few general accounts of it. And they tend to see it as an attempt by a layer of intellectuals living in the absolute monarchies of western Europe to learn from the supposed civilised tolerance of the gentry-run constitutional monarchy set up by the 'glorious' English revolution from above of 1688.

The great forerunner of the Enlightenment is often then portrayed as being John Locke, especially by liberal columnists for the *Guardian* (who deliberately seem to ignore his support for and profiting from slavery, his backing for superstitious belief in miracles, and his denial of freedom of speech to atheists). Along with this view goes the claim that Spinoza, the most consistent materialist of the 17th century, had no influence during the Enlightenment decades.

Jonathan Israel destroys both these claims. He shows that there were two Enlightenments. Alongside and preceding the 'Moderate Enlightenment' of Locke and his heirs was a 'Radical Enlightenment' which challenged old prejudices and superstitions to the core. Its adherents risked the sack, imprisonment or even being condemned to death for their views.

Spinoza, writing in the third quarter of the 17th century and in the immediate aftermath of the Dutch and English revolutions, was far from being a marginal figure. He drew on the scientific discoveries of the previous century and a half (especially Copernicus, Kepler and Galileo) to develop an account of the world in which everything had a material cause.

Nature as a whole was like a great machine operating according to the newly discovered laws of physics, with human ideas as one expression of its operation. 'God' in the sense of an ever-present, all-knowing, self-caused entity could only be the machine itself, nature. There was no room for some divine being who would break the laws of nature to change things at the bidding of priests and prayers.

This was in reality a form of atheism (although Spinoza did not describe it as such) and was not only a challenge to superstition and witch-burning (against which it played an important role).

It also challenged the witchery of the established Catholic, Lutheran and Calvinist religions that consecrated kings, justified social hierarchies and blamed the misery of much of humanity on original sin. And its logic was to move on from challenging religious superstition to challenging the social organisation within which religious superstition flourished.

Spinoza only went part of the way in this.

He was a republican, but held that revolution did more harm than good, and some of his followers, coming from the upper classes themselves, held similar views. But others followed the logic through to the end, and laid the basis for a critique not just of the absolutist societies of continental Europe at the time, but of all class societies.

Spinozism then became, like Marxism in the 20th century, something the moderates were continually reacting against while claiming not to take it seriously. But its influence persisted as the real core of the Enlightenment challenge to the existing order. And in the diluted form in which it appeared in the writings of Voltaire and Rousseau it inspired those who took to the barricades between 1789 and 1794. The product of one wave of revolutions helped inspire the next.

Nor was that the end of the matter. The wave of reaction after the French Revolution nearly buried the Enlightenment even in its moderate form as the victorious bourgeoisie preferred the obscurantism of the old order to the threat of insurrection in the streets. But the ideas of the Radical Enlightenment were still able to spur a new generation of intellectual revolt. Karl Marx's doctoral thesis was on the ancient Greek philosophers Democritus and Epicurus who influenced Spinoza, and he admired the mainstream Enlightenment philosophers most in the Spinoza tradition, Holbach and Helvetius.

Postmodern and postcolonial theories of recent years have been disparaging about the Enlightenment, blaming it for the dehumanisation of capitalism or even for totalitarianism. And it is true that some Moderate Enlightenment thinkers were complicit in oppression and racism. But Jonathan Israel shows the Radical Enlightenment as a project of courageous people aiming to further human emancipation.

This is an important book, even if, like the author's previous history of the Dutch Republic, somewhat long (I tired sometimes towards the end of the 800 pages). Anyone who is interested in the history of ideas in the age of revolutions should read at least its early chapters.

The other Moses

John Rose

A review of Edward Said, ***Freud and the Non-European*** *(Verso, 2004), £8*

This masterpiece was first delivered as a lecture to a spellbound audience at London University's School of Oriental and African Studies.

Edward Said, Palestine's greatest intellectual, has taken the final and troubled essay, *Moses and Monotheism*, of one of modern Judaism's greatest intellectuals, Sigmund Freud, and, as it were, flicked the switch that releases Freud's Moses as the ghost to haunt that distortion of modern Judaism we call Zionism.

And this cannot be dismissed as an Edward Said interpretation. Here we have not the least fascinating aspect of this essay. Edward Said's postmodernism had moved on, dare it be said, before he died, to a dialectical plane. The reader's historical and cultural context and the writer's historical and cultural context may provide two distinctive meanings, but an objective historical reality does connect them. Said describes a power to Freud's writing which allowed him 'to instigate new thought as well as to illuminate situations that he himself might never have dreamed of'. In other words it is Freud's Moses, not Said's interpretation of him, that casts a shadow on the way modern Israel's creation depended upon the exclusion of the non-European 'other'.

Said also celebrates Freud's *Spatstill*, 'late style', and compares it to Beethoven's late works. I sense we are going to read a lot more about this concept but we cannot do it justice here. One of Edward Said's last essays was devoted to it in the *London Review of Books*. Suffice to say it describes a release of creative albeit rather disorganised power as 'old age' beckons (I wonder if it can apply to ageing organisations?). A penetrating nugget of insight, like a genie released to assist the storming of barricades.

The crux of Freud's argument is that Moses was an Egyptian. Obviously a non-European; less obviously a non-Jew. Repeat: the founder of the Jewish religion was not a Jew. His monotheism was derived from the great Egyptian pharaonic tradition associated with Akhenaton. Freud 'grants that Jews eliminated sun-worship...but further undercuts Judaic originality by noting that circumcision was Egyptian...and that the Levites... were Moses's Egyptian followers'.

Freud doesn't much like his discovery. He hasn't developed it 'gladly or carelessly'—in Freud's own words 'especially by one belonging to that people'. He can already hear the Nazi jackboot and he wants to identify with his people. Still, it's the 'truth', and because of that, says Freud, it's more important than what are 'supposed to be [our] national interests'.

Here was implicit prophecy but Freud didn't know it. He did not live to see Israel 'countervene, repress...cancel [his] carefully maintained opening out of Jewish identity towards its non-Jewish background. The complex layers of the past [were] eliminated by official Israel. 'In excavating the archaeology of Jewish identity, Freud insisted that it did not begin with itself...but rather with the other...'

A last point. Edward Said calls Frantz Fanon, author of *The Wretched of the Earth*, one of the greatest books in defence of the revolutionary violence forced on the non-European 'other', not least by Zionism, 'Freud's most disputatious heir'. A further incentive to buy this remarkable little book is to discover why.

I'm all lost in the supermarket

James Woodcock

Supermarkets are hugely influential in 21st century corporate globalisation and capital accumulation. Wal-Mart (which owns Asda) is the world's biggest corporation, and the British multinational Tesco is one of Britain's biggest companies, worth around £40 billion in 2002.

During the last 30 years supermarkets have been a dominant force in transforming what we eat, how we shop, how our food is produced, our high streets and our countryside, and almost all the changes have been for the worse. They have also contributed to massive local and global environmental destruction. Supermarkets feature prominently in the powerful road lobby. They are aggressively targeting poorer countries and are taking over small shops in Britain, while still pushing for mega out of town stores.

Unsurprisingly there are many voices opposing supermarket domination. They range from large multinational food producers and processors (who object to supermarkets squeezing their profits) to the real victims, such as immigrant workers in 19th century conditions in Lincolnshire or near the Costa del Sol.

Wal-Mart is the superpower of supermarkets, and in the US there are many local groups opposing it. An entertaining little book is *How Wal-Mart is Destroying America (and the World) and What You Can Do About It,* by 92 year old Bill Quinn. Mainly written from a petty (and not so petty) bourgeois perspective, it does have the merit of suggesting practically how towns can organise to stop Wal-Mart. It's very US focused, but a new edition due this year may be more international.

For a much more detailed history of the Waltons, there is *In Sam We Trust* by Bob Ortega. Wal-Mart grew up in the much smaller towns ignored by the big retailers. It built huge out of town stores, destroying the town economy, sometimes later moving on to a bigger store further away. Wal-Mart is a truly scary organisation. It pays wages that mean staff often survive on food stamps, it has fired staff for inter-racial dating and it bans material considered to offend 'family values'—while being the biggest seller of alcohol and guns, and forcing staff to work on Sundays.

Asda, now part of Wal-Mart, was originally modelled on it. Working there is described like a cross between being at school and a Maoist re-education centre, with wages to match.

More specifically for Britain, three recent books all cover quite similar ground, and are all accessible but eye-opening reads: *Sold Out: The True Cost of Supermarket Shopping*, by William Young; *Not On the Label*, by Felicity Lawrence; and *Shopped*, by Joanna Blythman.

Felicity Lawrence, a *Guardian* journalist, provides the most research into the conditions of agricultural migrant workers in England and Spain, including interviews with union activists. Her book is also probably the most likely to put you off your chicken, pre-packed salad or loaf. She covers food rather than just supermarkets, and describes the adulteration of food on an industrial scale. She shows how immigration laws benefit supermarkets and gangmasters, who exploit their workers' vulnerability and shop them to avoid paying their wages. The latest high-tech supermarket production and distribution processes need cheap labour, and cheap labour in excess: 'The link in the chain that connects fluctuating orders to casual labour around the world is the supermarket.' She also undermines the supermarket illusion of choice: the same ingredients (usually high salt, high sugar and processed fats) are repackaged in a hundred different ways.

Joanna Blythman probably best understands the ideology of the supermarkets and what they have planned for us: the total retailing experience. Supermarkets are expanding into other areas, including health services, weddings, births, MPs' surgeries, restaurants, as well as banking, insurance, internet and even legal services. They now try and replace, in a far more corporate form, the community life they have destroyed, just as they get industrial farmers to dress up with twee wicker baskets for photoshoots. Blythman does not really examine the transport issues around 'food miles', but she undercuts very clearly the idea that we get cheap food from the supermarkets. It's overpriced, and often tastes of little more than its plastic wrap. Despite their control of the sector, supermarkets still resent having to deal with fresh food—they'd much rather we bought their frozen meals, which keep for years and have a much higher profit rate.

Supermarkets would like us to think that their dominance is driven by customers' needs for cheap food and convenience. These books show how the supermarkets put their needs before ours—and the two are incompatible. Food is transported long distances, it is processed when unripe, and the varieties chosen are those with a long shelf life—all of which are at odds with customers' desires for tasty and healthy food.

Sold Out gives good coverage of the food miles and the creation of food deserts (areas with few shops and little fresh food available), but it has less vision and is more based on reports than the other two. All are good for understanding what is happening to farmers, including extracts from submissions to the UK Competition Commission report from 2000.

Many of the reports mentioned in these books are available free online. The New Economics Foundation have done a really useful series of reports on 'Ghost Town Britain' and 'Clone Town Britain', highlighting the death of the high street and the role of supermarkets and economic globalisation in this (see also the article by Alex Law and Gerry Mooney in this journal). These reports go much wider than the supermarkets, but the supermarket is seen as the biggest retail force in this. They highlight some of the other harms, and have started a localist campaign.

There is also the Sustain: Eating Oil report on food miles, at http://www.sustainweb.org/chain_fm_eat.asp, which is not available for free, although there are extracts at http://resurgence.gn.apc.org/issues/jones216.htm

http://www.sustainweb.org/poverty_index.asp is a project on food poverty, currently without funding.

Farmers, NEF, Banana Link, Friends of the Earth and other organisations are supporting an Early Day Motion http://edm.ais.co.uk/weblink/html/motion.html/ref=187 to produce binding legislation in place of the current voluntary code.

Corporate Watch have a good report, available for free, which gives much of the information you need to know: http://www.corporatewatch.org.uk/pages/whats_wrong_suprmkts.htm

Opposition to supermarkets is often limited through being on a consumer or petty bourgeois basis, but socialists have a real chance to broaden and harden these campaigns, organising migrant workers, defending local communities, and organising in supermarkets. In the US unions already play quite a role in opposition to Wal-Mart: http://www.walmartwatch.com/index.cfm is connected with the United Food and Commerical Workers Union International.

Where Capital came from

Judy Cox

A review of Isaac Ilyich Rubin, ***A History of Economic Thought*** *(Bertram), £19.99*

Rubin was active in the Russian revolutionary movement of 1917 as well as being an academic and writer. He became a victim of Stalin's counter-revolution in the late 1920s when he was put on trial and disappeared in exile. But his history of economic thought, which, thanks to new printing techniques, is now easily available on demand, stands as a testimony to his faith in the Marxist method of understanding how society works. Rubin analyses how economic developments, specifically the emergence of capitalism in Europe in the 18th and 19th centuries, gave rise to new schools of economic thought which then fed back into developments in society. At the heart of his fascinating account is the emergence of the labour theory of value, which was to become a cornerstone of Marxist economics.

Rubin intended *A History of Economic Thought* to be a course of study for students of economics. This means it is structured in easily digestible chapters. The book pinpoints the key figures and key debates in the unfolding discipline of political economy. And it reveals how changes in economic production led to tensions in the accepted understanding of economics which created the potential for innovative thinking and deeper understanding. When so much of contemporary economics taught in today's universities is based on mathematical formulae, divorced from history or social context, Rubin's book is invaluable.

Rubin explains how economic theories arise in a context. They are forged out of social conflicts. Economists often act as the 'arms bearers' for different social classes; their theories are 'ideological weapons' carried in defence of different interests. The 16th and 17th centuries saw the rise of merchant capital. The merchant capitalists had to assert their power against the guild systems that controlled production and pricing in feudal Europe. Their strivings gave rise to a literature which championed trade.

Alongside this strand of political economy a more philosophical school of thought developed, including writers such as John Locke and David Hume. These philosophers attempted to penetrate beneath the day to day workings of the economy and get to grips with what determined the value of goods and money when they were not fixed by the guild authorities but by the spontaneous workings of the market. They debated whether goods were more or less valuable because they were rare or plentiful, or because of the need they satisfied, or because of what they cost to produce. In the most important contribution made by the Mercantilist philosophers, William Petty argued that the 'natural price' of a product was determined by the quantity of labour spent on producing it.

After the Mercantilists came the Physiocrats, a school of French economists who emerged in the 1760s. The Mercantilists had reflected the concerns of the developing bourgeoisie in England. The Physiocrats were rooted in French society and sought to improve the dire state of French agriculture by promoting the agricultural bourgeoisie against the great feudal landlords. They argued that capital should be switched from industry to agriculture because only agriculture could create a 'net product' or 'revenue', their terms for surplus value. They based their theories on the productivity of soil, rather than labour. However, the Physiocrats had to fall back on appealing to the crown, the pinnacle of the ancient regime, to carry through their programme of reform as the agricultural bourgeoisie were too weak to push through new methods of production. The Physiocrats, and the class interests they represented, were defeated by the forces of the king and the aristocracy.

By the 18th century Britain was home to the establishment of new forms of production when the cottage industries gave way to manufactories. Adam Smith emerged as the key advocate of the new factory system and the founder of modern economics. Smith understood how the division of labour, embodied in the techniques of the new factories, made possible a rise in the productivity of labour. He conceived the whole of society as a giant workshop in which everyone labours and exchanges the products of their labour with one another. To understand how this web of relationships could work, Smith developed Petty's labour theory of value.

Smith argued that commodities derived their value from the amount of labour spent on their production or on the amount of other people's labour that could be purchased for the product. Smith also identified the three main classes in society—landlords, industrial capitalists and wage labourers—and the source of their income: rent, profit and wages respectively. But Smith's theory of value was incomplete. Rubin argues that a distinction must be made when considering value in a capitalist economy. Commodities do not actually exchange simply according to the amount of labour in them. They are sold for a profit, above and beyond that quantity of labour. So the basic value of a commodity is based on the amount of labour power spent on producing it, not the amount of labour it will purchase when exchanged. Smith confused the two which meant he could not explain where profits came from. He moved away from the labour theory of value and talked instead of 'production costs', where the value of a product was determined by the various costs of producing it.

David Ricardo, the theorist of Britain's industrial revolution, developed Smith's theories. Unlike Smith, Ricardo reasserted that the amount of labour spent on producing a product is the measure of value of that product. If new machines mean a product is produced with less labour, then the value of that product falls. But other factors also play a role in determining the value of a commodity when it is exchanged. Ricardo argued that the exception to the law of value was the general rate of profit operating in the economy. Profit, he said, was the portion of the value left after wages have been deducted. Ricardo also developed his understanding of rent and argued that agricultural prices rose as poorer land was drawn into cultivation, requiring more labour to be spent on producing the crop.

Ricardo acknowledged the inevitability of class conflict in an industrial society. That conflict erupted in the field of economics where a school developed which sought to apologise for capitalism. From the 1830s onwards the vulgar school of economics set out to prove that value had nothing to do with the labour of the working class. Some argued that capital itself created profits. Others argued that the capitalists' profits were a reward for their 'abstinence' from consumption for personal pleasure. In response to them developed the Utopian Socialists and later the scientific socialism of Karl Marx and Frederick Engels who laid out the labour theory of value and put the emancipation of the working class as the act of the working class at the centre of their economic theory.

Pick of the quarter

Pride of place this quarter must go to the devastating critique by Vivek Chibber (whose book, *Locked in Place*, John Game has reviewed in this issue of *IS*) of Niall Ferguson's much-praised glorification of the British Empire, *Colossus* (http://www.marxsite.com/goodEmpire.pdf)

The latest issue of **Science and Society** had not arrived in England at the time of writing. But it looks as if it could be the best for a very long time. A special issue, guest edited by Martha Gimenez and Lise Vogel, promises a restatement of the Marxist-feminist case in opposition to postmodernism and locates women's oppression within the dynamic of capitalist society. Keep a look out for it.

If you've read our transcript of the debate between John Holloway and Alex Callinicos, you might be interested in the spring 2005 issue of **Capital and Class**. It contains an extensive discussion on the arguments, with contributions from Holloway, Callinicos, Michael Lowy and others. In the same issue Tony Weiss provides a useful account of the economic and politics of Jamaica.

The November-December issue of **New Left Review** contains a very useful piece by Gérard Duménil and Dominique Levy on trends in inequality in the US, and the January-February issue an informative piece on Spain since Franco by Carlos Prieto, with particular attention to the national question.

Against the Current's January issue contains a very good account of the Shia resistance in Baghdad's Sadr City by Michael Schwartz, who has also written stuff for **ZNet** web magazine.

The publication of Pierre Broué's history of the German Revolution of 1918-23 in English (to be reviewed in the next issue of *IS*) will make some readers want to go into the debates of the period. **Revolutionary History** (vol 8, no 4) provides translations for the first time of the views of one of the important actors in the events of 1923, August Thalheimer.

Gavin Capps reports that the latest **Historical Materialism** contains articles by 'the best Marxists writing on Africa'. But prepare for some difficult reading, since much of the language is excessively abstract and academic.

For readers of French, the most recent issue of **ContreTemps** is a bit of a treat. It takes up the discussions which have erupted in France over secularism, religion and the state since the ban on the hijab, with contributions avoiding the Islamophobia of so much of the French left.

Of particular note are the article by Jean-Pierre Debourdeau and Samy Joshua (on the history of socialist debate on religion and the state); by Patrick Simon (on how the 'universalism' of the French state excludes ethnic minorities); by Michael Lowy (on Marxism and religion); and by Mohamed-Cherif Ferzani and Sadri Khairi (on trends and contradictions in Islamism today). As well as these there are pieces by Gilbert Achcar and myself.

Readers of Spanish should look at the new Argentinian journal **Socialismo Revolucionario**, which can be read on-line. It contains a thorough and convincing analysis by Martin Ogando of how Argentinian capitalism and its state survived the uprising of three and a half years ago http://www.sr.org.ar/index.php?id=2

CH

A question of perspective

Daphne Lawless

A comment on the experience of the Alliance Party in New Zealand

Harman's otherwise extremely useful article in *International Socialism* 104, 'Spontaneity, Strategy and Politics', contained references to the experience of the Alliance Party in New Zealand. Although his outline of the history of this is correct, it missed some vital elements in the Alliance experience. He writes:

'The disaster in New Zealand was not the creation of the new party [the Alliance] under the aegis of a figure [former Labour Party president Jim Anderton] who still accepted a basically reformist perspective. It was the lack of an organised revolutionary tendency within the party, working with him in a united front so long as he offered a focus to the left to disillusioned Labour supporters, but also trying all the time to win people to a perspective that would enable them to resist any backsliding.'

But there were initially several 'organised revolutionary tendencies' in the Alliance—or at least the founding group which split from Labour, the NLP. Matt McCarten, its president and then a major figure in the Alliance, tells how he saw their talk of 'revolution' at the founding conference as an electoral liability:

'The day before our poll rating was 17 percent; after the public saw the conference on TV our poll rating crashed to 3 percent... We naively had an open session where anyone could speak. Everyone in the press gallery couldn't believe their good luck... Sure enough on Sunday night TV it was wall-to-wall revolution. The impression viewers got was that it looked hysterical and nutty... At future conferences I insisted there was delegated attendance and the affair was well controlled. When we had our first Alliance conference a few years later it was completely stage-managed'.[1]

This statement shows just how far to the right New Zealand's political climate had swung by 1989. The country had been transformed from the most regulated advanced capitalist countries to one of the most free for capital in less than five years, by a Labour government, no less. In this atmosphere a conservative social democrat and successful small capitalist such as Jim Anderton was regularly described by the capitalist media and political opponents as a dangerous radical or even a Stalinist. Given this, the existence of open revolutionaries in the NLP was pure gold for those wishing to discredit the political project. In response to this, McCarten and Anderton drove out two 'entrist' groups. Most of the revolutionary socialists left in the NLP—and many other leftists—thereafter resigned, drifted away, went silent or were marginalised. There was no opportunity for any organised revolutionary current to establish itself within the NLP or, later, the Alliance.

The growing complaint of all opposition tendencies within the Alliance during the 1990s was the fundamentally undemocratic nature of the party. In part this was due to its origin as a federation of parties, of which only the NLP and the Green Party had any mass base. The three minor Alliance parties had little in common with the NLP or Greens apart from opposition to neo-liberalism. They were, for the main part, petty bourgeois and conservative, with tiny memberships. But they had a veto on the Alliance ruling council.

The defeat of the former NLP members who described themselves as socialist was finally ensured by the massive authority exercised within the party by Jim Anderton, as the party's most articulate spokesperson and electoral 'drawcard'. As long as Anderton continued to soar in the preferred prime minister opinion polls, he was untouchable, although personal conservatism and antipathy to the socialist left were never a secret. It was only after the Alliance support base collapsed during the 1999-2002 coalition, mainly because of Anderton's refusal to distance his party from Labour's 'soft' neo-liberalism, that the Alliance left was able to challenge his authority—and by then it was too late. As far as political programme went, the Alliance showed the correctness of John Rees's observation that the important question about socialists participating in alliances with other political forces is not:

'whether there was an alliance but whether it was the working class and socialist elements...that determined the political direction of the alliance... The fault of the popular front was that it subordinated the radical forces to the political priorities of the most conservative forces in the alliance'.[2]

The Alliance certainly recapitulated the failings of popular front politics—with, of course, the vital difference that it was an anti neo-liberal rather than an anti-fascist bloc. Harman is right that, once Labour retreated from hard neo-liberalism, 'there was immense pressure on the Alliance Party to dilute its opposition to Labour so as to get the right out'.[3] But, given the political climate and the balance of forces within the Alliance, the socialist left had no realistic chance to intervene in a manner that would have prevented this drift rightwards.

The Communist Party of New Zealand, which later formed the basis of our Internatonal Socialist Tendency organisation, had this to say about the Alliance in 1994: 'The left wing of the NLP can think socialist thoughts and even whisper socialist words in back rooms, but they cannot act as socialists through the Alliance, which is committed to managing capitalism... And without collective action, socialist ideas are merely empty wishes.'

Harman is probably correct that the Alliance might have been saved from disaster if it had included an organised revolutionary tendency. This was, sadly, an objective impossibility. But the fate of the Alliance should show how decision-making structures which allow small cliques undue influence, and excessive internal deference to a popular leader figure, can make such political formations impossible for socialists to work within.

NOTES

1: M McCarten and C Casey, *Rebel in the Ranks* (Random House, 2002). My personal memory of the television coverage of that conference accords with McCarten's.

2: 'Socialism in the 21st Century', *International Socialism* 100 (autumn 2003), pp30-31.

3: An observation also made by Matt McCarten in *Socialist Worker Monthly Review*, December 2004.